THE CONSTITUTION OF ROMANIA

In December 1989, Romania became the last Eastern European communist country to break with its communist dictatorship, the most powerful in the region at the time. It has struggled ever since to overcome the transition to democracy and to become a 'full-time' member of the Western democratic community of states. This book provides a contextual analysis of the Romanian constitutional system, with references to the country's troubled constitutional history and to the way in which legal transplantation has been used. The Constitution's grey areas, as well as the gap between the written constitution and the living one, will also be explained through the prism of recent events that cast a negative shadow upon the democratic nature of the Romanian constitutional system.

The first chapters present a brief historical overview and an introduction to Romanian constitutional culture, as well as to the principles and general features of the 1991 Constitution. The chapters which follow explain the functioning of the institutions and their interrelations—Parliament, the President, the Government and the courts. The Constitutional Court has a special place in the book, as do local government and the protection of fundamental rights. The last chapter refers to the mechanisms and challenges of constitutional change and development.

Cover description

Romania: Turbulence and Triumph

The colours of Romania's national flag (blue, yellow and red) underpin the foundation of the composition. An anthology of icons from Romania's coat of arms symbolises independence and unity. In the outer perimeter are the golden eagle with a cross in its beak, the bull,* the sun, a crescent moon and star, a sword and dexter, a rose, a lion, a bridge of Apollodorus of Damascus and twin dolphins. At the heart of the composition can be seen the wooden spire and roof of the Maramures church, which rises from the Palace of Parliament, with 1991 etched on its facade. The juxtaposition of the two buildings represents both Romania's orthodox tradition and commemorates historical churches demolished for the construction of the Palace, where the Constitutional Court now sits. 1991 records the year the current constitutional system was inaugurated. To the left, the Fleur-de-Lis serves as a reminder of French influence. At the base, the Great Assembly of Alba Iulia held on 1st December 1918 stands for unification and the formation of Great Romania, while the twin cupolas from Bran Castle celebrate Romania's idiosyncratic architecture.

Putachad, Artist

* inspired by Picasso

Constitutional Systems of the World
General Editors: Peter Leyland, Andrew Harding and Benjamin L Berger
Associate Editors: Grégoire Webber and Rosalind Dixon

In the era of globalisation, issues of constitutional law and good governance are being seen increasingly as vital issues in all types of society. Since the end of the Cold War, there have been dramatic developments in democratic and legal reform, and post-conflict societies are also in the throes of reconstructing their governance systems. Even societies already firmly based on constitutional governance and the rule of law have undergone constitutional change and experimentation with new forms of governance; and their constitutional systems are increasingly subjected to comparative analysis and transplantation. Constitutional texts for practically every country in the world are now easily available on the internet. However, texts which enable one to understand the true context, purposes, interpretation and incidents of a constitutional system are much harder to locate, and are often extremely detailed and descriptive. This series seeks to provide scholars and students with accessible introductions to the constitutional systems of the world, supplying both a road map for the novice and, at the same time, a deeper understanding of the key historical, political and legal events which have shaped the constitutional landscape of each country. Each book in this series deals with a single country, or a group of countries with a common constitutional history, and each author is an expert in their field.

Published volumes

The Constitution of the United Kingdom; The Constitution of the United State; The Constitution of Vietnam; The Constitution of South Africa; The Constitution of Japan; The Constitution of Germany; The Constitution of Finland; The Constitution of Australia; The Constitution of the Republic of Austria; The Constitution of the Russian Federation; The Constitutional System of Thailand; The Constitution of Malaysia; The Constitution of China; The Constitution of Indonesia; The Constitution of France; The Constitution of Spain; The Constitution of Mexico; The Constitution of Israel; The Constitutional Systems of the Commonwealth Caribbean; The Constitution of Canada; The Constitution of Singapore; The Constitution of Belgium; The Constitution of Taiwan

Link to series website
http://www.hartpub.co.uk/series/csw

The Constitution of Romania

A Contextual Analysis

Bianca Selejan-Guțan

·HART·
PUBLISHING
OXFORD AND PORTLAND, OREGON
2016

Published in the United Kingdom by Hart Publishing Ltd
16C Worcester Place, Oxford, OX1 2JW
Telephone: +44 (0)1865 517530
Fax: +44 (0)1865 510710
E-mail: mail@hartpub.co.uk
Website: http://www.hartpub.co.uk

Published in North America (US and Canada) by
Hart Publishing
c/o International Specialized Book Services
920 NE 58th Avenue, Suite 300
Portland, OR 97213-3786
USA
Tel: +1 503 287 3093 or toll-free: (1) 800 944 6190
Fax: +1 503 280 8832
E-mail: orders@isbs.com
Website: http://www.isbs.com

Hart Publishing is an imprint of Bloomsbury Publishing plc.

British Library Cataloguing in Publication Data
Data Available

Library of Congress Cataloging-in-Publication Data

Names: Selejan-Gutan, Bianca, 1973– author.

Title: The Constitution of Romania / A Contextual Analysis / Bianca Selejan-Gutan.

Description: Portland, Oregon : Hart Publishing, 2016. | Series: Constitutional
systems of the world | Includes bibliographical references and index.

Identifiers: LCCN 2015049496 (print) | LCCN 2015050109 (ebook) |
ISBN 9781849465137 (pbk) | ISBN 9781782259589 (Epub)

Subjects: LCSH: Romania. Constitutia (1991) | Constitutional law—Romania. |
Constitutional history—Romania.

Classification: LCC KKR2064.51991 .S45 2016 (print) | LCC KKR2064.51991
(ebook) | DDC 342.498—dc23
LC record available at http://lccn.loc.gov/2015049496

ISBN: 978-1-84946-513-7

Typeset by Compuscript Ltd, Shannon

Acknowledgements

I am deeply indebted to Richard Hart, who commissioned this book, as well as to the outstanding editors of the series, Andrew Harding and Peter Leyland, for the interest they have expressed in the Romanian constitutional system, for their trust in me as an author and for including this book in their editorial plans. The book editors, Benjamin Berger and Rosalind Dixon, were of invaluable help in the revision process. Without their careful and prompt feedback and guidance, this project would have been an impossible mission.

My warmest gratitude goes to my husband, Manuel Guțan, for understanding and sharing my determination to carry on this editorial project. His thoughtful suggestions helped me to add insight and improved my work all along. I thank him and my loving children, Anastasia and Radu, for bearing with my lack of time and with my long absences during the writing of this book.

Last but not least, my thanks go to the Max-Planck Institute for Public International Law and Comparative Law in Heidelberg, and especially to Professor Anne Peters, for offering me a perfect research and writing environment, a second home where this book was shaped and revised.

Bianca Selejan-Guțan
December 2015

Contents

Acknowledgements v
List of Abbreviations xv
Table of Cases xvii
Table of Legislation xix

INTRODUCTION AND HISTORICAL OVERVIEW 1
  I.   Introductory Remarks...1
  II. Brief Overview of Romanian Modern
      Constitutional History 2
      A. The Rise and Fall of Romanian Liberal
           Constitutionalism 2
          i.   The Dawn of Romanian Constitutionalism 2
          ii. The Organic Regulations (1831–58) 5
          iii. The Birth of the Modern Romanian State
               and the Reign of Alexandru Ioan Cuza...................7
          iv. The Constitutional Monarchy (1866–1938) 10
          v.   The Right-wing Dictatorships (1938–44)..............15
      B. The Communist Period...17
      C. The 1989 Revolution and the Post-Communist
           Period..19
          i.   The 1989 Revolutionary Moment..........................19
          ii. The Constitution-making Process 22
  III. Conclusion: The Dynamics of the Romanian
      Constitutional Culture 24
      A. The Pre-Communist Period 25
      B. The Communist Period...27
      C. The Post-Communist Period 28
  Further Reading 30

1.   CONSTITUTION, NATION AND STATE...........................33
  I.   Constitution and Constitutional Law 33
      A. The Constitution: Formal and Substantive....................34
      B. Organic and Ordinary Laws...34

    C. Government Ordinances (*Ordonante de Guvern*) 35
    D. International Treaties: A Monist Incorporation............36
    E. Complementary Sources: Case Law of the
        Constitutional Court and the European
        Court of Human Rights 37
    F. Marginal Sources: Ordinary Case Law, Doctrine,
        Travaux Préparatoires 38
    G. EU Law in the Source System 38
  II. Romanian Nation, Sovereignty and Citizenship 40
    A. The Romanian People as Sovereign 40
    B. Citizenship 43
       i. Citizens and Nationals 43
      ii. Constitutional and Legal Aspects of
          Romanian Citizenship: Acquisition,
          Loss, Specific Rights 45
      iii. Political Rights of Citizens 46
      iv. Referendums 47
  III. The State and its Features 52
    A. General Characteristics of the State 52
       i. National State 52
      ii. Unitary and Indivisible State 53
      iii. Democracy and the Rule of Law 54
      iv. The Republic 56
      v. Social State 57
    B. The Institutional Architecture and
        the Separation of Powers 58
       i. The Separation of Powers 58
      ii. Semi-presidentialism 59
      iii. Legislature and Executive 60
      iv. The Judiciary 61
      v. Other Key Institutions of the
         Constitutional System 62
    C. Conclusion 63
  Further Reading 63

2. THE ROMANIAN PARLIAMENT 65
  I. Introduction 65
  II. The Struggle For Parliament: Political Parties
     and Elections 66
    A. Political Parties 67

B. Parliamentary Elections 72
C. The Structure and Internal Organisation
   of Parliament..76
   i. Bicameralism...76
   ii. Internal Organisation: Groups,
       Committees, Speakers.............................78
   iii. Sessions and Sittings.............................81
D. Status of Members of Parliament...................82
   i. Protection of Members of Parliament:
      Incompatibilities, Immunity....................83
E. The Opposition...87
F. The Legislative Process..................................88
   i. Legislative Initiative...............................88
   ii. The Legislative Council...........................89
   iii. Introduction to the Competent Chamber...........90
   iv. The Committee Stage..............................90
   v. Plenary Debate and Adoption.................91
G. Parliamentary Resolutions 92
H. Other Functions: Control and Supervision.................93
I. Dissolution of Parliament..............................95
J. Budgetary and Financial Powers....................96
   i. Adoption of the Budget.........................96
   ii. Financial Control Through the Court
       of Auditors...97
K. Conclusion..98
Further Reading...99

3. **THE DUAL EXECUTIVE AND THE AVATARS
   OF ROMANIAN SEMI-PRESIDENTIALISM** 101
   I. Introduction.. 101
   II. The President.. 102
      A. The Origins of the Presidential Function
         in Romania.. 102
      B. The Design of the New Presidential Institution....... 104
      C. The Election of the President................... 105
      D. The Presidential Term of Office.............. 106
      E. Role and Powers of the President............. 107
         i. Representative of the State................. 109
         ii. Mediator and Guarantor of the
             Constitution..................................... 110

F.   Relationship with the Government 112
    i.   Appointment and Reshuffle 113
    ii.   Cohabitation and its Effects 116
G.   Relationship with the Parliament 118
H.   Foreign Policy and Defence Powers 119
I.   Accountability of the President 120
    i.   Incompatibilities and Immunity 120
    ii.   Suspension from Office 120
    iii.   Impeachment for High Treason 124
J.   Vacancy of Office 125
K.   Acts of the President 125
L.   Conclusion 126
III.   The Government 126
A.   Appointment of the Government 127
B.   Structure, Competences, Functioning 128
    i.   Structure 128
    ii.   Functions and Competences 128
C.   The Prime Minister 130
D.   The Relationship Between the Government
    and the Parliament 131
    i.   Legislative Delegation 131
    ii.   Political Accountability of the
       Government 133
    iii.   Motion of Censure 134
    iv.   Engagement of Responsibility 135
E.   Criminal Accountability of the Members
    of the Government 137
IV.   The Public Administration 139
A.   Public Office and Lustration 139
B.   Ministerial Administration 141
C.   Autonomous Administrative Agencies 141
D.   Conclusion 144
V.   Conclusion 145
Further Reading 146

4.   **LOCAL GOVERNMENT** 147
I.   Brief Historical Overview 147
II.   Constitutional Principles of the Current System
    of Local Government 149
A.   Decentralisation and Deconcentration 150

  B. Local Autonomy... 152
  C. The Sensitive Issue of Linguistic Pluralism................ 154
 III. The Relationship Between Central and Local
      Government: A True Autonomy?.. 155
  A. The Prefect... 155
  B. Financial Autonomy 157
 IV. Conclusion... 159
 Further Reading 160

5. **THE CONSTITUTIONAL COURT.**
   CONSTITUTIONAL ASPECTS OF THE
   JUDICIAL SYSTEM.. 163
  I. The Constitutional Court.. 163
   A. The Foundations of the Romanian
       Constitutional Court... 163
   B. Composition of the Court: Appointment
       of Constitutional Judges, Independence
       and Impartiality 167
       i.   Composition and Appointment........................... 167
       ii. Independence and Impartiality
            of the Court.. 169
   C. The Constitutional Court's Powers 171
       i.   Abstract Review... 172
       ii. Concrete Review.. 173
       iii. Other Powers 176
  II. The Judicial System and its Constitutional
      Role... 181
   A. General Remarks on the Romanian
       Judicial System.. 181
   B. Constitutional Principles of the Judiciary.................. 182
   C. Organisation of the System and the Status
       of Magistrates... 183
       i.   How the Judicial System is Organised 183
       ii. Recruitment, Appointment and Status
            of Judges: Guarantees of Independence 184
   D. The Particular Situation of the Prosecution.
       The National Anti-corruption Directorate................. 185

      E.   The High Court of Cassation and Justice 189
          i.   Consistency of Jurisprudence 190
          ii. HCCJ and RCC: Dialogue or Conflict? 191
      F.   The Superior Council of Magistracy 193
  III. Conclusion 197
  Further Reading 201

**6. CONSTITUTIONAL PROTECTION
OF FUNDAMENTAL RIGHTS** 203
    I. National and International Foundations of
      the System of Fundamental Rights 203
      A.   National Foundations 205
      B.   International Foundations 207
   II. Constitutional Principles of Rights 209
      A.   Equality 209
      B.   Priority of International Law 211
      C.   Proportionality and Limitation of Rights 214
  III. Content of Rights 216
      A.   Access to Justice 217
      B.   The Pillars of Democracy: Rights to
           Free Speech, Association and Assembly 218
      C.   Personal Protection: Rights to Freedom of
           Conscience and Religion 221
      D.   Personal Freedoms: Rights to Liberty
           and Security of the Person, Respect
           for Private Life 222
      E.   Minority Protection and the Right
           to Identity 223
      F.   Economic, Social and Cultural Rights 227
      G.   The Right to Property 228
      H.   Fundamental Duties 230
  IV. Institutional Guarantees of Rights 231
      A.   Fundamental Rights in Romanian Courts 231
      B.   The Ombudsman 233
   V. Conclusion 236
  Further Reading 237

7. THE PROCESS OF CONSTITUTIONAL
    CHANGE: MECHANISMS, LIMITS
    AND FUTURE DEVELOPMENTS 239
    I. Contextual Mechanisms and Dynamics of
        Constitutional Change 239
        A. Formal Changes 241
        B. Informal Changes 244
    II. Limits.. 246
        A. Formal Limits 246
        B. Substantive Limits and 'Eternity Clauses'................... 248
    III. Future Developments 249
        A. Major Themes of Debate in the Context
            of Post-Communist Constitutional Change............... 249
            i.   Parliamentarism v Semi-presidentialism 250
            ii. Other Themes of Debate on
                 Constitutional Change 252
            iii. Constitutional Models 254
        B. International Benchmarks of Constitutional
            Change 255
        C. Conclusion 257
    Further Reading 259

Index.. 261

List of Abbreviations

ANI	National Agency for Integrity
CD	Chamber of Deputies
CNCD	National Council Against Discrimination
CNSAS	National Council for Studying the Former *Securitate* Archives
CR	Constitution of Romania
CSAT	Supreme Council of National Defence
CSM	Superior Council of Magistracy
CVM	Cooperation and Verification Mechanism
DNA	National Anti-corruption Directorate
ECHR	European Convention on Human Rights
ECtHR	European Court of Human Rights
EGO	Emergency Government Ordinance
ESC	Economic and Social Council
EU	European Union
GO	Government Ordinance
HCCJ	High Court of Cassation and Justice
ICCPR	International Covenant on Civil and Political Rights
MEP	Member of the European Parliament
MP	Member of Parliament
NGO	non-governmental organisation
NSF	National Salvation Front
RCC	Romanian Constitutional Court
SCJ	Supreme Court of Justice (1991–2003)
UDHR	Universal Declaration of Human Rights
Venice Commission	European Commission for Democracy through Law

Table of Cases

European Court of Human Rights

Archip v Romania App no 49608/08 (27 September 2011) 237
Atanasiu (Maria) v Romania App nos 30767/05 and 33800/06
 (12 October 2010) 230
Brumărescu v Romania App no 28342/95 (28 October1999) 230
Cumpănă şi Mazăre v Romania App no 33348/96
 (17 December 2004) 219
Pantea v Romania App no 33343/96
 (3 June 2003) 187, 209, 222, 242
Partidul comuniştilor (nepecerişti) and Ungureanu v Romania
 App no 46626/99 (3 February 2005) 70
Stângu şi Scutelnicu v Romania App no 53899/00
 (31 January 2006) 219
Vasilescu v Romania (1996) Reports 1998-III 212
Vlad v Romania App nos 40756/06, 41508/07 and 50806/07
 (26 November 2013) 233
Zelca v Romania, admissibility decision, App no 65161/10
 (6 September 2011) 193

Romania

CSM Plenum Ruling 981 of 2 October 2008 197
HCCJ, Decision no 39/2005 232
HCCJ, Decision no 1414/2005 232
HCCJ, Decision no 3221/2005 232
HCCJ, Decision no 8/2010 192
HCCJ, Decision no 4211/2012 of 18 October 2012 140
RCC, Decision no 27/1993 58
RCC, Decision no 9/1994 58
RCC, Decision no 81/1994 166
RCC, Ruling no 2/1996 107
RCC, Decision no 123/1996 166
RCC, Decision no 279/1997 232
RCC, Decision no 34/1998 132
RCC, Decision no 76/1999 216
RCC, Decision no 186/1999 232
RCC, Decision no 209/1999 58
RCC, Decision no 73/2000 216

RCC, Advisory Opinion no 1/2007 ....111, 121
RCC, Decision no 62/2007 192
RCC, Decision no 356/2007 115
RCC, Decision no 992/2007 191
RCC, Decision no 51/2008 143
RCC, Decision no 1557/2009 180
RCC, Decision no 61/2010 75
RCC, Decision no 415/2010 143
RCC, Decision no 820/2010 141
RCC, Decision no 1431/2010 ....136, 180
RCC, Decision no 1525/2010 181
RCC, Decision no 1560/2010 191
RCC, Decision no 53/2011 ....92, 178
RCC, Decision no 54/2011 178
RCC, Decision no 766/2011 173
RCC, Decision no 799/2011 177
RCC, Advisory Opinion no 1/2012 123
RCC, Resolution no 3/2012 51
RCC, Decision no 51/2012 137
RCC, Decision no 682/2012 ....75, 245
RCC, Decision no 683/2012 110
RCC, Decision no 727/2012 177
RCC, Decision no 729/2012 ....81, 93
RCC, Decision no 731/2012 50
RCC, Decision no 972/2012 84
RCC, Decision no 196/2013 196
RCC, Decision no 206/2013 167
RCC, Decision no 231/2013 179
RCC, Decision no 334/2013 51
RCC, Decision no 447/2013 133
RCC, Decision no 471/2013 51
RCC, Decision no 2/2014 86
RCC, Decision no 80/2014 ....245, 254
RCC, Decision no 265/2014 191
RCC, Decision no 284/2014 111
RCC, Decision no 418/2014 167
RCC, Decision no 669/2014 222
RCC, Decision no 678/2014 120
RCC, Decision no 761/2014 160
RCC, Decision no 17/2015 167
RCC, Decision no 75/2015 68
SCJ, Judgment of 9 March 1993 229
SCJ, Judgment (full court) of 2 February 1995...229
SCJ, Decision no 1813/1999 175

Table of Legislation

International

Association Agreement between Romania and the
European Union 38
European Charter of Local Self-Government
(Council of Europe, 1985) 153
European Convention on Human Rights 1950 .... 36, 37, 186, 203,
207, 208, 212–15,
218, 232, 233, 242
Art 3 .... 187, 237
Art 5 242
(1) 187, 222
(3) 187
(3)–(6) 187
Art 6 .... 217, 218
(1) 187, 230
Art 11 70
Art 15 214
Protocol 16 237
International Covenant on Civil and Political Rights 1966
Art 4 214
Art 14 218
Art 27 224
North Atlantic Treaty 1949 242
Paris Convention 1858 .... 8, 9
Treaty of Adrianopolis 1829 5
Treaty of Berlin 1878
Art 44 209
Treaty on Minority Protection 1919 223
Preamble 223
Universal Declaration of Human Rights 1948 212
Art 10 218

European Union

Commission Decision 2006/928/CE establishing a mechanism
for cooperation and verification of progress in Romania
[2006] OJ L354/56 .... 39, 142
Preamble (4) 39

National Legislation

Belgium

Constitution 1831 11

France

Constitution 1791 4
Constitution 1852 8
Constitution 1958 104
Constitution 107
Constitutional Charter 1814 6
Constitutional Charter 1830 6
Republican Constitution 1848 6

Germany

Basic Law 206
  Art 1 206

Portugal

Constitution 80

Romania

Civil Code 1864 45
Civil Code 35, 79
Code of Civil Procedure 35, 38, 183, 190, 191, 233
  Art 329 193
  Art 517 §4 38
Code of Criminal Procedure 35, 38, 120, 183, 186, 187, 191
Constitution 1866 .... 11, 14, 33, 65, 72, 97, 134, 137, 209
  Art 7 209
  Art 10 209
  Art 132 148
Constitution 1923 ....14, 15, 17, 24, 33, 65,
                                                                        89, 97, 134, 164, 205,
                                                                        209, 210, 223, 257
  Art 8 210
Constitution 1938 .... 16, 209, 224
  Art 5 210
Constitution 1948 .... 17, 210, 224
Constitution 1952 .... 17, 18, 67, 224
Constitution 1965 .... 18, 20, 67, 102, 103, 204, 224, 250

Constitution 1991

Title I	206
Title II	206
Art 1	52, 54, 66, 68
§2	56
§3	28, 54–56, 67, 206, 242
§4	59, 101
§5	34, 37
Art 2	41
Art 3	150
§4	43
Art 4	42, 44, 53, 206, 210
§2	210, 220
Art 5	45
Art 6	53, 206
Art 7	44
Art 8	67, 68
Art 11	212
§2	36
Art 16	206, 210
§1	210
§2	55
Art 17	45
Art 20	207, 208, 212, 232
Art 21	186, 217, 218
§1	217
§2	217
Art 23	222, 242
Art 25	223
Art 26 §1	223
§2	223
Art 27	223
Art 28	223
Art 29	221
§5	221
Art 30 §1	218
Art 31	220
Art 39	220
Art 40	68, 220
§3	46
Art 41	210
Art 44	210
§4	228
Art 48	210

Art 50.. 210
Art 53.. 210, 214, 215, 218, 220
  §2 215
Art 61.. 46
  §1 ....66, 191
Art 62.. 73
Art 71.. 83
Art 72...84, 120
Art 73 §1 34
  §3 ....34, 225
Art 75... 77
Art 80.. 107
  §4 107
Art 84 §1 110
  §2 120
Art 85 §2 ....114, 115
Art 87 §1 129
Art 91 §3 119
Art 92 §1 107
Art 96... 124
Art 103 116
Art 107 130
  §2 ....116, 130
  §3 131
  §4 115
Art 109 §2 ....134, 137
Art 114 ....135, 180
Art 115 131
  §1 132
  §4 ....36, 131
  §6 132
Art 120 ....150, 152
  §2 ....154, 225
Art 123 156
Art 124 183
Art 125 §1 185
Art 126 §1 183
  §5 ....183, 184
Art 128 §1 183
  §2 225
Art 131 §1 186
Art 133 §6 193
Art 141 58
Art 146 a... 254
  l) 176, 177

Art 147 192
§1 175
Art 148 §2 38
Art 151 167
Art 152 .... 57, 182, 246, 248
§1 67
Criminal Code 35, 79, 86, 166, 167, 192, 204, 219
Art 398 124
Decree-Law no 8/1989 68
Decree-Law no 92/1990 on the Election of Parliament
and of the President of Romania... 20, 107, 165
Diktat of Vienna 1940.. 16
EGO no 25/2008 140
Emergency Ordinance 2014.. 159, 160
Fiscal Code..97, 157
Law no 2/1973 97
Law no 21/1991 on Romanian Citizenship 45
Law no 60/1991 on Public Assemblies 220
Law no 47/1992 on the Constitutional Court 173
Law no 94/1992 on the Court of Auditors 97
Law no 27/1996 on Political Parties 68
Law no 115/1996 on the Statement and Control of the
Assets of Public Officials... 143
Law no 115/1999 on Ministerial Responsibility 138
Law no 187/1999 Law on Access to Personal Files and the
Disclosure of the 'Securitate'... 139
Law no 188/1999 Law on the Status of Public Servants...................... 139, 156
Law no 189/1999 on Popular Legislative Initiative 89
Law no 3/2000 on the Organisation of the Referendum.......................... 49
Law no 90/2001 on the Organisation of the Government.................... 128
Law no 215/2001 on Local Government..152, 225
Law no 14/2003 on Political Parties 68
Law no 303/2004 Status of Magistrates Law 185
Law no 304/2004 on Judicial Organisation 182, 183–85, 189, 194
Law no 370/2004 Law on the Election of the President 105
Law no 96/2006 on the status of the Deputies and Senators.................... 82
Law no 195/2006 on Decentralisation 150
Law no 334/2006 on the Financing of Political Parties.....................68, 71
Law no 489/2006 on Religious Freedom and Cults 2006.................... 221
Law no 35/2008 on Parliamentary Elections 73
Law no 217/2008 on the Court of Auditors 97
Law no 1/2011 on National Education.. 136
Law no 113/2015 on Changing the Law on Financing of
Political Parties.. 71
Law no 114/2015 on Parliamentary Elections 69

Law on Primary Education 1924 224
Law on Administrative Unification 1925 224
Law on the General Regime of Religious Cults 1925 224
Organic Regulations (Regulamentele Organice) 1831–32 .... 6–8, 65, 67, 147
Resolution of the Great National Assembly, Alba Iulia 1918 14
Statute Developing the Paris Convention 1864 .... 9, 65
Timişoara Proclamation 140

Spain

Constitution
  Art 10 §2 37

Introduction and Historical Overview

Constitutional Culture – Constitutional Transplant – Authoritarianism – Democratic Traditions – Communism – Post-Communism

I. INTRODUCTORY REMARKS

ROMANIA HAS AN intricate and troubled political and constitutional history, which it is essential to depict in order to understand what the country and its Constitution have become today. This introductory chapter attempts to explain, on the one hand, why the Romanian constitutional system is worth reading about and, on the other hand, how this system reached its present stage. Because of its greater influence on the present constitutional development, only the modern part of Romanian history will be explored in this chapter. It will be shown that the current Romanian system was not the result of an organic and constant evolution, as in other contemporary democracies, but a process with many ups and downs, contradictions of all kinds, with a high degree of instability, partly dominated by the lack of legal and constitutional self-esteem.

The development of the Romanian system is outlined over three main periods: the building and the decay of liberal constitutionalism, the communist period and the post-communist period. This evolution reveals several particular aspects of the Romanian constitutional culture, as well as the various internal and external contexts that influenced it. Most of these particularities were perpetuated by and can be traced in the present constitutional system, the last section of the chapter emphasising this process: the role of constitutional transplant, the external influence and pressures, the recourse to history.

Within this framework, the development of Romanian constitutionalism has been primarily influenced by the following cultural and constitutional factors: an appetite for legal and constitutional transplant, especially from French law and legal culture; a characteristic tendency towards ethnocentrism; the focus on the creation of institutions rather than on their actual functioning; a partial incapacity to apply the principles of democratic constitutionalism in practice. To what extent have these factors evolved and changed over the last 25 years? How can they be traced within the current constitutional system created after 1989? The attempt to answer this question was one of the reasons this book was written.

II. BRIEF OVERVIEW OF ROMANIAN MODERN CONSTITUTIONAL HISTORY

Romanian modern constitutional history can be roughly divided into three periods: the rise and fall of liberal constitutionalism (from the beginning of the nineteenth century until 1945), the communist period (1945–89) and the post-communist period (1990–present).

A. The Rise and Fall of Romanian Liberal Constitutionalism

i. *The Dawn of Romanian Constitutionalism*

The 'constitutional imperialism' of the great European powers in the nineteenth century, as well as the Romanian political elite's appeal for massive constitutional transplant, determined all major changes in Romania's modern constitutional history. Hence, this period saw a remarkable break with almost any previous constitutional tradition.

At the beginning of the nineteenth century, Romanians were politically organised into two separate autonomous entities: Wallachia (*Ţara Românească*) and Moldavia (*Moldova*), both having been, for centuries, under Ottoman suzerainty. However, the two Principalities did not account for all the Romanians living in the area to the north and the west of the Carpathians, in Transylvania and Banat—two provinces that were successively under Hungarian, Ottoman and Austrian rule— Romanians of the Orthodox Christian religion formed the majority population. Northern Moldavia, known as Bukovina, occupied in 1774 by Austria, and the territory between the Rivers Prut and Dniester, known as Bessarabia (obtained by the Russians following the Bucharest peace of 1812), were also inhabited by Romanians.[1] However, being the only Romanian *political* entities, the two small Principalities played a catalysing role in the process of future consolidation of an independent nation state. They became the core of the modern Romanian nation and, from a political point of view, the central and stable element in the unification and building of the future state. This role was somehow natural, given that the overwhelming majority of the Romanian population lived in that territory (over 85 per cent).

The beginning of the nineteenth century also meant the end of 110 years of Phanariot rule in the Romanian Principalities (1711–1821). Despite the fact that the Ottoman Empire had recognised the region's political, administrative, fiscal and judicial autonomy since the fifteenth century, from 1711 the Sublime Porte started to directly appoint princes (*domni*) to the thrones of the two small Romanian states. This was justified by the increasing threat from the annexing offensive of the Russian and Austrian Empires, which were both keen to expand in south-eastern Europe. This appointment process meant, on the one hand, reducing each state's internal autonomy, by preventing the Romanian nobility from acceding to the throne, and, on the other, the enthroning of princes of Greek origin, recruited by the Turks from the rich inhabitants of the Phanar/Fener district of Constantinople.

The Phanariotes' rule and the increased political and economic control of the Ottomans represented a 'dark age' of pre-modern Romania, which lasted for more than a century. From a constitutional point of view, the old medieval customs, which relatively limited the powers of the prince, continued to exist formally, but actual political power was gradually taken over by the Phanariot princes. Consequently, the princes' power went from an arbitrary authoritarianism to absolutism, with accents of oriental despotism.

---

[1] It is important to mention here that by 'Romanians' we mean a population speaking the Romanian language despite territorial separation. The Romanian language has no dialects: all Romanians speak the same language with slightly different accents. The language developed homogeneously across these territories, despite the fact that they were politically separated from each other and subjected to other, different linguistic influences.

The whole period was dominated by extreme instability and a complete lack of interest in the public well-being. The thrones were actually bought from the Ottoman sultan, therefore the princes were at first changed every three years and then yearly: in order to raise more money themselves, the princes sold high nobility titles; and members of the great nobility sold inferior nobility titles. The result was a general lack of concern for the actual administration of the public interest, instability in public positions and an endemic lack of professionalism in the public administration. Paradoxically, although taking place in an absolute monarchy, Phanariot despotism and corruption prevented the formation of a professional and loyal public service. Corruption and nepotism, as well as the typical Turco-Phanariot superficiality, extended throughout the state apparatus. This was the age in which the Romanian 'modern' civil service was born, inheriting two flaws that continued to affect its evolution: on the one hand, the public service was seen as a means of social climbing, and on the other hand, it was exploited as a means of illegal enrichment.

Economically, the Romanian states were suffocated by the taxes imposed by the Ottomans. The requests increased exponentially over the years and were amplified by the already endemic corruption, with catastrophic results for the Romanian economy and society. Although enormous amounts of money were raised by the states, nothing was invested in their development. The lion's share of these amounts went to Constantinople, or fed the treasuries of the princes or of the great nobility. The economy was largely based on a medieval agriculture model, and external trade was restricted. At the end of the eighteenth century and beginning of the nineteenth century, the despotic Phanariot absolutism became too oppressive for the local political class, and the nobility started to address letters and requests to the Ottoman, Russian and French powers. They proposed a diverse range of political and state formulae, from the 'aristocratic republic' to the constitutional monarchy. These projects had a common goal: to counteract authoritarianism, either by eliminating the institution of the princes, or by subordinating it to the interests of the aristocracy.

An important part of the struggle for constitutional reforms was using ideas, principles and concepts based on French constitutionalism, and proposing institutions borrowed from the different French constitutions of the time (especially the 1791 Constitution). This demonstrated the influence that European liberal constitutionalism was starting to have on the new Romanian political elite, and saw the first signs of constitutional import from the French model. However, this did not mean that the values, ideals, principles and institutions of liberal constitutionalism entered the Romanian Principalities via a political class converted to liberalism. Although liberal concepts were used (human rights, representative government, separation of powers, etc), they were merely instruments to maintain, paradoxically, a feudal basis for the political power. Sovereignty was not transferred to the nation and the 'representative government' was based on the medieval structures of the Estate assemblies. In the end, the only concrete result of all these reformation efforts was the end of Phanariot rule in 1821 and the return of the local aristocratic families, with constitutional structures that preserved the medieval coordinates of political power.

ii. The Organic Regulations (1831–58)

The Russian occupation, which started in 1828 after the Turco-Russian War, accelerated the pace of constitutional reform. As a Protecting Power, Russia assumed the role of moderniser, which obscured its true intention of annexing the Romanian Principalities. However, the effects of Russian domination, in the sense of modernising Romanian society, were remarkable. Beyond the changes relating to the everyday life of the upper classes (fashion, cuisine, manners), due to the Russian military elite, the French language became the language of the privileged and French culture a landmark of modernisation. Thus, an overwhelming trend representing direct contact with French civilisation had started. By the Treaty of Adrianopolis (1829), Russia obtained freedom of trade for the Romanian Principalities and a more consolidated autonomy, which led to a more open Romanian economy, and to a civilisation and culture leaning towards Western Europe. The growth of a national consciousness, and the wish to remove the huge gulf between the Romanians and Western civilisation, transformed the contact with France into an almost mythical relationship with 'the Latin older sister'. This cultural context had an immense influence on the region's constitutional evolution, French liberal constitutionalism becoming, due to the numerous members of the Romanian aristocratic elite being educated in French universities, the main model to be transplanted. Starting in 1820, French liberal constitutionalism gradually became a serious alternative to the political attempts of the conservative aristocracy to limit the princes' authoritarianism by an oligarchy.

However, from the formal point of view, the instruments of constitutional reform in the period—the Organic Regulations (*Regulamentele Organice*)—were introduced by Russia. These instruments neither expressed the reformatory wishes of the Romanian political and aristocratic classes (conservative or liberal), nor applied the Tzarist constitutional model. They were the expression of an indirect constitutional borrowing from the French Constitutional Charter of 1814.

The Regulations entered into force in 1831–32 and lasted until 1858. They were a mixture of constitutional and administrative rules, transposing the principles of a limited monarchy similar to that in place following the French Restoration, but within an institutional machinery with local peculiarities. The Prince (*Hospodar*) was elected for life from the aristocracy, and he was the holder of the sovereignty by divine right; the apparent division of powers only referred to the extent to which the prince was prepared to yield the exercise of power. The parliament (Elective Assembly/*Adunarea Electiva*), dominated by the different levels of the nobility, did not have true legislative power. The independence of the judiciary was not even a theoretical goal. Moreover, the Regulations ignored the idea of fundamental rights of citizens, which pushed them even further away from the idea of liberal constitutionalism. In these circumstances, the Principalities (and especially Moldova) evolved towards neo-absolutism.

All of these factors led to increasing protest from the supporters of the principles of liberal constitutionalism, which culminated in the revolutionary movements of 1848. Values and principles such as limited government, national sovereignty, representative government, separation of powers, social justice, equality and the supremacy of the Constitution were in opposition to the existing monarchic authoritarianism.

Consequently, beyond the interest in ideas, principles and values, an increasing trend toward the actual transplantation of constitutional institutions can be identified. As an official reform initiative was impossible in the context of Ottoman and Russian control, this process was achieved by memoranda addressed to the Great Powers and by individual reform projects, which multiplied considerably in the context of the 1848 revolution. The overwhelming influence of the French model was clear, as these projects resorted to the specific structures and mechanisms of the French constitutional charter of 1830, and of the republican Constitution of 1848, with great difficulties, however, especially as regards the transposition of foreign ideas and principles into a coherent constitutional text.

Besides the issue of the limitation, by liberal solutions, of the Prince's authoritarian power, political life was marked by the gradual development of a Romanian political discourse focused on the goals of national unity and of the unitary nation state. After 1848, a nationalist type of constitutionalism, with ethnocentric accents, gradually developed, conflicting with the values of liberal constitutionalism.

iii. The Birth of the Modern Romanian State and the Reign of Alexandru Ioan Cuza

The Organic Regulations regime ended in the context of the diplomatic negotiations that followed the Crimean War (1853–56). Russia ceased to be a protecting power, and the Principalities came under the collective guarantee of the European powers. As a result, the influence of the Ottoman Empire as suzerain was considerably reduced, but this did not lead to internal constitutional reform, as had been requested in 1848. The European powers decided to send a committee to the Principalities, in order to take the pulse of Romanian society as regards political and administrative reorganisation. In 1857, on the basis of a popular vote, the so-called Ad Hoc Assemblies were established in Wallachia and Moldavia, in order to express the wishes of the Romanians. The main topic of debate, expressed by all the Romanian representatives, was the unification of the Principalities into a national unitary state, a favourite subject of all internal reform proposals since 1848.

The first problem was that of appointing a common head of state. The Ad Hoc Assemblies had expressly asked for a foreign prince, which seemed illogical in the context of the obsession with national unity and nation statehood. However, this preference for an external candidate was the result of the troubled history of the Romanian monarchy from the fourteenth to the nineteenth centuries, dominated by intense struggles for the throne between the local ruling houses. With a few important exceptions, most princes reigned for very short periods of time, and their deaths resulted in protracted fights between their successors. This was caused by the historical lack of established rules of succession: while the male-preference principle was well-defined, the rule of primogeniture was absent. Thus all legitimate and illegitimate sons of the late ruler had access to the throne and fought for it.

The reinstatement of local rule in 1821 reopened the matter, interrupted during the Phanariot reign. A section of the Romanian political class was conscious that a return to this state of affairs would endanger the national unitary state project. Therefore, the idea of a foreign prince within a hereditary monarchy, based on the primogeniture principle, was considered the best solution.

As regards the organisation and exercise of power, the Ad Hoc Assemblies of 1857 requested a parliamentary constitutional monarchy, contrasting with the extremely negative experiences of the neo-absolutist period and the arbitrariness of the Organic Regulations princes. The parliamentary regime thus became the desired political and legal tool to limit monarchical power, and also a constitutional solution designed to create a modern executive controlled by the parliament.

The result of the consultation of the Ad Hoc Assemblies was the *Paris Convention of 1858*, which ended up putting in place all that the Romanian political class wished to reject. The Convention was a classic expression of constitutional imperialism, and of the interests of and negotiations between the European Great Powers. As Turkey, Austria and Great Britain strongly opposed unification (fearing the eventual independence of the Principalities), they imposed a constitutional organisation that maintained two separate states with only a limited degree of integration.

The Convention, partly inspired by the French Constitution of 1852, was very far from expressing Romanian wishes for constitutional reform: instead of a national unitary state under the rule of one prince, the Convention set out plans for two states led by separate princes, united only at the level of certain secondary institutions; instead of a constitutional parliamentary monarchy, the Romanians were given a French-inspired authoritarian regime (caesarism);[2] instead of a foreign hereditary prince, they were given an elected Romanian prince; instead of a weak monarch, they were given a prince with exorbitant powers, head of the executive and with an absolute power of veto; instead of a strong parliament capable of limiting the monarch, they obtained a parliament with limited legislative powers. As a result, the other principles of liberal constitutionalism (national sovereignty, separation of powers,

---

[2] See for details, *Du césarisme antique au césarisme moderne* (Aix-en-Provence, Presses Universitaires d'Aix-Marseille, 1999) 80.

individual rights and freedoms, etc) were lost in the authoritarian constitutional design.

Nevertheless, the spirit of unification was so strong that it managed to put a stop to any separatist trend. The union was gradually achieved, through the policy of *fait accompli*. On 24 January 1859, the assemblies, appointed to elect two new princes, elected Colonel Alexandru Ioan Cuza as Prince (*Domn*) of both Principalities. In a tense diplomatic context, the Great Powers recognised the new association of states only for the duration of Cuza's reign. For his part, Prince Cuza favoured an intensely unionist policy. Thus, the Romanian national state was born: in December 1861 and January 1862 the two parliaments and governments merged. The capital of the new state was established in Bucharest.

As regards the internal political regime, Prince Cuza, a moderate liberal, endorsed the important ideological stream favouring the parliamentary regime. However, he did not manage to apply the principles of a parliamentary regime correctly, as he wished to recruit members of government according to his own political preferences. As a result, he appointed moderate-liberal governments led by prime ministers faithful to his own reformatory views. This generated a conflictual regime, marked by Cuza's permanent wish to politically control the Government and by the steady opposition of the Parliament, usually dominated by the Conservatives.[3]

Initially, Cuza accepted this situation, but the tensions grew, leading to institutional blockages: the need for a new constitutional solution became clear. As the Paris Convention could not be abolished, Cuza attempted its reform, but not in the spirit of a parliamentary regime, as the Prince had started to manifest authoritarian views, being an admirer of Napoleon III. As a result, the *Statute Developing the Paris Convention*, adopted by plebiscite in May 1864, almost literally transplanted the French constitutional model of the Second Empire. A central part was played by the Council of State (which copied its French counterpart) and by the *Corp Ponderator* (the future Senate), attached to the Elective

---

[3] The political structure of the successive parliaments was due to an electoral law that was annexed to the Convention and established a census of sex and a relatively high wealth census of voters and candidates. This led to the continuous domination of the parliaments by the great landowners who, although they had lost their titles and rank, remained the faithful successors of the former aristocracy.

Assembly as a second chamber, whose members were appointed by the Prince. The Government was completely subordinated to the Prince, and was given the right to rule by extraordinary legislation (decree-laws/*decrete-lege*) when the Parliament was not in session. New electoral laws were enacted, which considerably extended the right to vote by allowing access to the elective assembly of the representatives of the bourgeoisie and of the peasants. Nevertheless, in order to exercise complete control over the Parliament, Cuza launched, by means of his governments, systematic pressure and electoral manipulation, which became a true mark of parliamentary elections in modern Romania. In this climate, however, most of the reforms that founded the modern Romanian state were achieved, and Cuza became, in a more or less inspired comparison, 'Romania's Napoleon I'.

Notwithstanding the important steps taken towards modernising the Romanian state and society, Cuza's reign demonstrated once again that, with immature civil and political societies, reform of the state could only be made under an authoritarian regime. Carrying on the process of authoritarian personalisation of power was not accidental. This time, it was done within a relatively modern institutional frame, which subordinated the legislature to the executive. It was clear that the urgency for reform and the backwardness of Romanian society did not allow the political elite to wait to reach their own maturity and for the parliamentary regime's mechanisms to become embedded within the system. Therefore, the Romanian unitary state was not founded on parliamentarianism but against it.

iv.   The Constitutional Monarchy (1866–1938)

a. The Reign of Carol I

Despite the remarkable reforms achieved during his reign, the Romanian political elite of all persuasions started to become dissatisfied with Cuza's policy. He was subsequently forced to abdicate in 1866. Although the situation was not identical to that in 1859, the Great Powers maintained their interest in returning to the pre-unification position. An essential role was played by the Romanian Liberal Party in solving this new crisis, which was the party most interested in reviving the reformatory agenda of 1857. Thus, it reiterated the request to elect a foreign prince, and managed to maintain the 1866 status quo, with Prince Carol of Hohenzollern-Sigmaringen ascending the throne (from 1881, King Carol I). This was considered a true diplomatic achievement, meant to offer political guarantees to the Europeans and to ensure the survival of the unitary state.

In 1866 the first Romanian Constituent Assembly was organised, with the aim of elaborating the first modern Constitution of the Romanian national unitary state. The 1866 Constitution reaffirmed the attachment, expressed in 1857 by the political class (especially the Liberals), towards the values and principles of liberal constitutionalism. The Constitution responded, from an institutional point of view, to the specific problems of Romanian political life, by a massive and faithful transplant of provisions from the Belgian Constitution of 1831. Thus, the interest in the stability of the monarchy was reflected in the establishment of male-preference rules of primogeniture; the interest in avoiding authoritarianism was expressed through the entrenchment of the monarch's irresponsibility; the interest in consolidating the representative system of government was achieved via the formal establishment of a second chamber of the Parliament, now renamed the Senate. At the same time, the 1866 Constitution reflected the need to consolidate an ethnocentric constitutionalism with strong religious accents: the interest of the Orthodox Christians in securing the primacy of the Orthodox Church, and the concern for national unity and the majority ethnic group in that period, were reflected in the refusal to grant citizenship to non-Christians.[4]

Although still under Ottoman suzerainty (until 1878), Romania had, for the first time, the chance to have its own constitutional and political life, based on a Constitution emanating from the nation through its representatives. However, the values, principles, institutions and mechanisms transplanted from the Belgian Constitution established expectations that were difficult to meet for a young and inexperienced political class. The new Constitution created a dualist parliamentary regime, which should have been based on a stable political balance between a monarch actively involved in political life and a strong Parliament, underpinned by a mature political class emerging from ideologically solid political parties. Unfortunately, Romanian society at that time did not have the resources necessary to ensure such a balance: the political

---

[4] See Ch 6.

class was still dominated by the great landowners, the bourgeoisie was almost absent from society and the number of intellectuals was insignificant. The great majority of the population (around 80 per cent) was still composed of illiterate peasants. Some of them were given land during Cuza's reign and had an indirect right to vote, but they were, due to the high-wealth census mentioned above, kept out of true politics.

The political elite thus was inexperienced and ideologically confused. The main parties—the National Liberal Party and the Conservative Party—officially created in the 1880s, as yet had no solid doctrines. Both parties were controlled by strong political figures willing to become government leaders. This was not necessarily beneficial in a political climate dominated by immaturity and disregard for the true national interest. The competition between the two parties was exacerbated by internal struggles, giving rise to extreme instability in political life.

Because the reform agenda was endangered by permanent government instability, King Carol I reached the same conclusion as Cuza: if the Romanian political class was not capable of respecting the rules of the game, those rules would have to be changed. With this goal in mind, he waited neither for the political class to mature, nor for the parliamentary regime to become functional within Western parameters; instead he discreetly interfered with political life, gradually dominating it. In order to obtain a stable and functional government, he started a 'governmental rotation', by alternately calling to power the two main political parties, Liberal and Conservative. By the intense politicisation of the local administration, the government party managed to manipulate the parliamentary elections to ensure an absolute majority in Parliament. Although the much-desired stability was achieved, the encouragement, by King Carol I, of such practices, led to the idea of representative government becoming discredited. The Parliament had become an instrument of the executive. The King was closely involved in governmental politics and, due to his absolute power of veto and considerable political authority, he influenced almost all governmental decisions. Individual rights and freedoms were also subject to meddling: the right to vote was transformed into a mockery, and the freedom of the press and freedom of assembly were frequently restricted in order to protect the system of governmental rotation.

The most important consequence was the compromising of the 1866 constitutional transplant and the departure from values of liberal constitutionalism. If the objective of the constitutional transplant was the adaptation and practice of liberal constitutionalism within a dualist parliamentary regime, it could be said that it was a failure. The Romanian constitutional and political regime evolved towards a particular type of constitutionalism based on the principle of monarchical sovereignty. The importance, prestige and authority of the monarch, and his decisive influence and control over the executive and legislative powers during this period, led to monarchical sovereignty's precedence upon the national sovereignty.

On the other hand, the functional political mechanisms, as they were shaped by Carol I with the support of very active prime ministers, ensured the political stability necessary to the reforms. During Carol's long reign (over 48 years), Romania's economy developed considerably, as did education, culture and research. However, it still remained a society of contrasts, due to the great discrepancy between the urban and the rural worlds, as seen from the miserable lives of the huge mass of illiterate peasants (according to a 1912 census, around 60 per cent of the population was illiterate). In 1877, after a successful military campaign against the Turks, in alliance with the Russian armies, Romania proclaimed its independence, and in 1881 it became a kingdom.

b. The Inter-war Period (1918–38)

All these evolutionary events deeply influenced the constitutional and political life of the inter-war period (1918–38). During these two decades, spectacular positive transformations occurred, but equally some negative aspects continued to be apparent.

The period started with the birth of what is called 'Greater Romania', created by the unification of all Romanian-inhabited territories on 1 December 1918. The territory of the old kingdom doubled in size (from 138,000 square kilometres in 1915, to 295,000 square kilometres in 1918, the sixth largest European country in terms of territorial size; the population doubled from 7.9 million in 1915 to 14.7 million in 1919), as a result of unification with the Romanian territories previously under Hungarian, Austrian and Russian rule: Transylvania, Banat, Bukovina and Bessarabia. In the context of the demise of the Ottoman and Austro-Hungarian Empires, the Romanians (representing the majority population in these territories) expressed their will to unite with the Kingdom of Romania.

The event was of overarching importance for Romanian society, marked for decades by the obsession with building a national state. The unification of Transylvania with Romania in particular produced enormous patriotic enthusiasm in the old kingdom, in the face of scepticism on the part of the Transylvanian Romanian cultural elite. At the same time, the return of those territories that had been under foreign domination for centuries brought about the incorporation into the Romanian nation of important ethnic minorities (Hungarians, German Saxons, Russians).[5] In the context of the Transylvanian ethnic dialogue, the Transylvania Romanians had promised, by the founding act of the Great Union—the Resolution of the Great National Assembly, given in Alba Iulia on 1 December 1918 (*Rezolutia Adunarii Nationale de la Alba Iulia*)—that they would respect the administrative autonomy as well as the cultural and linguistic identity of the minorities. The Romanians from the old kingdom, displaying a remarkable ethnic homogeneity, were less willing to promote the interests of the ethnic minorities and more concerned with consolidating the unitary national state.

In this context, the unconditional application of the 1866 Constitution to the new territories was to be avoided. Greater Romania had to draw up a Constitution for the whole nation. As a result, a new Constitution was enacted in June 1923. More than 60 per cent of the new Constitution's text was taken from the 1866 Constitution, so it was more a constitutional amendment than an entirely new document. Some institutions that had been created by case law,[6] such as constitutional review, were included in the new constitutional text, as were institutions that featured in the specific context of the old kingdom after 1866, like land reform (distribution of land to peasants) and universal male suffrage. There were no provisions regarding the administrative autonomy or linguistic identity of national minorities. Generic equality before the law was granted, including on ethnic grounds, but the whole constitutional text promoted the interests of the ethnic majority, including from a religious point of view (the national Church).

Formally, the 1923 Constitution preserved all liberal constitutional values, as they had been intertwined, ever since 1866, with those of

---

[5] In 1910, the main ethnic composition of Transylvania was as follows: 53.8% Romanian, 31.6% Hungarian and 10.8% German (L Boia, *De ce este România altfel?* (Bucharest, Humanitas, 2013) 71).

[6] See Ch 5, section I.

nationalist, ethnocentric constitutionalism. The attachment to national sovereignty, representative government and a parliamentary regime was reiterated by the Constitution. But did constitutional life of the period reflect these values? The social, economic and political context was different from that in 1866, and the political class was no longer dominated by the descendants of the former aristocracy. But it must be emphasised here that although, after the 1989 Revolution, the interwar period was regarded as the 'golden age' of Romanian democracy, in reality it was far from that. Although the population doubled in size, and universal male suffrage considerably increased the number of voters, the political immaturity of the citizens was still remarkable, mainly because of the low level of education of the majority of the population. The clash between the rural and the urban worlds was illustrated by the high level of illiteracy in the former, and the situation did not improve until mid-twentieth century (until which point around half the population was illiterate or had completed only three school grades at most). Economically, things had evolved, but the urbanisation of Romania still lagged far behind the European average of the time. Even in the most prolific years of the pre-communist era (1938–39), the Romanian economy was among the least developed in Europe.

In these circumstances, the effects of such economic backwardness on the political life of Romania were serious and irreversible. Political pluralism and fresh political movements originating in the 'newer' parts of the country (Transylvania) could not change old customs left over from the pre-World War I period. The struggle for power took place within the same parameters serving group interests, with negative consequences for representative democracy: the mass of voters continued to vote for the governing party, who organised the elections without sparing resort to any means of pressure in order to reach its goals. The parliamentary majorities continued to be subordinated to the executive, whereas power continued to be personalised, centring around a unique, 'charismatic' leader (either the king or prominent prime ministers).

v. The Right-wing Dictatorships (1938–44)

In 1938, King Carol II instated what is now called the 'royal dictatorship', which meant the end of a failed democratic experiment in

Romania.[7] Political parties were abolished and a single official party was created—the National Rebirth Front. The new Royal Constitution of 1938 transferred rule of the country to the King. Paradoxically, the positive cultural and economic evolution of the period 1938–40 consolidated the new institutional context and prepared the ground for the launch of the 'cult of personality' in twentieth-century Romania.

In September 1940, the King abdicated in favour of his son, King Michael I. This did not mean the end of authoritarianism, however: the 1938 Constitution was suspended and power was seized by a military commander, Marshall Ion Antonescu, who ruled by decree. Officially declared 'Leader of the State', he justified his internal policy (with an anti-Semitic dimension) and his pro-German foreign policy by the wish to reunify the national territory, forcibly wrenched apart by the 1940 Diktat of Vienna. While the prerogatives of King Carol II had been extensive, King Michael I, although the holder of executive power, in practice had no control over the Government. He retained the right to appoint the President of the Council of Ministers, but this was exercised under pressure, which transformed the prerogative into a mere act of confirmation. The King was still politically irresponsible, all his decrees being countersigned by the Leader of the State. Thus, with the exception of a few symbolic powers of the King (head of the army, right to confer decorations), the Leader of the State appropriated all state powers, which transformed him into the centre of Romanian political life. In practice he exercised both legislative and executive powers, but, in contrast with the German *Führer* (whose model he copied), the Romanian Leader held no judicial power. This regime meant the end of the Romanian inter-war democratic era. The rise of the right-wing, pro-German dictatorship entailed the suspension of fundamental rights and the promotion of the ideas espoused by the Nazi regime in Germany, especially anti-Semitism, which was made concrete through discriminatory legislation, deportations and the killing of over 400,000 Jews.[8]

---

[7] An important part of the Romanian public law doctrine of the time (like Paul Negulescu) considered that the way in which liberal constitutionalism and parliamentarianism evolved in Romania, starting in 1866, only perpetuated the unfortunate combination of Western-imported constitutional forms with an unprepared Romanian substance (P Negulescu, *Tratat de drept administrativ român* (Bucharest, Atelierele Grafice ale Fundaţiei Culturale Voevodul Mihai, 1930) 93, at 106).

[8] *Report of the International Committee for the Study of Holocaust in Romania*, 11 November 2004. However, in 1942, the Romanian Government decided to reject the application of the 'Final Solution' in Romania.

B. The Communist Period

On 23 August 1944, Romania joined the allied forces against Germany, but the return to democracy was further away than ever. Although a decree of August 1944 restored the most important principles of the 1923 Constitution, the country was occupied by Soviet forces, and this led to the gradual establishment of a communist dictatorship. Under Soviet pressure, the communist Government of Petru Groza was installed on 6 March 1945. In 1946, this regime dissolved the Senate, and the elections for the Deputies' Assembly, organised later that year, were controlled and subsequently won by the communists. In the summer of 1947, the historic political parties were dissolved, and on 30 December 1947 King Michael I was forced to abdicate and the republic was proclaimed, under the official name 'The People's Republic of Romania'. The 1923 Constitution was abrogated and a new law was enacted to replace it until the adoption of a new fundamental law.

The country was run by a collective organ, Soviet-inspired, named the 'Presidium of the Republic', which comprised five members and had head-of-state-specific competences. Meanwhile, a new Parliament was elected, with a unicameral structure and named 'the Great National Assembly' (*Marea Adunare Nationala*, MAN), a body that was entrusted to prepare the draft of a new Constitution to embrace the newly installed order. There is little evidence about how the Assembly actually worked, but the 1948 Constitution was adopted one week after the start of debates on the draft. The text was drafted in emphatic language, specific to the communist propaganda, and proclaimed the existence of the 'people's state', born 'from the people's fight against fascism, reaction and imperialism'. One of the declared goals of the new Constitution was the elimination of the 'exploiting classes' and the 'building of socialism'. The Constitution ensured a legal basis for the nationalisation of industry, trade and of private property in buildings and lands, as 'land belongs to the ones who work it' and 'the means of production belong either to the state or to the cooperative organisations'.

In 1952, a new Constitution was enacted, to reflect other newly established realities. The nationalisation of buildings and land had been completed, and for the first time the 'leading roles' of the working class and of the Communist Party (officially named the 'Romanian Working Party') were constitutionally recognised. The new regime was defined as a 'popular democracy', and the power belonged to 'the workers from towns and villages, who exercise it through the Great National Assembly and the Popular Councils'. Although rights and freedoms were listed in the Constitution, they were not actually respected—especially as regards the freedoms of thought, of speech and of assembly. It was the period in which the most prominent representatives of the inter-war elite were arrested, accused of acting against the socialist order, and incarcerated in communist prisons, where they were subjected to a regime of extermination. Previously, starting in 1945, under Soviet influence, tens of thousands of Romanian citizens of German origin were deported to work camps in the USSR, and tens of thousands of Romanians from the Soviet-occupied territories were deported to Siberia.

The last communist Constitution was enacted in 1965, and it coincided with the final establishment of a totalitarian regime in Romania, based on the elimination of private property, on the installation of the single party as 'the political leading force of the entire society' and on serious violations of virtually all first-generation human rights. The state was given a new name—the Socialist Republic of Romania—and was defined once again as 'state of the workers from towns and villages'. The state organisation was similar to that established in the previous Constitutions, with two 'supreme' organs: a Great National Assembly as 'supreme organ of state power and sole legislator', and a Council of State as 'supreme organ of state power with permanent activity'. In 1974, the position of President of the Republic was created[9] and the personal dictatorship of Nicolae Ceauşescu commenced, leading to the most atrocious Eastern European totalitarian regime of the time. With the help of the political police—*Securitatea*—Ceauşescu and his close collaborators, including his wife, who was promoted to the highest political and state positions, instigated a regime of terror, a cult of personality and human rights violations. The centralised economy was producing mainly for external markets, while the population was deprived of food and basic facilities like electricity, heating and running water, all rationalised for the purpose of paying the external debts of the country. Constitutional rights and freedoms existed only on paper, as there was no free press, no free speech (an elaborate system of censorship was established) and no private life (as the political police had created a sophisticated surveillance system in order to identify potential

---

[9] See Ch 3.

'enemies' of the regime). According to the official report of the Commission that investigated the crimes of the communist regime in Romania,[10] there were over 2 million victims.

All these constitutional and institutional developments took place in the context of a deeply divided and antagonised society. The old saying used by the communists, 'whoever is not with us, is against us', was unfortunately applicable throughout the whole of Romanian social life: the political activists and appointees from the nomenklatura, who had access to all facilities, versus the ordinary citizens, who had to stand in line for hours to buy the bare necessities; the political dissidents, repressed by the regime, versus the 'official' intellectuals—members of the Communist Party, some of whom were collaborators with the political police; the majority of the population versus those Romanians who managed to escape the country; the workers and peasants versus the intellectuals, etc. The mindset encouraged by such stark discrimination was unfortunately perpetuated after the fall of the Iron Curtain, and is still characteristic of the Romanian society on different levels and with different subjects, but all with the same passion. This was the broad picture of Romania at the end of 1989, when, due to political changes all over the world and to the new policy of the Soviet Union under Mikhail Gorbachev, the country was touched by the wind of change and the December Revolution started.

C. The 1989 Revolution and the Post-Communist Period

i. The 1989 Revolutionary Moment

The December 1989 Revolution was the ultimate response of Romanian society to the abuses of the communist regime. Romanian was the last Eastern European nation to rise up against tyranny. Although it started as a reaction to the repression of the Timisoara anti-communist demonstrations of 16–17 December 1989, the Revolution was not, at the beginning, altogether anti-communist. The first and most important goal was the overthrow of Ceauşescu and his regime. But the

---

[10] *Report of the Presidential Commission for the Study of the Communist Dictatorship in Romania*, 2006, available at http://www.presidency.ro/static/ordine/RAPORT_FINAL_CPADCR.pdf.

popular movement, backed by the 'coup-d'état'-type involvement of former communist leaders (like Ion Iliescu, who became the first post-revolutionary president of the country) in the revolutionary stream, rapidly shifted to a profound anti-communist message and transformed it into a massive cry for freedom. This was a wholly natural evolution, as Ceauşescu's regime was so intimately linked with communism that it was impossible to overthrow one without the other. Therefore, the first revolutionary declaration of 22 December 1989, the 'Address to the Country of the National Salvation Front' (*Comunicatul către ţară al Frontului Salvării Naţionale*),[11] proclaimed immediately after the flight of the dictator and his entourage from the governmental palace, expressly called for, as well as the 'fall of the Ceauşescu clan', the installation of a pluralist democratic regime, based on the separation of powers, to grant individual freedoms and to integrate Romania with the 'united Europe'.[12] The Address also proclaimed the dissolution of the old power structures and the abolition of the 1965 constitutional establishment, with emphasis on the need to adopt a new constitution.

A 'mini-constitution' and electoral law were adopted by Decree-Law no 92/1990 on the election of Parliament and of the President of Romania, which also covered the rules on the organisation of the elected organs and provided that the newly elected Parliament should adopt a new constitution. The first democratic and free elections were organised in May 1990, and were based on the principle of proportional representation, which gave the NSF a huge advantage. There was a huge turnout rate (over 86 per cent of the voters). The NSF won over

---

[11] The National Salvation Front (NSF) was an ad hoc organisation of the revolutionaries, with territorial branches, which became a political party in January 1990. As a result of the other political parties' protests against the dangers of a new single-party system, the provisional legislative organ created in December 1989, the 'Council of the National Salvation Front', changed its name and structure and became the 'Provisional Council of National Union' and continued to adopt decree-laws until May 1990, when the first post-communist Parliament was elected. For further details of the NSF's transformation into a political party, see R Weber, 'Constitutionalism as a Vehicle for Democratic Consolidation in Romania' in J Zielonka (ed), *Democratic Consolidation in Eastern Europe* (Oxford, Oxford University Press, 2001) 213–17.

[12] Available at http://www.historia.ro/exclusiv_web/general/articol/comunicatul-ara-al-consiliului-fsn-22-decembrie-1989.

70 per cent of the seats, which would have allowed it to impose any constitutional text. However, it was decided to follow a more transparent and pluralist procedure, involving all political forces represented in Parliament. Two months later, a constitutional committee started work on the new constitutional draft.

The period following was marked by great political and social instability, exacerbated by serious economic problems (inflation, failed attempts to 'privatise' the former public enterprises, bankruptcies, high levels of unemployment and impoverishment) and by anti-democratic movements like the miners' riots in Bucharest in June 1990 (the miners were allegedly called by the President Iliescu to help in repressing the civil society protests against Iliescu and the NSF, which lasted for months in the University Square) and in September 1991. The rising extreme-left nationalist movements attempted to discourage from participation in public life any 'outsiders' who did not 'eat soya salami'[13] (ie politicians and intellectuals who had returned from exile, including the members of the Royal House of Romania). The antagonistic and conflictual character of the communist society was preserved, with periodical shifts of emphasis on different controversial issues. This inevitably affected political life, including the law- and constitution-making process. The rapid adoption of the Constitution was seen as a solution to these difficulties, as it was considered a 'ticket to democracy' and to international recognition of the new Government's legitimacy.

Because of all of these factors, Romania was left behind, in the race to be accepted into the European organisations, by other Eastern European nations—post-communist countries with better economic and political situations at the start of the transition process, like Poland, Hungary or the Baltic states. The long-awaited accession to NATO, in 2004, and to the European Union (EU), in 2007, should have officially completed the transition, but the existence and preservation of the European Commission's Cooperation and Verification Mechanism (CVM)[14] seems to prove that, on the contrary, the main problems are still there and Romania has to make more efforts to solve them.

---

[13] The epitome of the hard life under communism, soya salami was an almost artificial food product that was (scarcely) made available to the population, in Ceauşescu's frenzy to pay all the country's external debts.

[14] See Ch 1, section I.G.

ii. The Constitution-making Process

Between 22 December 1989 and 8 December 1991, Romania did not have a constitution. Following the May 1990 elections, the new Parliament (and Constituent Assembly at the same time) adopted rules for the constitution-making process. First, a Committee for Drafting the Project of the Constitution was elected. The Committee comprised 21 members—deputies and senators from all parties represented in Parliament (the great majority thus belonging to the NSF) and, without voting rights, five experts in public law.

The Committee decided to undertake a two-phase process: first, to develop the so-called 'Draft Articles of the Constitution'—a set of ideas, principles and mechanisms to be submitted to the debate of the Constituent Assembly; and, secondly, based on the results of the first debate, to develop the 'Project of the Constitution'—again to be debated and adopted by the Assembly. The third stage was the approval referendum, as provided by the electoral law.

There were no round-table negotiations concerning the Constitution Project, but the composition of the Drafting Committee—representatives of all parliamentary parties, dominated by the NSF, which had an absolute majority in both chambers—as well as its presidency (the independent senator Iorgovan, professor of public law) did not support claims that all the ideas included in the 'Draft Articles of the Constitution'/*Tezele Proiectului de Constitutie* and in the final project were imposed by the political majority.

Those drafting the Constitution included democratic principles and ideas in the first proposal submitted to the Assembly, which, for whatever reasons (commitment to democracy or eagerness to improve the image of the new regime)[15], accepted them, including some amendments suggested by the political minority. In spite of the lack of power enjoyed by the opposition and pressure in political circles (especially from President Iliescu and the Government), the Committee managed to tackle most major controversial issues and to put together a well-documented proposal, not least because the independent experts were highly respected and their voices were heard. This was also due to the contacts the Committee had developed with foreign experts, non-governmental organisations (NGOs) and international organisations.

---

[15] Weber (n 11), at 218.

In July 1990, a request was sent to the Council of Europe to send experts to Romania in order to assist in the constitution-making process.[16] A delegation, comprising members of the European Commission for Democracy through Law (the Venice Commission) and law professors from European universities, arrived in October 1990. United Nations experts from Geneva also acted as advisers. Members of the Committee made official visits to public institutions in Italy, France and Spain in order to collect information and possible sources of inspiration. The Draft Articles were almost simultaneously translated into French, in order to be subsequently presented at the meetings of the Venice Commission. Therefore, a spirit of openness, and at the same time a wish for the approval of the European bodies, was obvious. Comparative law, in rather empirical forms, was also used in the drafting process, and constitutional texts of other post-communist countries from the same period were considered.

The most controversial issues the Committee had to tackle (and the subject of subsequent pressure and constraints) were: the form of government (monarchy *or* republic) and, in the latter case, the type of republic (parliamentary *or* semi-presidential); the structure of the Parliament (bicameral *or* unicameral); the relationship between the legislative and the executive (subordination *or* equality); the powers of the President; the establishment or not of a Constitutional Court; and the catalogue of rights (how extensive it should be). If in most cases there was room for negotiation (eg the solution for judicial review), the form of government, involving the preservation of the republic, was imposed by the NSF. Another extremely controversial issue was the request by the representatives of the Hungarian minority to introduce rights of autonomy for 'national communities'. The amendment was rejected by an overwhelming majority, as it was contrary to the national and unitary character of the state. However, the right to identity, including political representation of persons belonging to national minorities, was accepted without amendment.

Regarding institutional design, tradition was fiercely invoked, but it did not find acceptance in all cases: it was accepted with respect to

---

[16] At the same time, Romania was subject to a monitoring process following its request to be accepted as a member of the Council of Europe. The Report produced by Alphonse Spielmann and Jochen A Frowein mentioned the cooperation with the Council of Europe in the process of constitution-making.

the bicameral structure of the Parliament, as a reconnection with the tradition of the pre- and inter-war periods, but was rejected in connection with constitutional review[17] (which, under the 1923 Constitution, was left to the supreme court of the land) or as regards the form of government.

The first phase undertaken by the Committee ended in November 1990, when the Draft Articles were submitted to the Assembly. The plenary debates took place in the first half of 1991. In July 1991 the Project was taken forward and the final round of Assembly debates started. On 21 November 1991, the new constitutional text was adopted by the Constituent Assembly with an overwhelming majority of 81 per cent. On 8 December 1991, a referendum was organised for the approval of the new fundamental law, which passed with 77 per cent of the votes cast.

The period 1991–2015 was dominated by three major themes that will be covered by the following chapters: (i) the obsession with European integration, (ii) European law as a source of constitutional law and (iii) the need to revise the Constitution. In 2003, this need was embodied in the first constitutional amendment law, which included, alongside changes made necessary by the coming accession to the EU, other changes determined by political interests. In 2011 and 2013, two amending projects failed to be adopted.[18]

III. CONCLUSION: THE DYNAMICS OF THE ROMANIAN CONSTITUTIONAL CULTURE

It is difficult to speak of a modern Romanian constitutional culture, born in the nineteenth century and maintained organically up to the present time. Throughout this time, Romania recognised three main periods from the point of view of constitutional evolution, which, without being completely isolated from one another, gave separate

---

[17] In this case, comparative law arguments, in the context of the widespread influence of the European model of constitutional review, were decisive. However, the potential political dependence of a Constitutional Court, as opposed to an ordinary supreme court, might have influenced the decision of the political majority in the Constituent Assembly. In any case, the Romanian reading of the Kelsenian model was, at the beginning, a truncated one (see Ch 5).

[18] See Ch 7.

meanings to the ideas, theories, values, mentalities and ideals, but also to the institutions and practices regarding the Constitution and constitutionalism: the period between the beginning of the nineteenth century and the first half of the twentieth century, the communist period and the post-communist period.

A. The Pre-Communist Period

The first period, which was also the longest, brought about remarkable transformations at all levels, marking the passage to modernity of a society deeply anchored in the feudal past. Under a strong Western influence, a modern constitutional culture was created, dominated by a few contradictions between conflicting trends. First of all, the tendency to gradually assume the principles and values of liberal constitutionalism, at the level of ideas, ideals and theories, especially those inspired by French ideas, contrasted with the practice of this constitutionalism. Principles and values like limiting the state's political power, representative government, the separation of powers, human rights and freedoms did not find a clear and strong correspondence in the constitutional-political praxis. On the contrary, systematic electoral manipulation and fraud, the lack of interest in actually guaranteeing individual rights and freedoms, the executive's domination over the legislature, ideological confusion and the lack of political consensus marked the Romanian constitutional and political culture of the time. Even in the period of maximum flourishing (1859–1938), decisive reforms were made not in the context of the reasonable functioning of the highly-praised parliamentary regime, but under a more or less authoritarian one. An ideological stream, developed at the highest level (Cuza, Carol I, Carol II) periodically supported the idea that, within a backward Romanian society, modernisation had to be achieved by a strong executive, dominated by an authoritarian monarch. Hence, while at the ideological level, the supporters of the parliamentary regime outnumbered those of the authoritarian regime, at the practical level, authoritarianism gained leverage.

Another contradiction within the Romanian constitutional culture of the time was that between the liberal constitutionalism of Western European origin (adopted by the Romanian elite by the mid-nineteenth century) and the deeply ethnocentric and religious nationalism manifested in the second half of the nineteenth century and the first half of the twentieth century. Certainly, influenced by the French ideas, Romanian constitutionalism of the first half of the nineteenth century had been born liberal. As the 1848 moment and its ideals were left behind, the interest in limiting political power and in the separation of powers decreased, in favour of the idea of building a strong nation state; the interest in rights and freedoms diminished in favour of the idea of national unity; the idea of a political community was replaced by the idea of a community united by blood, language, history and (especially) religion: the ethnocentric Romanian constitutionalism had, until the inter-war period, a strong Orthodox Christian tone. The presence on the Romanian throne of a foreign prince from a European dynasty, originally meant to increase the international legitimacy of the new nation state, had become more important than any constitutional reform aimed at limiting monarchical authority.

All of these evolutions of Romanian constitutional culture can be understood better in the context of another contradiction: that between the mechanisms and outcomes of the constitutional transplant, on the one hand, and its presumed goals, on the other. The entire constitutional evolution of modern Romania depicts the central part played by legal transplant in building a modern body of constitutionalism. Although at first it was determined by the weak socio-political and economic context, constitutional transplant gradually became a central feature of Romanian constitutional culture and an explanation for further transformations. Even today, the 'importing mindset' explains a certain inconsistency in the Romanian constitutional identity.

Constitutional transplant as a defining element of Romanian constitutional culture was at first highly irrational. The Romanian political elite of the nineteenth century had very often transplanted constitutional institutions too swiftly and too slavishly from the French constitutional tradition, as well as more than was necessary, when they could have looked for solutions within the system. Nevertheless, this type of transplant had been the expression of an inner need of Romanian society of the time: rapidly overcoming its backwardness and radically modernising the state necessitated the adoption of the values and principles of Western constitutionalism. On the other hand, at the international level, the same approach had been justified by the urgency of consolidating the young state, which was permanently threatened by dismantling and annexation, as well as by the need to legitimise its new constitutional architecture.

The irrational character of the constitutional transplant is also reflected in the imbalance between expectations and actual consequences. The reforming elite deemed it sufficient to import institutions and norms (forms) in order to magically transform the Romanian substance and bring it closer to the cultural background of the exporting society (France). Thus, the constitutional transplant was successful as regards its external goals, but as for its internal ones, it was permanently doomed. Adapting newly imported Western institutions to the Romanian cultural background ultimately meant the significant distortion of the former, without the significant positive transformation of the latter.

Last but not least, there was a contradiction between the values, principles and institutions of Western constitutionalism and Romanian constitutional traditions. In the Romanian mindset of the time, it was more important to adopt a new institution from the West, in order to confer legitimacy on the system, than to perpetuate a Romanian constitutional institution to which Western circles might have objected. This approach did not exclude, however, the valuing of Romanian constitutional tradition to a certain degree, especially when trying to find roots for a new institution in Romania's constitutional past. However, even when it existed, the interest in constitutional identity could not eliminate the interest in constitutional import, and so finally a compromise occurred: the national constitutional identity consisted of the manner in which the imported institutions were adapted to the Romanian background.

B. The Communist Period

A significant part of the pre-communist constitutional culture was abandoned or 'frozen' during almost 50 years of communist rule. Although a certain continuity (especially as regards the transplanting mindset, the tendency to authoritarianism and ethnocentrism) can be detected, important transformations occurred. Thus, for instance, unlike the pre-communist political elite, who waited for the imported institutions to influence Romanian society, the communist elite carried out intense 'cultural engineering' by rapidly imposing on Romanian society the values and principles of soviet constitutionalism.

This process was based on forced 'education' and re-education, with a highly propagandist character, but it was efficient, with the aid of repression, to inculcate the 'new values' into society: the former attachment to the monarchy became an attachment to the republic, the parliamentary regime was replaced by the 'popular regime', political pluralism by single-party ideology, etc.

C. The Post-Communist Period

After 1989, the revolutionary basis of the new constitutional order meant radical changes in the perception and evolution of the constitutional culture: rejecting communism and its totalitarian facets led to the rejection of every value, principle, ideal, mindset or practice, significant under communism. New democratic principles and values, inspired by contemporary Western constitutionalism, were introduced into the public discourse and called for a new constitutional architecture. However, even if we were to consider these revolutionary expectations as the roots of a post-communist constitutional culture, it could hardly be depicted as a brand new one after 1989: the old, pre-communist constitutional traditions were reactivated to fill the cultural and ideological void created by abrogating the former constitutional order.

The 'ideals of the Revolution', however, were not constitutionally recognised until 2003, more than a decade after the adoption of the new Constitution. At the same time, Article 1 §3 of the Constitution was amended in order to introduce, alongside the 'ideals of the Revolution', another 'common denominator' to interpret the most important constitutional values—the 'democratic traditions of the Romanian people'—both of them intended to outline a post-communist constitutional culture. However, at least at the level of constitutional practice, one of of the 1989 ideals was not reflected: if we count among those ideals a total break with the totalitarian past, including forbidding former members of the higher communist political structures to occupy public positions in the new democracy, this was never achieved in contemporary Romania. Furthermore, there has been no coherent public, nor even academic, discourse regarding what pre-communist constitutional tradition might mean: as can be observed from above, the 'unorthodox' evolutions from the pre-World War II period deserved a more critical approach than being placed on a golden pedestal. Even the

Constitutional Court, since 2003, has made very few references to these traditions. Therefore it is legitimate to claim that their inclusion in the Constitution had a mere declarative meaning, a formal acknowledgement of the existence of a Romanian constitutional identity, and that it was not the expression of certain particular and effective constitutional features. As before, the Romanian political elite were more interested in the idea of a constitutional identity than in its actual content.

As in other countries in the region, after the demise of communism the direction of the new constitutional culture in Romania was hesitant and inconsistent. The building of a new constitutional culture has been influenced by multiple factors like, for instance, the need for a truly democratic adjustment of political behaviour. In reality, from the outset, the main feature of the 'new' political class was mimicking commitment to the rule of law and democracy, and the expected contribution of the judiciary and of the Constitutional Court was tentative and feeble.

In terms of constitution-making, borrowing principles, values and institutions from the West was the main trend. In the presence of an importing mindset and of the rebirth of the older inferiority complex, as well as of the urgent need for international legitimisation (increased-doubled by recent pressures from Western powers), recourse to constitutional transplant was once more inevitable. The result was not a perfect Constitution but the best that the drafters could create at that moment, in that uncertain context and with the tools available:

> [T]he 1991 Constitution was the best that could be done. Given the political climate in 1994 or 1995, when nationalist-extremist parties were not only in parliament but also in the government and when the ruling party acted more and more in an authoritarian way, it seems clear that a more liberal constitution could not have been adopted.[19]

The constitutional text is, therefore, an imperfect compromise between the traditional nationalist constitutionalism, with ethnocentric shading, ideologically attached to the idea of the nation state, and the requirements of contemporary pluralist constitutionalism.

Over the years, the Constitution and national constitutional culture suffered from the same problem encountered in virtually all post-communist countries, politicisation of constitutional interpretation,

---

[19] Weber (n 11), at 241.

which sometimes went 'against the very grain of constitutionalism'.[20]
Exacerbated by the politicisation of the potential rectifier of unconstitutional behaviour—the Constitutional Court—this led to a constitutional system with numerous contradictions and malfunctions. Setting
constitutional limits has always been a problem, but also a necessity, in
order to ensure that Romanian decision-makers observe the constitutional and legal rules. On the other hand, contradictions mark the functioning of the key constitutional institutions: the Romanian Parliament
is constitutionally designed as the supreme organ of the country, but in
practice it prefers a secondary role—to rubberstamp legislation made
by the Government; the office of President is designed to be weak, but
in practice the President has often assumed an active role in politics
('player-president'), rather than the 'referee' role attributed by the Constitution; the judiciary was given a tool to render inapplicable legislation
contrary to human rights, but it did not use it for two decades; the Constitutional Court is designed as a Kelsenian 'negative legislator', but it
interfered actively with law-making work, exceeding its jurisdiction. All
these aspects will be explored in the following chapters of this book,
with an in-depth analysis of the context in which they became apparent.

FURTHER READING

A Albi, *EU Enlargement and the Constitutions of Central and Eastern Europe*
(Cambridge, Cambridge University Press, 2005).

D Deletant, *Romania under Communist Rule* (Oxford, Center for Romanian
Studies, 1999).

T Gallagher & V Andrievici, 'Romania: political irresponsibility without
constitutional safeguards' in R Elgie & S Moestrup (eds), *Semi-presidentialism in Central and Eastern Europe* (Manchester, Manchester University Press, 2012).

M Guṭan, 'The Challenges of the Romanian Constitutional Tradition: II.
Between Constitutional Transplant and (Failed) Cultural Engineering'
(2013) 26 *Journal of Constitutional History* 217.

——, 'The Challenges of the Romanian Constitutional Tradition: I.
Between Ideological Transplant and Institutional Metamorphoses'
(2013) 25 *Journal of Constitutional History* 223.

---

[20] R Ludwikowski, 'Constitutional Culture in the New East-Central European
Democracies' (2000) 29(1) *Georgia Journal of International and Comparative Law* 21.

——, 'Le droit comparé contemporain et l'actualité de la théorie des "formes sans fond" en Roumanie' (2013) 3 *Revue de droit international et de droit comparé* (Bruxelles: Bruylant, 2013) 427.

——, 'Building the Romanian Modern Law—Why is it Based on Legal Transplant?' (2005) biss *Acta Universitatis Lucian Blaga, Seria Jurisprudentia*, English edn.

K Hitchins, *A Concise History of Romania* (Cambridge: Cambridge University Press, 2014).

——, *Romania 1866–1947* (Oxford: Clarendon Press, 1994).

AE Dick Howard, 'Constitution-Making in Central and Eastern Europe' (1994) 28 *Suffolk University Law Review* 5.

B Iancu, *Constitutionalism in Perpetual Transition: The Case of Romania, in The Law/Politics Distinction in Contemporary Public Law Adjudication* (The Hague, Eleven International Publishing, 2009).

F Julien-Laferrière, 'La Constitution roumaine de 8 décembre 1991 ou le difficile apprentissage de la démocratie' (1993) 5 *Revue du droit public et de la science politique en France et à l'étranger* 1217.

RR Ludwikowski, 'Constitutional Culture of the New East-Central European Democracies' (2000) 29(1) *Georgia Journal of International and Comparative Law* 21.

ES Tănăsescu, 'Modern Romanian Constitutionalism under the Influence of EU Accession' (2011) I *Rivista di diritto pubblico comparato ed europeo* 225.

T Verheijen, 'Romania' in R Elgie (ed), *Semi-Presidentialism in Europe* (Oxford, Oxford University Press, 1999).

R Weber, 'Constitutionalism as a Vehicle for Democratic Consolidation in Romania' in J Zielonka (ed), *Democratic Consolidation in Eastern Europe* (Oxford, Oxford University Press, 2001).

1

Constitution, Nation and State

———◆◆◆———

Constitutional Sources – Sovereignty – Referendums – Citizenship – The National State

I. CONSTITUTION AND CONSTITUTIONAL LAW

THE CONSTITUTION OF Romania (CR) is the supreme law of the land and lies at the centre of the Romanian legal system. As in most Romano-Germanic legal systems, the constitutional system itself is a very formal one, based almost entirely on written norms and with little legal weight given to custom and judge-made law. The origins of this formalism, as has been shown in the historic introduction to this book, can be traced back to the first 'modern' constitutional acts, especially starting with 1864 and then with the first Romanian Constitution of 1866. The hierarchical structure (with the Constitution as the supreme law) was not obvious from the beginning, as the constitutional review of legislation was not expressly provided for by the 1866 Constitution but introduced by the courts in 1912 and then formally by the 1923 Constitution. This chapter will provide introductory ideas on the sources of the constitutional system, as well as on its main foundational concepts and principles: nation, people and sovereignty. The main features of the state will be examined (nation state, democracy, rule of law) and, in the last section, a brief overview of the institutional architecture will be provided.

A. The Constitution: Formal and Substantive

The hierarchical structure of the constitutional system does not exclude recognition of a French-inspired distinction between the formal and substantive Constitution. Thus whereas the 'formal' Constitution means the actual document, adopted by a special organ, using a special procedure and with a superior binding force, the 'substantive' one represents the ensemble of rules relating to the existence and exercise of state power: constitutional norms, electoral laws, international human rights rules, constitutional case law. This formal–substantive distinction also covers the matter of the constitutional source system. The formal hierarchy of sources, entrenched and praised by Hans Kelsen in his general legal theory, is not only reflected in the system, but also expressly provided for in the constitutional text: 'the observance of the Constitution, of its supremacy and of the laws is compulsory' (Article 1 §5). The term 'supremacy' introduces the idea of a hierarchy, which also results from other constitutional and legal rules.

B. Organic and Ordinary Laws

Laws are understood as the acts of Parliament, situated at the second level of legal binding force below the Constitution. However, several constitutional texts refer to 'organic laws' as a special category. They are considered to be laws of greater importance, regulating broader or essential fields, designed to complement the Constitution by regulating in detail the regime of the most important institutions. The nature of this category is neither explained nor defined, but is to some extent inspired by French law. The organic laws are simply mentioned in Article 73 §1 CR, which states that 'Parliament enacts constitutional, organic and ordinary laws'. The similarity with French organic laws ends here, as there are neither detailed procedural requirements for introducing such laws, nor any compulsory *a priori* constitutional review.

The Romanian Constitution does not set a general ordinary law domain/*domaine de la loi*. This means that the Parliament is not limited in its legislative competence. The Constitution only establishes the fields of organic laws in the third paragraph of Article 73. The list is quite heterogeneous, covering: essential fields on the political stage, such as the electoral system and the political parties, the regime applicable to states of siege, war and emergency; and general fields like property, education and 'the organisation of local public administration', but also more particular issues like administrative litigation and labour relations. In one field no organic law has yet been enacted (the status of national minorities). The list is open-ended, as it acknowledges that there are other fields which may be regulated by organic law, as referred to in the Constitution (such as the Romanian citizenship, the Constitutional Court, the Ombudsman etc).

The special nature of organic laws also results from their adoption procedure. The majority required for their adoption by Parliament is higher than in the case of ordinary laws, being the majority of the total number of the members of the two chambers of Parliament (whereas only a standard majority is required to pass ordinary legislation, ie 50 per cent plus one of the Members of Parliament (MPs) present in session).

Organic laws are supposed to be more stable and therefore less subject to political whims, but they are still in need of evolution and updating. The most recent important organic laws are the new codes (Civil Code, Criminal Code, Code of Civil Procedure and Code of Criminal Procedure), which entered into force in a very short period of time (around two to three years, after a long period of drafting) and replaced the old codes (amongst which were the Civil Code, enacted in 1864, and the Criminal Code from 1965).

C. Government Ordinances (*Ordonante de Guvern*)

Delegated legislation is considered a 'necessary evil' in contemporary democracies. Romania is no exception, and the Constitution provides for two types of delegated legislation: Government Ordinances (GOs) and Emergency Government Ordinances (EGOs). Both types are acts adopted by the Government based on direct or indirect delegation from Parliament. As a result, the ordinances have the legally binding force of laws. Government Ordinances are adopted by virtue of an enabling law, enacted by Parliament and expressly giving the Government this competence. Emergency Government Ordinances do not need an enabling law; they are adopted by the Government by virtue of a constitutionally granted power, but theoretically only 'in exceptional cases, the regulation of which cannot be postponed, and [the Government has] the obligation to give the reasons for the emergency status within their contents' (Article 115 §4 CR). In practice, the emergency requirement has frequently been disregarded by the Government, and EGOs have been used simply to circumvent Parliament. As both types of ordinances are submitted to parliamentary approval, this 'vice' of many EGOs has merely been covered by a subsequent parliamentary vote.[1] The use and abuse of ordinances was criticised on various occasions by the European Commission in its CVM reports,[2] as well as by the Venice Commission in its opinions. For instance, the adoption of over 140 ordinances in only one year (2011) was considered by the Venice Commission to demonstrate a clear 'abuse of this instrument'.[3]

D. International Treaties: A Monist Incorporation

Romania chose the monist method of incorporating international law: by the automatic effect of the law of ratification, any international treaty becomes a part of domestic law (Article 11 §2 CR). The Constitution maintains its primacy, and no international treaty may be ratified if contrary to its provisions, unless the Constitution itself is amended. This once again proves the monist vision, as ratification is subject to the domestic legal hierarchy. Ratified human rights treaties have a privileged position: besides being a part of domestic law, they have priority over infra-constitutional legislation. Moreover, constitutional provisions on fundamental rights and freedoms must be interpreted and applied according to the international treaties on human rights ratified by Romania. It is common in most post-communist countries' constitutions to give precedence to international human rights law, with a special emphasis on the European Convention on Human Rights (ECHR). Post-communist Romania followed this trend, inspired by the French

---

[1] See Ch 3.

[2] See section I.G. below. COM(2013) 47, *Final Report from the Commission to the European Parliament and the Council on progress in Romania under the Cooperation and Verification Mechanism,* Brussels, 30 January 2013, 3.

[3] CDL-AD(2012)026, European Commission for Democracy through Law (Venice Commission), *Opinion on the compatibility with constitutional principles and the rule of law of actions taken by the government and the parliament of Romania in respect of other state institutions,* Venice, December 2012, §11.

(but not entirely, as France gives priority to all ratified international treaties) and Spanish models.[4] The priority of international law of human rights is subject to the principle of subsidiarity (ie is applicable with the exception of more favourable provisions of internal law). Such treaties are considered to have a supra-legislative binding force but an infra-constitutional one.[5]

E. Complementary Sources: Case Law of the Constitutional Court and the European Court of Human Rights

Two sources complementary to the constitutional law system have gained importance over recent years. Although they do not formally have normative binding force, they have managed to become a part of the interpretative source system. These are: the decisions of the Constitutional Court,[6] due to their general binding effect (*erga omnes*); and the decisions of the European Court of Human Rights (ECtHR), due to the ECHR's priority in domestic law and to the importance of the Strasbourg Court's case law in defining Convention terms. The status of these complementary sources is now so high that, in the current process of constitutional change, they have, along with the opinions of the Venice Commission, been the sources most frequently cited to underpin the necessity for changing constitutional texts. However, this started to happen only after 2003, when the Constitution was amended to expressly provide for its own direct applicability (Article 1 §5) and the mandatory *erga omnes* effects of the Constitutional Court's decisions on unconstitutionality. The judges were also initially quite reluctant to apply the case law of the ECtHR. It can be said that, although the Constitution is monist as regards international law, Romanian judges are dualist, even in implementing the national Constitution.[7]

---

[4] Art 10 §2 of the Spanish Constitution states that 'the rules referring to fundamental rights and public freedoms recognised by the Constitution shall be interpreted in conformity with the Universal Declaration on Human Rights and with the treaties and agreements ratified by Spain'.

[5] See Ch 6.

[6] See Ch 5.

[7] See also chs 5 and 6.

F. Marginal Sources: Ordinary Case Law, Doctrine, *Travaux Préparatoires*

Judicial decisions of ordinary courts (ordinary case law) do not have the force of precedent in the Romanian legal system. For a long time, judicial decisions (jurisprudence) were applied *inter partes litigantes*, having no binding force apart from in the cases in which they were pronounced, even as regards the same court. Only in the last few years, under pressure following a few judgments from Strasbourg, has judicial consistency been considered by Romanian courts, as well as judicial precedent, but even then only as having persuasive force. The only decisions having a compulsory effect on all ordinary courts in the system are two types of High Court decision: preliminary rulings on 'solving a matter of law' (newly introduced by the new Codes of Civil and Criminal Procedure), at the request of lower courts, on the interpretation of certain legal matters; and decisions on 'appeals on points of law' (*recurs in interesul legii*).[8] The effect of such decisions is, therefore, to unify divergent jurisprudence on a specific point of law, as the solution to the specific legal problem found in such decisions must be followed in all courts.[9]

Legal doctrine and the *travaux préparatoires* are still very marginal sources of legal interpretation. Law specialists are often called to form committees for drafting legislation, or to advise parliamentary committees, but actual legal doctrine is rarely used in constitution- and law-making, or in decision-making by the courts. The same is true as regards *travaux préparatoires*, which are mostly used by scholars and are rarely cited by the Constitutional Court in its reasonings.

G. EU Law in the Source System

Starting in 1993, as a result of the Association Agreement with the EU, Romania was trying to adopt the *acquis communautaire* and to 'Europeanise' its national law from an integration perspective. After joining the EU in 2007, Europeanisation became an obligation. The supremacy of EU law over national laws is provided for in Article 148 §2 CR, which

---

[8] See Ch 5.
[9] Art 517 §4 New Code of Civil Procedure.

states that, '[a]s a result of the accession, the provisions of the constituent treaties of the European Union ... shall take precedence over the [contrary] provisions of the national laws'. However, the text is not sufficiently clear on the status of EU law vis-à-vis the Constitution. In Europe, other strong constitutional courts decided this matter in favour of the national constitutions,[10] despite the view of the European Court of Justice that EU law should take precedence. The Romanian Constitutional Court (RCC), when confronted with the issue of the supremacy of EU law over national law, adopted the view taken by other member states' constitutional courts, invoking an 'authority argument', not analysing the opportunity for such a solution in the Romanian case: 'the RCC judges assumed the *Solange*-type solution, but not the *Solange* mentality'.[11] This means that the Constitutional Court has not actually been concerned with the problem of Romanian constitutional identity, but only to find a technical solution to placing EU law within the legal system. Thus, EU law has, indeed, an infra-constitutional position, but a supra-legislative one.

Ever since its accession to the EU, Romania has been subject to a monitoring process—the CVM[12]—which aims to help the new member state to tackle its existing shortcomings and to achieve its most important aims in consolidating the democracy: independence of justice system and the fight against corruption. One of the main reasons for establishing the mechanism was that

> whilst noting the considerable efforts to complete Romania's preparations for membership, [the Commission] has identified remaining issues ..., in particular in the accountability and efficiency of the judicial system and law enforcement bodies, where further progress is still necessary to ensure their capacity to implement and apply the measures adopted to establish the internal market and the area of freedom, security and justice.[13]

---

[10] In Germany and Italy.

[11] For an in-depth analysis of the RCC's decision from a legal-cultural perspective, see M Guțan, 'The Infra-constitutionality of the European Law in Romania and the Challenges of the Romanian Constitutional Culture' in R Arnold (ed), *Limitation of Sovereignty by European Integration* (Heildelberg, Springer, forthcoming 2016).

[12] Commission Decision of 13.12.2006 establishing a mechanism for cooperation and verification of progress in Romania to address specific benchmarks in the areas of judicial reform and the fight against corruption, available at http://ec.europa.eu/enlargement/pdf/romania/ro_accompanying_measures_1206_en.pdf.

[13] ibid, preamble, (4).

The introduction of this supervisory mechanism as regards two new member states—Romania and Bulgaria—was a first in the history of the EU. The process is ongoing, and in Romania the results have started to show. The European Commission's annual reports are among those documents most eagerly awaited by politicians and civil society. The CVM itself has become an important informal source of legal changes, and is extremely influential on political and constitutional life. However, many politicians, especially parliamentarians, perceive the CVM as a strong irritant, mainly because of the strengthening of the anti-corruption system and the obvious influence of the mechanism on the increase in the number of high-level politicians convicted for corruption offences.

II. ROMANIAN NATION, SOVEREIGNTY AND CITIZENSHIP

A. The Romanian People as Sovereign

The Romanian Constitution makers of 1991, keen to achieve a strong democratic constitutional text, put the Romanian people at the centre of the constitutional architecture: the people are the locus of 'national sovereignty', wording that still exhibits an air of 'mystery', as it brings together two similar concepts: 'people' and 'nation'. In this context, the term 'people' was designed to mean the holder of sovereignty at a specific moment (ie the citizens of Romania, within or outside the national borders), whereas the 'nation' and 'national sovereignty' were seen as historic concepts, embodying the whole 'package' of traditional constitutional achievements so far.[14] Defining the people as the holder of power was not an easy mission because, from 1947 onwards, the term 'the people' (understood primarily as 'the working class') was used by the communist governments to underpin their totalitarian ideologies, depending on the historical context: during the 1950s the 'enemies of the people' had to be annihilated; all private property was nationalised and given to 'the people'; even the name of the country was, between 1947 and 1965, 'the Romanian People's Republic'. Paradoxically, the

---

[14] I Muraru, 'Articolul 2' in I Muraru & ES Tănăsescu (eds), *Constituția Romaniei. Comentariu pe articole* (Bucharest, CH Beck, 2008).

omnipresent 'people' had no actual rights within the constitutional and political regime, being completely subordinated to the power, decisions and repression of the Communist Party. In December 1989, the people rose up and overthrew the regime, during the now-constitutionalised Revolution. Therefore, 'the people' had to be awarded its rightful place in the new Constitution (Article 2), that is, as the holder of sovereignty, capable of exercising power through free and fair elections or by referendum.

The word 'nation' does not appear throughout the Constitution, which uses the broader term 'people' (all citizens, including those persons belonging to national minorities). However, the term 'national' is used around 40 times as a determinant of other concepts, but with different meanings. For example, 'national' primarily determines the state: Romania is a national state (*stat national*);[15] the sovereignty that belongs to the people as supreme constitutional actor is also 'national' (the same meaning is used in connection with 'national territory', 'national day', 'national anthem', 'national security', 'national budget' and even 'national interest'). Therefore the nation, although not expressly mentioned anywhere in the Constitution, remains the foundational concept for both the state and the people.

In the expression 'national minorities', the word 'national' is used to indicate the ethnic origin of the persons belonging to such minority groups, as opposed to a 'national majority'. 'National culture' refers to the whole cultural heritage of the country, including minority cultures, which are recognised as part of the right to identity.

In this context, some explanations should be offered as regards the ethnocentric language of the Constitution. At the constitutional moment in 1991, anxiety about totalitarianism was exacerbated by another strong national concern regarding the threat to the unity and territorial integrity of the state. This concern was amplified during the constitutional drafting process, and was added to the historical reasons for invoking national unity as the 'identity mark' of the Romanian state. Therefore, it triggered the wish to emphasise, in the constitutional text, the national character of the state, the unity of the people, and the integrity and indivisibility of the territory, and to carve them in stone for future generations via the limitations on constitutional amendment.

---

[15] See III.A.i. below.

This mentality, which is now partially extinct, was dominant amongst the politicians in 1991. It was inherited from a strong tradition, born during the historic struggle of Romanians to affirm and acquire national identity and statehood, of identifying everything that referred to the state with the nation in the ethnic sense. Therefore, the constitutional drafting committee

> had an extremely difficult task: to satisfy at the same time the wish of the majority to consolidate the nation state, the wish of the Hungarian minority to have territorial autonomy based on ethnic criteria and the wish of international society, that the post-communist countries would become post-modern states.[16]

As a result, the constitutional texts are a mixture of ethnocentric ('national' sovereignty, 'national' state) and pluralistic language (right to identity of persons belonging to national minorities, political representation of national minorities). The 2003 constitutional amendments added the right of persons belonging to minorities to use, in certain conditions, their mother tongue in their interaction with local civil services, but only as a result of political pressure from minority groups and negotiations. Even the inclusion, by the same 2003 amendments, of the words 'solidarity of the citizens … regardless of their ethnic origin' (Article 4) as one of the foundations of the state, was not the result of a change of mentality but of a compromise between the representatives of the Hungarian minority, who requested the removal of the expression 'national state' from the Constitution, and the political majority, who would not agree to that. Therefore, despite the more open-minded constitutional language, the ethnocentric mentality is still present, especially among the political class.[17]

In 2003, 'democratic traditions' were also included in the Constitution, as interpretative filters for the supreme constitutional values.

---

[16] DC Dănişor, *Libertatea în capcană* (Bucharest, Universul Juridic, 2014) 44.

[17] A significant example was the 2014 electoral campaign for the presidential elections, in which the governing party candidate (Acting Prime Minister Ponta) used the electoral slogan 'Proud to be a Romanian' and transmitted a strong message focused on his Romanian ethnicity and Orthodox Christian religion, as opposed to his main competitor, the Liberal politician Klaus Iohannis, of German Transylvanian origin and the Protestant religion. Iohannis was accused, by Ponta's supporters, of being a 'foreigner', of not being Orthodox and mainly of 'not being Romanian'.

These related more to 'national traditions' than to the functioning of democracy: to say otherwise would literally mean that Romanian identity is exclusively past-orientated, 'limiting any axiological option of future generations. By this, the living, dynamic, character of the constitutional culture would be destroyed'.[18] To increase the confusion, in the same apparent ethnically-protective tone, the Constitution prohibits, in Article 3 §4, foreign populations being displaced or colonised on the territory of the Romanian state. However, the constitutional text is not, all in all, ethnocentric in itself: it allows an opposite, pluralistic interpretation. What must be changed, therefore, is not the constitutional text but the ethnocentric mentality.

B. Citizenship

i. *Citizens and Nationals*

Those drafting the Romanian Constitution preferred the term 'citizenship' instead of 'nationality', the latter being more frequently used by other constitutions. In the inter-war period, nationality was defined as 'the unity of race, language, religion'[19] within a territorially and spiritually-defined nation. Therefore, nationality was seen as an individual ethnic feature, shared with other persons, whereas citizenship was a legal status: in other words, citizenship, as opposed to nationality, can be lost or withdrawn. This distinction has been maintained, with the nation as a foundation of the state and defined as the group of persons having in common the same nationality.

Because, during the communist age, the concepts 'co-inhabiting nationalities' and 'nationality' referred, including in official papers, to ethnic or national origin, in 1991, in order to avoid any discriminatory meaning, the constitutional legislator preferred to use the word 'citizenship' to describe the status of an individual in relation to the

---

[18] M Guțan, 'Transplantul constituțional și obsesia modelului semiprezidențial francez in România contemporană (I)' (2010) 5 *Pandectele Române* 53.

[19] P Negulescu, *Curs de drept constituțional român* (Bucharest, Alex T Doicescu, 1927) 70.

state. Thus, citizens of all 'nationalities' are part of the people and of the 'nation' as the foundation of the state. At the same time, Article 4 CR came with an important provision, with a view to eliminating any discriminatory interpretation: the state is based on the 'unity of its *people* and on the solidarity of its *citizens*' and 'Romania is the common and indivisible homeland of all its *citizens,* without any discrimination on account of race, *nationality, ethnic origin*' (emphasis added). Despite the understanding (common among the Romanian political class when the Constitution was drafted) of 'nationality' and 'ethnicity' as synonymous, the Constitution's drafters tried to overcome this mentality and avoid express references to it. The rather evasive wording that has been adopted was recently criticised by the Venice Commission, which stated that '[unity of the people] is a rather outdated notion, typical for instruments of the system prevailing in the country prior to its democratic transformation'.[20]

A particular feature, which comes from the same need to 'compromise' between *ethnos* and *demos,* is the constitutionalisation of a dual obligation of the state: to support all Romanians living abroad, regardless of their citizenship, and to protect all Romanian citizens abroad, regardless of their ethnic origin. On the one hand, a text written in an ethnocentric key underpins the relationship between the state and all ethnic Romanians: 'The State shall support the strengthening of links with the Romanians living abroad and shall act accordingly for the preservation of their ethnic, cultural, linguistic and religious identity' (Article 7).[21] This text emphasises a purely ethnic link between the state and its citizens, and is reminiscent of the nineteenth-century idea of 'nation' in the wider sense, which includes all persons having certain common 'national' features: ethnicity, culture, language, religion. This 'nation' cannot be mistaken for the 'people' who is the holder of sovereignty, as the latter excludes those Romanians living abroad who no

---

[20] CDL-AD(2014)010 Venice Commission, *Opinion on the Draft Law on the Review of the Constitution of Romania,* Venice, 21–22 March 2014, at 8.

[21] Art 7 served as constitutional basis for the legal provisions granting citizenship to all Romanians living abroad, who had never held Romanian citizenship but who could prove that their ancestors were Romanian citizens (up to the third degree of parentage). This was particularly so in the case of ethnic Romanians, citizens of the Republic of Moldova (formerly Bessarabia, part of the territory of Romania between 1918 and 1940).

longer hold Romanian citizenship. On the other hand, Article 17 CR sets forth the obligation of the state to protect all its citizens living or travelling abroad, regardless of their ethnic origin.

ii. Constitutional and Legal Aspects of Romanian Citizenship: Acquisition, Loss, Specific Rights

Romanian citizenship is considered the strongest expression of the bond between state and individual. Nevertheless, Article 5 CR makes only passing reference to the institution—'Romanian citizenship can be acquired, retained or lost as provided by the organic law'—and establishes the principle that the citizenship acquired by birth may not be withdrawn. The organic Law no 21/1991 established the *ius sanguinis* principle for acquisition of citizenship, a traditional principle in Romania, introduced by the 1864 Civil Code and maintained in subsequent legislation. The first detailed law on citizenship was adopted in 1924, and it perpetuated the inequalities established by the Civil Code (especially between men and women), as well as the possibility of acquiring the citizenship by way of marriage. The equality of men and women, as well as of children born in or out of wedlock, in matters of citizenship, was established in 1948, when marriage ceased to produce any legal effects upon citizenship. The following laws on citizenship were enacted in 1952 and 1971, the latter year introducing most of the principles that can be found in the present law.

There are two *de iure* ways of acquiring citizenship: by birth and by adoption (plus the special case of 'children found on the Romanian territory', who are presumed citizens by birth). Acquisition is also possible on request, in which case the legal requirements differ as between persons who have never held Romanian citizenship and persons who held it in the past but lost it. In order to be naturalised, for instance, a person must, among other requirements, such as a period of eight years' residence in Romania, know the Romanian language, prove sufficient knowledge of Romanian culture and civilisation, and know the provisions of the Romanian Constitution.

The status of citizen used to offer an extensive package of exclusive rights and duties. These rights were considerably nuanced following the country's accession to the EU in 2007. Thus, the right to vote and the right to be elected to some public positions, such as local representatives or Members of the European Parliament, no longer belong only to Romanian citizens but to EU citizens too. The right to acquire property in land, initially an exclusive right, was also affected by the accession: foreign citizens and stateless persons may only acquire private property in land under the terms resulting from Romania's accession to the EU and other international treaties to which Romania is a party, on a mutual basis, on the conditions stipulated by an organic law, as well as by lawful inheritance.[22] Since 2003, the right to be appointed to public office may belong to a person with dual citizenship. The right to vote in referendums still belongs exclusively to citizens, as do the duties of fidelity to the country and of defending the country. As a constitutional principle, Romanian citizens benefit from the state's protection abroad, but are still bound to fulfil those of their duties that are not incompatible with their absence from the country.

iii. Political Rights of Citizens

Romanian citizens have the right to vote, from the age of 18, when they acquire full legal capacity. Mentally disabled persons, placed under judicial interdiction, as well as persons subject to disenfranchisement by a final judgment, cannot vote. According to Article 61 CR, suffrage is universal, equal, direct, secret and freely expressed. These characteristics apply to all electoral calls: for Parliament, President, local authorities and European Parliament. Since Romania joined the EU in 2007, the right to vote has been extended from the strict category of 'Romanian citizens' to other EU nationals too, in the case of elections for Members of the European Parliament and local elections.

The right to be elected is subject to more requirements than the age of majority and legal capacity. These requirements differ depending on the body for which the right is being exercised. The only general exception from the right to be elected set by the Constitution is that of persons who are forbidden to join political parties according to Article 40 §3, that is, judges of the Constitutional Court, the ombudsman, magistrates, active members of the armed forces and of the police.

---

[22] This provision, although introduced in 2003, has been applied in full only since 1 January 2014; prior to that, the conditions imposed on foreign citizens acquiring land were more restrictive.

iv. Referendums

In contemporary democracies, the participatory dimension has become a *sine qua non*, even in the most conservative countries. The possibility to get involved in the legislative process, as well as to be consulted on matters of public interest, is now a regular part of the public status of citizens. The 1991 Romanian Constitution introduced, as tools of participatory democracy, direct democracy-related rights, that is, the rights to popular legislative initiative[23] and to vote in a referendum. The latter is a point of interest here as, although it has been used several times, the will of the people has not always been respected.

There are two kinds of referendum provided by the Constitution: consultative and binding. The new law on local administration also provides for the possibility of organising local referendums in certain circumstances.

A consultative referendum may be convened by the President, to ask the people to express their will on 'matters of national interest'. The Constitution is silent on the content of the notion: no matters are excepted from the possibility to call a referendum. It is certain, however, that such a referendum would not be constitutional if it were called to approve a law, as Parliament is the sole legislator according to the Constitution. This type of referendum has no binding effect, although it may be argued that, being an expression of the national sovereignty of the people, the 'will' expressed thereby should bind Parliament.

The second type of referendum is the binding (compulsory) one. Its compulsory nature applies both to its organisation and its effect: it must be organised in certain situations prescribed by the Constitution and its effect is legally binding. The two circumstances in which such a referendum must be organised are:

1. for approval of draft constitutional amendments (the so-called 'constitutional referendum'); and
2. to decide on the dismissal of the President, following a suspension procedure.[24]

In both cases, the effects of the referendum are binding: if the necessary majority is met, the constitutional amendment is approved or the President is dismissed.

---

[23] See Ch 2.
[24] See Ch 3, section II.I.ii.

The consultative referendum has been used only twice since 1991. The first such referendum, organised in November 2007, aimed at consulting the people as regards a change to the electoral system involving the introduction of the uninominal type of scrutiny in parliamentary elections. This was a recurring theme of political debate, as the existing system (a proportional representation system based on list scrutiny) was considered inadequate from the point of view of the relationship between the candidates and the voters. The political parties had no common understanding of the new system, and although two bills were on the Parliament's agenda, neither was adopted prior to the autumn of 2007 because of a lack of consensus as to the type of uninominal scrutiny to be introduced. In this context, President Băsescu decided to call for a referendum, which was organised simultaneously with the elections for the European Parliament. Despite the fact that all the political actors had declared the great interest of the people in changing the electoral system, the turnout was very low (only 26 per cent, three percentage points less than the turnout for the elections) and the referendum was invalidated. The uninominal system was eventually introduced by a new electoral law adopted by the Romanian Parliament in 2008.[25]

In November 2009, President Traian Băsescu decided to call for a consultative referendum, organised simultaneously with the presidential elections, on two 'matters of national interest': to change the Parliament's structure from bicameral to unicameral; and to reduce the number of parliamentarians to a maximum of 300. The referendum was used as a strong element of propaganda during President Băsescu's election campaign, the President's image being used extensively on the posters promoting the referendum. This was contested by three prestigious NGOs—Pro Democracy, Centre for Legal Resources and Transparency International—as arguably interfering with the electoral campaign, but the Bucharest Court of Appeal rejected the claim. The contested posters displayed, next to the President's picture, the message, 'They will not escape what they're afraid of' and the number '300'. The posters used the same colours as were used in the presidential campaign, and the simultaneity of the two ballots was also a source of confusion. With a 50.56 per cent turnout, the referendum was validated. Over 77 per cent of the voters were in favour of the President's affirmative answers

---

[25] See Ch 2.

to both referendum questions. However, since it was considered to be a non-binding referendum, Parliament took notice but no action. A constitutional amendment initiative introduced by President Băsescu in 2011 was rejected by a two-thirds majority in 2013.

The decision not to follow the result of the referendum may appear contradictory to the principle of democracy, although the referendum is consultative only.[26] It may be argued that even in such a case, the representatives should be bound by the result. However, in the particular case of the 2009 consultative referendum in Romania, the context in which it was organised was very problematic. The subject matter of the referendum has never been discussed in an objective manner, and the goal of establishing a unicameral parliament was presented, on the one hand, as establishing a 'lower-cost' legislator and, on the other, as a tool of the President to 'take his revenge' on the institution that had suspended him from office in 2007.

The compulsory (binding) referendum has an even more tortuous history, as the law establishing its conditions kept changing, every time motivated by political interests. Its compulsory character means that such a referendum must lead to a final decision of the people. The Constitution set out neither a turnout quorum, nor any other requirements for the referendum's validity, leaving this to the subsequent organic law.[27] This lack of precision in the constitutional text ensured controversies in practice in the 'versatile' Romanian political context. The law was changed back and forth several times, and even the Constitutional Court interpreted it inconsistently, especially as regards the referendum's validity.

The debate on the necessity for a turnout quorum in order to validate a referendum ignited the Romanian political and constitutional scene in 2012 and 2013. Theoretically, a compulsory referendum is very clearly intended to produce legal effects, in order to settle the matter as regards which its calling is mandatory. Therefore, theoretically, such a referendum should not be invalidated, as this would mean that it will produce no effects. Moreover, the Constitution provides for neither the possibility nor the consequences of invalidation, only for a vote rejecting the

---

[26] Ş Deaconu, 'Articolul 90' in I Muraru & ES Tănăsescu (eds), *Constituţia României. Comentariu pe articole* (Bucharest, CH Beck, 2008) 848.
[27] Law no 3/2000.

proposal. The Venice Commission clearly disapproved of the establishment of such a quorum in the event of any kind of referendum: 'It is advisable not to provide for … a turnout quorum, because it assimilates voters who abstain to those who vote no …'[28]

Given the silence of the constitutional text, the logical interpretation would be not to establish a supplementary validity quorum by law. In Romania, the referendum law provided for no such quorum until March 2012, when the governing Democrat-Liberal Party (PDL) introduced a turnout quorum for the referendum organised regarding the dismissal of the President. This came in a special context: the opposition, which was gaining a majority in Parliament, was threatening the suspension of President Băsescu. Once in power, a couple of months later, the new majority once again amended the referendum law, returning it to its initial form, by eliminating the validity quorum. A group of PDL MPs addressed the Constitutional Court, claiming the unconstitutionality of this amendment. In July 2012, the Court gave its ruling, in which said, among other things, that

> this is an essential condition for the referendum to be able to express in a real and effective way the will of the citizens, constituting the premise of authentically democratic manifestations of sovereignty by the people … Participation in the referendum of the majority of the registered voters represents an act of civic responsibility, by which the electoral body will decide to sanction or not the President of Romania, having the possibility to revoke him or to maintain him in office.[29]

The suspended President called at first for participation in the vote, but he later changed his message and encouraged voters to boycott the referendum. In August 2012, the Constitutional Court rubber-stamped the presidential call and gave a new reading of the meaning of sovereignty, stating that not voting in the referendum might produce effects and is even advisable in a democracy:

> Expressing a political option may take place not only by participating in the referendum, but also by abstaining [from participating], especially in situations when the relevant legislation imposes a certain turnout quorum.

---

[28] Venice Commission CDL-AD(2007)008, *Code of Good Practice on Referendums*, at 14 and 23. This document was recommended as a 'guideline for the public authorities of the member states' in 2008, by the Committee of Ministers of the Council of Europe.

[29] RCC, Decision no 731/2012.

This way, a blockage majority may be created, by reference to the number of a country's citizens … [T]he absence from [voting in a] referendum … is also a form of expressing the political will of the citizens and of participation in political life.[30]

This ruling contradicts the Court's previous case law as, in 2007, in an identical situation, following another suspension of the President, the referendum organised according to the law in force at the time had no required turnout quorum (and achieved a turnout of 44.45 per cent) and was validated by the Constitutional Court. In 2012, with a 46 per cent turnout and with over 80 per cent of the votes cast in favour of the dismissal, the referendum was declared invalid.

One year after these events, the Parliament elected in December 2012 adopted other amendments to the referendum law, especially as regards the turnout quorum, which was lowered to 30 per cent of the total number of registered voters, with a supplementary condition that at least 25 per cent of the votes should be valid. In June 2013, a group of 83 opposition MPs challenged the law before the Constitutional Court. The Court took its fourth major decision on the referendum law since 2007, and again reversed its jurisprudence:

By analysing the constitutional texts and of international documents in the field, the Court states that the Constitution … does not expressly impose a certain turnout threshold. The Court has not identified any text imposing or recommending a turnout quorum for the referendum. … As a consequence, regulating or changing the conditions on the validity of a referendum is of the exclusive competence of the legislator.[31]

The entire reasoning of the Court focused on the 'stability of legislation', in the context of a forthcoming constitutional amendment by

---

[30] RCC, Resolution no 3/2012.

[31] RCC, Decision no 334/2013. See also the Decision no 471/2013. Moreover, whereas in 2012 the Court completely disregarded the Venice Commission Code of Good Practice on Referendums, which clearly disapproved the imposition of a turnout quorum, in the present decision this Council of Europe document underpins the entire argument: 'In the Code of Good Practice on Referendums of the Venice Commission the recommendation was established not to provide for rules applicable to quorums. … These recommendations … cannot be ignored, although they do not have a compulsory character'. See also B Selejan-Guţan, 'One Year After: How the Romanian Constitutional Court Changed its Mind' *International Journal of Constitutional Law Blog*, 14 July 2013, available at http://www.iconnectblog.com/2013/07/oneyearafter.

referendum (a process initiated by the same political majority against which the Court ruled in 2012).

Although referendums play a significant role in any democracy, in Romania this seems to happen only in theory, because of the instability of the legislation. This has created a negative 'public image' regarding referendums. Except for the first two constitutional referendums (the one for the adoption and the one for the 2003 revision), all the others organised so far have been used as weapons in political fights rather than as democratic tools.

III. THE STATE AND ITS FEATURES

A. General Characteristics of the State

The 1991 Constitution-makers tried to free the state from the bleak corner into which had been backed, in the eyes of public opinion, by the communist regime, which used it as an instrument of oppression. The 'new' Romanian state was endowed with a generous set of principles and features, designed to determine its new position in its relationship with the international community, with the individual and with society as a whole: sovereign, independent, national, unitary and indivisible, rule-of-law-based, democratic, social and, last but not least, republican. Article 1 CR was amended in 2003, when two paragraphs were added— one expressly establishing the separation of powers and one affirming the principle of legality.

i. National State

The constitutional establishment of the 'national' character of the state stems from the history of and the struggle to create the modern Romanian state. Although it is singular among the constitutions of the European democratic countries, the expression 'national state' (*stat national*) must be acknowledged as a mark of the historical context rather than of some extremist views. 'National' in this case is not the same as 'nationalist' but can be traced back to President Wilson's 'nationality principle', which, at the end of World War I, led to the actual creation of the Romanian state. Therefore, the national character of the state expresses the unity of the nation, its right to self-determination as a foundation of the state, its continuity and cohesion. The historical process that led to the nation state was long and very difficult, from the pre-1848 struggle for national identity to the first Romanian unitary state in 1862, independent since 1877 and reunited with the outer provinces of Transylvania, Bukovina and Bessarabia on 1 December 1918—now declared the National Day.

Since 1918, the nationalities principle has not meant the exclusion of other minority groups, as it resulted from the peace treaties of 1919–20 themselves. The contemporary Romanian national state recognises diversity and protects national minorities, according to Article 4 CR as well as Article 6, 'The Right to Identity'.[32] Romania as a nation state recognises and applies the principles of non-discrimination, minority protection and the 'solidarity of citizens'.

In the present international context, most contemporary nation states (as they exist, even though they do not call themselves such) are confronted with important legal and political challenges: the emergence of supra-national political and legal systems, like the EU, and economic challenges to the very sovereignty of the state (such as the agreements with financial international institutions and their conditions, in the context of the recent economic crisis). Another major challenge, especially in Central Europe, but also in Spain or in the United Kingdom, is the existence of minority national or ethnic groups, which have become very vocal in their claims for cultural and territorial autonomy within the state. The nation state's sovereignty is therefore challenged from both the outside and the inside, and the correct response to these challenges is, at least in the case of Romania, still to be found.

ii. Unitary and Indivisible State

Romania has been a unitary state since 1862, which means that there has always been a single state structure, with a single set of central authorities, a single citizenship and Romania acting as a unique subject of international law. Since 1918, when full Romanian political and territorial unity was accomplished, the national character has been strongly linked to the unitary and indivisible character: this excludes federalism

---

[32] See Ch 6.

and any kind of territorial or cultural autonomy.[33] These characteristics of the state may not be the object of any constitutional amendment.

iii. Democracy and the Rule of Law

Article 1 §3 CR sets the core of the constitutional system. The principles of democracy and rule of law were the first to be proclaimed by the new Romanian political regime after the fall of the dictatorship in 1989, and also the first to be included in the new Constitution. This constitutional establishment was a natural consequence of the declared shift of political orientation, and also a requirement for the country's acceptance as a potential member of the European organisations. In 2003, two peculiar 'sources' of these principles and values were added to Article 1 §3:

> Romania is a democratic and social state, based on the rule of law, in which human dignity, the citizens' rights and freedoms, the free development of human personality, justice and political pluralism, represent supreme values, in the spirit of the democratic traditions of the Romanian people and the ideals of the Revolution of December 1989, and shall be guaranteed.

The founding principles are thus the source and safeguard of the supreme values of the state, which, in their turn, are deemed to stem first from the 'democratic traditions of the Romanian people'.

As shown in the introductory chapter, Romania had a quite short democratic history as an independent state, roughly between 1866 and 1938, less than 80 years. Some of the values listed in Article 1 were either non-existent or less important to the state in that period. Political pluralism and justice are the only values that can be identified as belonging, in a certain measure, to the 'Romanian democratic tradition'. Even 'democracy' was understood in a peculiar way (an 'absurd parliamentary system',[34] in which Parliament was the 'emanation' of the Government and not vice versa, as in a regular democratic regime). Human dignity, in the contemporary sense, human rights and freedoms, and the 'free development of the human personality' were placed on a secondary

---

[33] See Ch 4.

[34] The opinion of the deputy and historian Dan Lăzărescu, expressed in the 1991 Constituent Assembly, in A Iorgovan, *Odiseea elaborării Constituţiei* (Tg.Mureş, Vatra românească, 1998) 35.

level. Society was deeply divided, marked by inequalities, hard to moder-nise, affected by poverty, corruption and illiteracy, and still indebted to the customs of the old semi-feudal regimes. As for the social state, the only tradition from which it could have stemmed was the communist regime, which introduced social and economic rights into the Constitu-tion, hand in hand with the entirely state-run economy.

The reference to the ideals of the 1989 Revolution is more realistic in the present context. It is interesting, first, that the 2003 drafters of the constitutional amendments wanted to settle the controversy surround-ing the nature of the 1989 events by conferring constitutional status on the 'Revolution'. Secondly, the supreme values listed in Article 1 §3 are far more likely to stem from the ideals of the Revolution, set out mainly in the 'Address to the Country of the National Salvation Front Council' of 22 December 1989:[35] a pluralist regime, free elections, the separation of powers, respect for human rights, a free market economy.

The democratic character of the Romanian state, as designed by the Constitution is therefore underpinned by the constitutional entrench-ment of political pluralism, national sovereignty stemming from the people, participatory democratic tools, and respect for fundamental rights and freedoms. Political pluralism (understood as a multi-party system, as opposed to the communist totalitarian system) was seen by the constitution-makers as the main landmark of democracy. Making reference to history is characteristic of the general Romanian context and mentality: any change, any initiative, must be justified either by its historical roots, or by reference to Western Europe or other models. These are the two formal landmarks of the Romanian constitutional establishment.

The Romanian concept of rule of law (*stat de drept*) was widely inspired, formally, by the French theory of *État de droit*. The rule of law, understood as the duty of all state authorities to obey the law, and embodied in another constitutional provision, 'no one is above the law' (Article 16 §2 CR), may be identified in rules covering such matters as access to justice, the independence of justice, the supremacy of the Constitution, the accountability of authorities for their acts, equality before the law, and constitutional review by the Constitutional Court by way of binding decisions. The 'substantive' rule of law, ie the actual

---

[35] See Introduction, section C.i.

observance of these rules, is the true problem, as will be shown in the chapters following: the institutions do not always function in the way prescribed.

iv. The Republic

Although often unnoticed, the first significant paradox within the Romanian constitutional system is to be found in the first article of the Constitution. Article 1 §2 provides that the form of government in Romania is a Republic. This is the only element maintained from the previous, totalitarian constitutional order. On the other hand, in Article 1 §3, the text refers to the 'democratic traditions of the Romanian people'. It is true that the democratic traditions are invoked here to uphold the supreme values consecrated by the Constitution, but still, the Constitution must be a coherent document, with a coherent ideology. Therefore, if the democratic traditions of the Romanian people must underpin the whole system of values, then certainly the republican form of government is not one of them. The Republic was established in Romania 'by Soviet tanks'—according to a popular saying—in 1947, and quickly developed into a totalitarian state—the 'People's Republic', governed by the 'proletariat dictatorship', and then the 'Socialist Republic', governed by a personal dictatorship, both under the patronage of a single political power, the Communist Party.

The preservation of the republican form of government was the political choice of the new revolutionary power, upheld by the people, who, after almost 50 years of dictatorship, were eager to be able to elect all their rulers directly. This was amplified by the negative propaganda disseminated against the monarchy and the Royal House of Romania during the 42 years of totalitarian republicanism and in the first post-revolutionary years.[36] Although the question has never been discussed separately, the large majority obtained by the draft republican Constitution in the December 1991 referendum was considered to have legitimised the preservation of this form of government.

Therefore, ironically, the new Romanian Constitution maintained a form of government that was imposed as a dictatorship, while

---

[36] Such as the alleged 'escape' of King Michael with 'trains' full of wealth, and the royal family's alleged treason as regards Romanian interests, etc—all fabricated stories, typical of communist propaganda.

acknowledging the 'democratic traditions of the Romanian people' as foundations of the supreme values of the state. Moreover, the republican form of government is an unamendable constitutional provision ('eternity clause') according to Article 152.[37]

Apart from that, the Republic might have functioned as a new democratic tradition, but unfortunately, due to an imperfect mechanism and to other imperfect legal transplants,[38] this has yet to happen.

v. Social State

Although some 'social' characteristics of the state—recognition of a wide range of social rights and benefits—seem to have been inherited from the past socialist regime, they were actually borrowed from the European constitutions that had inspired the constitutional drafters in 1990–91: Germany, Spain, Portugal, etc. The expression 'social state' mirrored the German doctrine established at the beginning of the twentieth century.[39] Although, it is, in theory, opposed to the 'market economy' characteristic of a liberal state, this did not flagrantly contradict the objectives of the social and economic transition Romania was about to undergo in 1991. Certainly, the social state entails a higher degree of intervention in the economy, but this has become more and more necessary, even in the most liberal states. In theory, the Romanian Constitution prescribed a state having as its main objectives the regulation of some economic activities, without actually affecting economic freedom. The social protection of disadvantaged categories (retired persons, the unemployed, persons with disabilities, etc), the principle of a minimum standard of living, the protection of young people and their education, the protection of the environment and of public health are some of the objectives that resulted from the constitutional provisions, but so did the stimulation of private initiative and of loyal competition. However, to a large extent, these have so far remained only ideals, as in the social field the results are not very encouraging. In 2015, Romania had the second lowest Gross National Product in the EU, and was among the countries having the lowest income and standard of living.

---

[37] See Ch 7.
[38] The semi-presidential regime. See Ch 3.
[39] W Heun, *The Constitution of Germany. A Contextual Analysis* (Oxford, Hart Publishing, 2011) 45.

From the institutional point of view, in 2003 the Constitution introduced the Economic and Social Council (ESC), inspired by the French model but tailored to the Romanian constitutional system, as a 'consultative' organ of the Parliament and Government in the fields established by its organic law (Article 141 CR). Even though it is a 'civic and social' establishment rather than a political one (due to its consultative nature), the ESC may act in the field of protection of social rights (the labour-related rights), as the trade unions are equally represented within its structure. The purpose of the Council is the achievement of a 'social dialogue' at national level, between employers, unions and government, with a view to achieving a climate of stability and social peace. It also has competence to ensure the conformity of Romanian legislation with international labour law and with the requirements of EU law. However, the social role of the Council in practice is virtually non-existent, all decisions in the social and economic field being made at a governmental level.

B. The Institutional Architecture and the Separation of Powers

i. *The Separation of Powers*

The principle of the separation of powers was amongst the first stipulated by the new political actors, during and after the 1989 Revolution, as one of the 'ideals' of the revolutionary movement. This principle had been totally disregarded during the totalitarian years, therefore it was meant to become a symbol of the new constitutional order. The 1990–91 constitutional drafters included it among the foundations of the state, but not expressly in the constitutional text. The initial version of the Constitution implicitly provided for a horizontal division of powers between the legislature, the executive and an ambiguously named 'judicial authority'. The Constitutional Court itself confirmed the existence of the separation of powers, from the silence of the text: 'although the Constitution does not state it *expressis verbis*, the principle of separation of powers results from the way in which the fundamental law establishes the public authorities and their competences'.[40] In 2003

---

[40] RCC, Decision no 209/1999. The separation of powers had been previously mentioned in Decisions nos 27/1993 and 9/1994.

the principle of separation of powers was expressly introduced into the Constitution, in order to clearly reflect the revolutionary ideals: 'the state shall be based on the principle of the separation and balance of powers—legislative, executive and judicial—within the framework of the constitutional democracy' (Article 1 §4).

Considering the intentions of the founding fathers, the whole division of powers system and the checks-and-balances mechanism have been designed to meet the requirements of a parliamentary regime endowed with a directly elected president. The expression 'parliamentary semi-presidentialism'[41] timidly tries to encompass this institutional interplay, born from the firm will of the political parties as well as institutions to maintain the republican form of government. However, a few dilemmas had to be resolved in these circumstances: How to preserve the republic and still avoid the risk of a too-powerful president? How to give the people a directly elected but less powerful president? How to find the right balance between the legislature and the executive in this fragile context? It was no easy task, but the founding fathers came up with a solution: they reserved primacy to the Romanian Parliament, making it the 'supreme' representative organ of the Romanian people. In addition, they set out a dual executive power, exercised by a directly elected president and a government endorsed by and politically responsible to Parliament. Therefore, although it is still considered incoherent as regards the role and position of the President—especially in light of the huge gap between his strong legitimacy and his weak constitutional powers—the Romanian system reveals its internal logic in the light of the Constitution drafters' ideals.

ii. Semi-presidentialism

The founding fathers' view of the division of powers was based on so-called 'aversive constitutionalism'.[42] It stemmed primarily from an aversion to the past and from the need to deny past institutions.

---

[41] See below section ii.

[42] For the meaning of the term 'aversive constitutionalism', see KL Scheppele, 'Aspirational and aversive constitutionalism: The case for studying cross-constitutional influence through negative models' (2003) 1 *International Journal of Constitutional Law* 300.

Thus, the founding fathers knew what had to be rejected in the Constitution better than they knew what was actually necessary in the post-communist, 'transitional' socio-economical and political context. All they did, intially, was to adopt solutions that were the opposite of those adopted in the past.[43] For example, knowing that the communist dictator Ceauşescu had been indirectly elected, in an abusive way, by the communist Parliament, a post-communist Romanian president had to be directly elected by the people. At the same time, considering the country's experiences under the head of state's authoritarianism, the post-communist president had to be a less powerful figure. Just as in France in 1958,[44] where 'aversive constitutionalism' led to the 'rationalisation' of the Parliament and to the present semi-presidential system, in Romania in 1991 a 'reversed' semi-presidentialism was born, as the institution which had to be rationalised was the President and not the Parliament. Nevertheless, France is considered, by most Romanian legal scholars, as the main source of inspiration for the present political regime. Hence, the Romanian President, a mix between a French President with narrower powers and a Spanish monarch, was primarily designed to play the role of mediator, leaving the actual governing to the Government. In this context, anxiety regarding the Romanian head of state's authoritarianism has become the most relevant element of the Romanian post-communist constitutional identity.

Following this game of 'negations', a semi-presidential regime was created without especially planning it. Consequently, in practice, Romanian semi-presidentialism shifts between presidentialism and parliamentarianism, with a strong tendency towards the former. The direct election of a President endowed with limited powers did not result in a better institutional balance, as will be shown in chapterthree.

iii. Legislature and Executive

The Romanian Parliament, composed of the Chamber of Deputies and the Senate, is defined by the Constitution as being the 'supreme representative organ of the Romanian people and the sole legislative

---

[43] M Guţan, 'Transplantul constituţional şi obsesia modelului semiprezidenţial francez în România contemporană (I)' (2010) 5 *Pandectele române* 54.

[44] S Boyron, *The Constitution of France. A Contextual Analysis* (Oxford, Hart Publishing, 2013) 51.

authority'. The bicameral structure can be traced back to 1864 and is one of the oldest democratic traditions of the Romanians. During the communist regime, the legislature was unicameral (the Great National Assembly). At present, the chambers are organised into committees and parliamentary groups. Until 2003, the legislative procedure was a parallel process, both chambers having the same competences. In 2003, differentiation was attempted, but the new mechanism amounted in practice to 'unicameral bicameralism'. Parliament can also delegate its legislative function to the Government, as will be shown in chapterthree.

The Government is composed of the Prime Minister and the Members of Cabinet (Ministers), each one in charge of a specific Ministry. The President appoints the candidate for the office of Prime Minister, who must obtain the vote of confidence from Parliament for the new list of Government. Once appointed into office, the Government becomes politically responsible to Parliament.[45]

A checks-and-balances mechanism is provided. The dual executive—President and Government—is accountable to Parliament in specific ways. Thus, the President can be suspended from office by Parliament and, following suspension, dismissed by referendum. The Government is politically responsible before the Parliament: it can be dismissed by a motion of censure adopted by Parliament (a vote of no confidence). The executive enjoys no powers corresponding to these rather wide powers of Parliament. The dissolution of Parliament is strongly rationalised: the President can only dissolve Parliament if it twice refuses to give a vote of confidence to a new Government within a period of 60 days. Therefore, in order for Parliament to be dissolved, there must be a common will shared by the three political authorities. To date, the Romanian Parliament has never been dissolved, but the President has been suspended from office twice (in 2007 and 2012) and the Government was dismissed twice by motions of censure, in 2009 and 2012.

iv. The Judiciary

The independence of justice is postulated as a constitutional principle as well as forming a limit on constitutional amendment, being considered a landmark of the rule of law. The executive has some competences relating to the judiciary: all judges are appointed by the President. This

---

[45] See Ch 3.

is a formal power, as the proposals are made by the Superior Council of Magistracy, a high judicial council inspired by the French *Conseil Supérieur de la Magistrature*, with an eclectic composition that includes the Minister of Justice as a representative of the executive. The Council has a corporatist organisation and large autonomous powers.[46]

The High Court of Cassation and Justice and the other courts form a classic Continental judicial system, without a common/administrative division. The High Court is the supreme court of the land, with the power to hand down binding interpretative decisions, with a view to unifying divergent jurisprudence. Judges are independent and cannot be removed from office. Prosecutors are considered 'magistrates', but they are not independent as they are placed under the authority of the Minister of Justice. The judicial branch does not have the power to review legislation. All of these particular aspects will be developed further in chapter five.

v. Other Key Institutions of the Constitutional System

The Constitutional Court and the Ombudsman are new institutions for the Romanian system. They were created by the 1991 Constitution in an attempt to add more guarantees to secure the rule of law. The Constitutional Court, an independent authority that is not part of the judiciary, is entrusted with the constitutional review of laws, government ordinances, parliamentary regulations and international treaties. Its role and impact on the constitutional system will be analysed extensively in chapterfive. The Ombudsman is an independent organ meant to secure the respect of fundamental rights by the administration.[47]

Both institutions, despite their relatively short history, have managed to become key factors in the rule of law. However, the Constitutional Court, due to the appointment of its judges by political authorities, was on the verge of becoming a political instrument in 2012–13, a risk which is still present. Although the European authorities, alerted during the events of July 2012, considered the Constitutional Court as the cornerstone of democracy in Romania, its incoherent and biased recent case law diminishes the authority of this essential institution, which should regain the position and esteem it truly deserves.

---

[46] See Ch 5, section II.F.
[47] See Ch 6.

C. Conclusion

It is not an easy task to define the present Romanian constitutional system. Is it a parliamentarised semi-presidential democratic republic? A parliamentary republic with a directly elected president? A presidentialised semi-presidential system? A unique hybrid regime? The answer is still unclear. Romania's past and present context—historical, social, political, economic—is not much help in this endeavour. With a relatively young constitutional tradition—actually starting in the second half of the nineteenth century, with a very short democratic period of less than 80 years—passing through several dictatorships, among them a soviet-imposed communist totalitarian regime which lasted 45 years, the country had little chance to achieve redress and rapidly create, after 1989, a perfectly functional, democratic constitutional system. Everything had to be changed—people's way of thinking, society, institutions, legislation. In the turmoil surrounding the transition, the 1991 Constitution was viewed with hope as a potential solution to all the country's problems. Unfortunately, the mere enactment of the Constitution was not enough: the established institutions and mechanisms need to function properly, the rights set forth should be respected, principles should be implemented. This has depended primarily on the emerging political elite and not on the dry constitutional text alone. The founding fathers did their best, with the help of Western expertise, to create, in theory, a functional system. Whether they succeeded, whether there were unforeseen evils, whether everything needs to be changed again, all will be examined in the next chapters of this book.

FURTHER READING

Constitution of Romania, text translated in English and available on the website of the Romanian Chamber of Deputies at http://www.cdep. ro/pls/dic/site.page?id=371.

A Albi, 'Some idiosyncrasies of CEE constitutions' in A Albi, *EU Enlargement and the Constitutions of Central and Eastern Europe* (Cambridge, Cambridge University Press, 2005) 18–35.

R Bercea, 'Doit-on encore réviser la constitution nationale pour répondre aux exigences du droit de l'Union Européenne?' (2013) 1 *Romanian Journal of Comparative Law* 7.

M Dogan, 'Romania, 1919–1938' in M Weiner & E Ozbudun (eds), *Competitive Elections in Developing Countries* (Durham, Duke University Press, 1987) 369.

M Guţan, 'The Infra-constitutionality of the European Law in Romania and the Challenges of the Romanian Constitutional Culture' in R Arnold (ed), *Limitation of Sovereignty by European Integration* (Heidelberg, Springer, forthcoming 2016).

——, 'Romanian Semi-Presidentialism in Historical Context' (2012) 2 *Romanian Journal of Comparative Law* 275.

L Heuschling, 'La Constitution formelle' in M Troper & D Chagnollaud (eds), *Traité international de droit constitutionel*, vol 1 (Paris, Dalloz, 2012) 265–96.

B Iancu, 'Separation of Powers and the Rule of Law in Romania: The Crisis in Concepts and Contexts' in A von Bogdandy & P Sonnevend, *Constitutional Crisis in the European Constitutional Area* (Oxford, Hart Publishing, 2015) 153–69.

F Julien-Laferrière, 'La Constitution roumaine de 8 Décembre 1991 ou le difficile apprentissage de la démocratie' (1993) 5 *Revue du droit public et de la science politique en France et à l'étranger* 1217.

ES Tănăsescu, 'Modern Romanian Constitutionalism under the Influence of EU Accession' (2011) I *Rivista di diritto pubblico comparato ed europeo* 225–35.

R Weber, 'Constitutionalism as a Vehicle for Democratic Consolidation in Romania' in J Zielonka (ed), *Democratic Consolidation in Eastern Europe* (Oxford, Oxford University Press, 2001) 221.

2

The Romanian Parliament

Parliament – Political Parties – Elections – Bicameralism – The Legislative Process

T HE ROMANIAN PARLIAMENT, as designed by the 1991 constitutional legislator, illustrates the appeal to the 'constitutional democratic traditions' of the pre-communist period. The principle of democracy is reflected by the electoral system, and system of political parties, both of which have undergone several fundamental changes over the past 25 years. This chapter will examine the principles of parliamentary legitimacy—the electoral system and the constitutional regime of the political parties—the bicameral structure of the Parliament (a controversial issue in very recent Romanian doctrine and practice) and the law-making process. Issues like the status of parliamentarians, immunity and the actual role of Parliament as a legislator and representative organ will be emphasised, as will Parliament's powers of control over the executive.

I. INTRODUCTION

Romanian legislative assemblies transformed themselves rather late in history, from typical Estate-Generals (the Elective Assembly from the Organic Regulations, 1831–32) into elected unicameral assemblies (1858–64). The first modern bicameral parliament was established by the 1864 Developing Statute of the Paris Convention, and was composed of the Elective Assembly and the *Corp Ponderator*. The bicameral tradition, established by the 1866 and 1923 Constitutions, was interrupted by the communist constitutions, which created unicameral parliaments (Great National Assembly), being reinstated by the 1991 Constitution. The Romanian Parliament is thus among the few existing institutions that is a part of the 'democratic traditions of the Romanian people', referred to in Article 1 CR. However, apart from the names of the chambers, there is no other similarity between the inter-war Parliament and the current one. The electoral system, the internal organisation of the Parliament and the law-making process are all different.

The 1991 Constitution defines the Parliament as 'the supreme representative organ of the Romanian people and the sole legislative authority of the country', but the assertion in Article 61 §1 CR is not entirely precise. The Parliament does not exercise the legislative power alone: certain competences also belong to the executive (legislative initiative, legislative delegation, promulgation of laws, power of veto) as well as to the people (approval by referendum of constitutional amendment laws). In practice, especially in the period 1999–2013, pieces of parliamentary legislation were outnumbered by GOs.[1]

The Romanian Parliament is free, in principle, to adopt and follow its own legislative policy. The only case in which an obligation is imposed on Parliament to act in a certain way is when the Constitutional Court declares a law to be unconstitutional before its promulgation. Such a decision imposes an obligation on Parliament to re-examine the law and bring it into line with the constitutional provisions.

II. THE STRUGGLE FOR PARLIAMENT: POLITICAL PARTIES AND ELECTIONS

In the constitutional drafting process of 1990–91, special attention was paid to the election of representative organs. Universal, direct, equal, free and secret suffrage was the goal for both chambers of Parliament. These features and the actual exercise of the electoral rights were developed by successive electoral laws. It must be emphasised from the start that there is no integrated electoral system in Romania. Every elected organ (Parliament, President, mayors, local councils, departmental councils, MEPs) has its own electoral law. Political parties play the most important role in the electoral process.

---

[1] For example, in 2000, 407 ordinances were adopted, compared with 233 laws.

A. Political Parties

Political pluralism and political parties were sensitive points to address and resolve during and after the 1989 Revolution. Obviously, the restoration of political pluralism, understood essentially as a multi-party political system, after over 40 years of totalitarian single-party regimes, was crucial for establishing the new democracy. The importance of political pluralism for the commitment to democracy was underpinned in the Constitution by its inclusion in the 'supreme values' of the state (Article 1 §3 CR) and among the unamendable provisions: no constitutional amendment may affect political pluralism (Article 152 §1 CR). Article 8 CR also defines pluralism as a 'condition and guarantee of the constitutional democracy', and affirms the key role of political parties in the democratic society as 'contributors to the definition and expression of the political will of the citizens, while observing national sovereignty, territorial integrity, the legal order and the principles of democracy'. As in most democratic societies, political parties are considered to be an important link between the state and the civil society, and Romanian legislation gives them a special status in this respect.

From an historical perspective, early forms of political parties appeared in the Organic Regulations period,[2] in both Moldova and Wallachia. During the 1848 Revolution, political groups took the name 'party' (*partida*), and in 1857 there were two established parties—conservative and national. However, modern political parties came into being only after 1869. In 1866, political groups and trends were well defined, and continued to develop during the entire 'democratic age' of modern Romania, until 1938. The National Liberal Party was officially created in 1875. In 1938, for the first time, the existing political parties were dissolved and banned by the royal dictatorship regime, and a single, official party was created (the National Rebirth Front). They reappeared after 1944, but for only a short period of time, as, in 1947, the single-party communist regime spelled the end of the political pluralism for almost half a century. During the communist era, the Romanian Communist Party was the only political party, defined by the 1952 and 1965 Constitutions as being 'the leading political force of the entire society'.

The multi-party system and the freedom to create political parties were reintroduced into the Romanian constitutional system by one of

---

[2] See Introduction and Historical Overview, section II.A.ii.

the first revolutionary acts, Decree-Law no 8/1989. Law no 27/1996 on political parties rationalised the conditions necessary to create a political party, and therefore the number of registered parties was significantly reduced. Presently, political parties are regulated by constitutional provisions, as well as by Law no 14/2003 on political parties and Law no 343/2006 on the financing of political parties, both amended in 2015.

The Constitution is extremely concise as regards political parties. Besides the principles set out in Articles 1 and 8, it also refers to membership and to the unconstitutionality of political parties. Political parties are defined as the result of the exercise of the freedom of association of the citizens. Article 40 lists the categories of persons who may not become members of political parties by reason of their profession, that is, magistrates, members of the police and military, judges of the Constitutional Court and Ombudsmen. The same article provides that 'parties or organisations which, by their aims or activities, militate against political pluralism, the principles of the rule of law, or against the sovereignty, integrity or independence of the country shall be unconstitutional'. The Constitutional Court is competent to declare such unconstitutionality, but has not been asked to do it so far.

The law sets forth the rules on political parties' registration, membership, limitations and dissolution. Political parties are considered by the current legislation to be 'public law legal persons', which means that their status is different from that of regular private law associations. The most important consequences of this status are that political parties can only cease to exist by the means established by law and that they may receive public funding subsidies. The law also establishes the main aspects of the internal organisation of political parties, which, though it is not expressly prescribed, must be in accordance with democratic principles.

It is interesting that in 1989–90, the minimum number of members required for a party to be registered was 251; in 1996 this number increased to 10,000; and in 2003 the figure was set at 25,000 (with a wide geographical distribution). In 2015, a Constitutional Court decision[3] fundamentally reversed the previous jurisprudence in favour of a wider scope for the freedom to create political parties. Thus, the requirement for a minimum 25,000 founding members was considered an excessive restriction of this right, and the provision was declared

[3] RCC, Decision no 75/2015.

unconstitutional. The unconstitutionality[4] was invoked by a representative of the 'Pirate Party', who was unable to register the party without the necessary signatures. The Court extensively quoted recent case law of the ECtHR, as well as opinions of the Venice Commission, and the decision was essentially based on the evolution of society and on the existence of strict regulation of parties' financing, which removed 'the risk of "depreciating" the idea of political parties, of fragmentation of parliamentary representation and of an excessive burden for the state budget'. Following this decision, in May 2015 the law was amended,[5] and the required number of founding members was reduced to three. In practice, since 1989, the number of the parties has varied, following a peculiar pattern: from 80 parties registered in May 1990, to 155 in May 1992, and finally to 28 registered parties in December 2012. Not all registered parties participated in elections. Other electoral competitors are the organisations of persons belonging to national minorities, which have the right to field candidates in elections but are not considered political parties.

Parties that meet the legal requirements, as recognised by a judicial court—the Bucharest Tribunal—are included in the Register of Political Parties, a unique document that contains all the relevant information required. A political party can cease to exist either by its own will (self-dissolution or reorganisation), or by one of two types of dissolution: judicial dissolution (by the Bucharest Tribunal) and dissolution by the Constitutional Court (when the party is dissolved on the ground of unconstitutionality). The reasons for judicial dissolution may be:

1. when the purpose or the activity of the party has become illicit or contrary to public order;
2. when the achievement of the goals of the party is pursued by illegal means or in a manner contrary to public order;
3. when the party pursues a goal different from that established by its statute and political program;
4. as a result of inactivity, established by the Bucharest Tribunal.

There is no formal preventive ban on specific political parties, based on ideological criteria, such as on communist or fascist parties in other countries. A proposal, made during the Constitution drafting process,

---

[4] See Ch 5.
[5] Law no 114/2015.

to prohibit the creation of parties on ethnic criteria, was not included in the final draft.[6] The Constitution does, however, generally ban parties that militate against political pluralism and against the basic principles of the state. In 2005, Romania was found in violation of Article 11 of the ECHR for its refusal to register a communist party on the grounds of disrespect for the constitutional order.[7]

A common practice in the Romanian political life is the creation of political associations and alliances. Electoral alliances are the most frequent (ie constituted only in order to participate in elections), but there are also permanent alliances (in which the parties also coexist between elections, but for a rather limited period of time). The most important alliances have been the Democratic Convention (1996–2000), the DA Alliance ('Justice and Truth'/*Dreptate și Adevăr*, which was created for the 2004 elections between the National Liberal Party and the Democratic Party, and lasted until 2007) and the USL Alliance (Social-Liberal Union/*Uniunea Social-Liberală*, which was created in 2012 between the National Liberal Party, the Social-Democrat Party and the Conservative Party, and lasted until March 2014).

The main political parties, which, in one form or another, under different names, have come to power in Romania since 1990 are the Social-Democratic Party (PSD, formerly the National Democratic Salvation Front and PDSR), the National Liberal Party (PNL), the Democrat-Liberal Party (PDL, formerly the Democrat Party, at present merged with the PNL), the National Peasant Party and the Democratic Hungarian Union. After the last elections, in December 2012, two alliances (USL and ARD), one small party (PPDD) and one national minority political organisation (UDMR, the Hungarian Democratic Union) entered Parliament by meeting the required threshold. The other minorities' organisations are represented by one deputy each, regardless of the number of votes cast for them.

The UDMR is a special case: it is not technically a political party, but it falls into the category of 'organisations representing the national

---

[6] The two main ethnic minorities—Hungarian and German—are not represented by parties but by NGOs (the Democratic Forum of the Germans from Romania (FDGR) and the Democratic Hungarian Union (UDMR)). The latter was, from 1996, with brief interruptions, a part of all governmental coalitions, regardless of their political orientation—see further below.

[7] *Partidul comuniștilor (nepeceriști) and Ungureanu v Romania* App no 46626/99 (ECtHR, 3 February 2005).

minorities'. Due to the high percentages of Hungarians in three counties, the UDMR has always managed to reach the electoral threshold and obtain more seats in Parliament than the Constitution allocates for minority organisations. As a result, it has always been a part of the governing coalitions, regardless of their political orientation; and although it has no clear political ideology, it has always pursued the interests of the Hungarian community. Invariably, the UDMR has used its position as a 'joker' within the successive coalitions (which could not form a majority without its parliamentarians) to promote minority interests to—and even impose them on—the Government.

The financing of the political parties is regulated by a separate organic law.[8] The maximum total amount that may be allocated to political parties from the state budget's income is 0.04 per cent. A privileged position is given to parties that promote women on their electoral lists to eligible positions: the allocated amount from the state budget will increase in proportion with the number of seats obtained in elections by women candidates. The law establishes two criteria for awarding public subsidies: the number of votes obtained in parliamentary elections and the number obtained in local elections. The subsidy is paid monthly, through the budget of the Permanent Electoral Authority. The law also expressly provides for eligible expenses from public subsidies. Payments can be suspended if these or other legal requirements are not respected. The Permanent Electoral Authority and the Court of Auditors control the use of funds and of public subsidies by political parties.

The private financing of political parties is also strictly regulated by the organic law, substantially amended in 2015. Besides the regular contributions of party members, other forms of financing are donations and loans. All contributions must be declared to the Permanent Electoral Authority and can only be used after declaration. The electoral campaign may not be financed by foreign citizens (except for EU citizens who are members of the party and residing in Romania) or by foreign legal persons. Outside the electoral campaign, donations may not exceed, in a fiscal year, 0.025 per cent of the state budget incomes foreseen in the budget for that year. Donations from trade unions and religious cults are forbidden, as are donations from foreign states,

---

[8] Law no 334/2006, amended by Law no 113/2015.

organisations or persons. For obvious reasons relating to neutrality, the law also forbids donations made to political parties by public authorities or institutions, state-owned companies or companies in which the state holds the whole or the majority of capital. Political parties are forbidden by law to deploy commercial activities, and they have the obligation to publish in the *Monitorul Journal* the total amount of their income from other sources.

The most famous case involving corruption in the field of electoral campaign financing is that of the former Prime Minister, Adrian Năstase. Using his influence as president of the governing party, Năstase received over €1.6 million for his 2004 presidential campaign. The money came from a symposium organised by the State Inspectorate for Constructions, for which 'participation fees' were paid by representatives of other state-owned companies or institutions. The collected sums were then directed to companies controlled by close acquaintances of the Năstase family, which redirected them to the presidential campaign. Adrian Năstase was sentenced to two years' imprisonment in 2012.

B. Parliamentary Elections

Universal suffrage for parliamentary elections was introduced in Romania in 1917, by revising the 1866 Constitution.[9] The previous legislation (of 1866 and 1884) established an unequal right to vote, based on wealth and sex censuses. The system was unified in 1926 by a new law that introduced a proportional system based on closed and blocked party lists. The elections from the whole pre- and inter-war period lacked democratic character, due to gross inequalities and manipulation of the votes.[10] During the communist regime, there were no free and democratic elections. The mandatory vote, combined with the single-party system, resulted in turn-out rates of 98–100 per cent, and in 99.96 per cent 'majorities' for pre-determined winning candidates.[11]

---

[9] Although, in practice, due to restrictive conditions, female suffrage was effectively applied only from 1929. See C Preda, *Rumânii fericiți. Vot și putere de la 1831 până în prezent* (Iași, Polirom, 2011) 159.

[10] See Introduction and Historical Overview.

[11] Preda (n 9) at 269.

After the fall of the dictatorial regime, the first parliamentary and presidential elections were organised in May 1990. These actually were the first free and democratic elections, based on a truly universal and equal suffrage, in the country's history, thus marking 'ground zero' of election-based democracy.

According to Article 62 CR, the Chamber of Deputies and the Senate are elected by universal, equal, direct, free and secret suffrage, according to the electoral law. Based on the first electoral laws of 1992, the first 'constitutional' post-revolutionary elections were organised in September 1992. Parliament was then elected through a party-list system, with closed and blocked lists,[12] the seats being distributed according to a mechanism of proportional representation. All parties that reached the minimum threshold entered Parliament, the allocated seats being counted in decreasing order, on a proportional basis (according to the score obtained by each party at the national level). These first elections remained famous for their high turn-out: over 76 per cent of the voters. As a result, eight parties were represented in Parliament, with no party gaining a majority.

Since 1992, the electoral legislation has been amended several times, but in 2008[13] it underwent a major change with the introduction of a new system,[14] combining the uninominal system with a proportional distribution of seats (the system was called 'mixed compensatory with a proportional end').[15] This mixed character came from the combination of proportional representation with a majoritarian system. Although each political competitor (party or alliance) fielded only one candidate per electoral constituency (electoral districts or 'colleges'), the candidate who obtained the highest number of votes cast did not necessarily gain the seat (as in the 'first-past-the-post' system). Another candidate would be elected if his or her party obtained a better score at the national level. Only candidates who managed to obtain the majority of the votes in the college would automatically win the seat; all other candidates went on to the second phase of the distribution.

---

[12] The voters could change neither the composition of nor the order of candidates on the list.

[13] Law no 35/2008 on parliamentary elections.

[14] C Preda, 'The Romanian Political System: after the Parliamentary Elections of November 30, 2008' (2009) 1 *Studia Politica. Romanian Political Science Review* 10.

[15] M Nica, *Drept electoral* (Craiova, Sitech, 2010) 276. See also Preda (n 9) at 9–11.

The 'uninominal vote', as it was named in the campaign for changing the previous law, was seen as a panacea for the multiple deficiencies of Romanian political life. The system was supposedly 'bringing the voters closer to their representatives', by creating the 'uninominal colleges' in which each party proposes one candidate, and therefore contributing to the improvement of the political class by increasing representativeness and the accountability of the elected. The rate of success would be assured, allegedly, by the relationship of the candidate with the voters from his or her college. However, because of the contradictory method of distribution,[16] which did not fully take into account the results within the constituency, candidates who obtained, for instance, 27 per cent of the votes in their college would enter Parliament, to the detriment of a candidate in the same college who obtained 48 per cent of the votes, but whose party obtained a lower score at the national level or did not meet the criteria above.

Moreover, according to a complicated mathematical algorithm, Parliament had a variable number of members, disregarding the representation quota prescribed by law. As neither the Constitution nor the electoral law establishes a fixed number of MPs, the numbers of deputies and senators should be established according to a fixed representation quota: one deputy to every 70,000 inhabitants, and one senator to every 160,000 inhabitants. In the 2008–12 Parliament had 471 members. After the last elections (2012), it had 588. As the total population of Romania actually decreased, the higher number was made possible as a 'perverse effect' of the seat-redistribution process. This is the result of the purely mathematical distribution of seats at the national level: a number of the seats were allotted directly if the candidates obtained a majority in their college, while the rest of the seats were allotted according to a multi-level distribution process, in proportion to the votes obtained by the parties nationally. This enhanced the electoral disproportionality, which had already, in earlier measurements, placed Romania among states like Venezuela, Costa Rica or Colombia, 'all three [being] considered as genuine examples of the mode in which can be perverted the proportional logic'.[17]

The Constitutional Court also criticised the 'deficiencies' or 'imperfections' of the new system, stating that

---

[16] See also Preda (n 14) at 10.

[17] ibid, at 15, citing A Lijphart, *Patterns of Democracy. Government, Forms and Performance in Thirty-Six Countries* (New Haven & London, Yale University Press, 1999).

the mechanism used for distributing the [parliamentary] seats consequently had results which did not correspond to a uninominal majoritarian system, as they were determined by the mathematical operations set forth by the law. Therefore, the appointment of some members of parliament was made based on such operations and not as a result of the expression, by vote, of the political choice [of the citizens].[18]

Nevertheless, in June 2012, the Constitutional Court refused to endorse a bill that tried to partly redress the above-mentioned shortcomings, on the grounds that, by changing the electoral law with less than six months to go before the elections, the principle of legal certainty would be infringed.[19] Among other provisions that allegedly would give rise to the unjustified increase in the number of MPs, the impugned law tried to correct the anomaly of attributing a seat to a candidate who did not obtain the highest number of votes in his or her constituency. In the Government's view, this was a response to criticisms of the previous case law of the Constitutional Court. The Court admitted, however, that

> even the present electoral legislation was modified with less than one year to go before the elections, but there were no criticisms raised before the Court back then, whereas this time, the Court has been called on to establish the consequences of a sudden change of the electoral legislation.

As a result of the Court's decision, the 2012 elections were organised according to the unchanged law, and their outcome was even more distorted[20] than in 2008 from the point of view of the votes–seats ratio, with over 100 MPs more than in the preceding Parliament.

In December 2014, the newly elected President of Romania called the main political parties to take part in consultations with a view to changing the electoral system once more. In July 2015, the new law was promulgated, and it marks a return to the previous party-list system. The representation quota was changed (one deputy for every 73,000 inhabitants and one senator for every 168,000 inhabitants) and the electoral threshold was subject to slight adjustments: 5 per cent for parties and a higher percentage for alliances (3 per cent added for

---

[18] RCC, Decision no 61/2010.
[19] RCC, Decision no 682/2012.
[20] The distortion came from the artificial increase in the number of seats, as the representation quota prescribed by law was not respected. In some colleges, redistribution resulted in the allocation of two seats, although the system is based on the principle 'one college–one candidate–one seat'.

the first member and 1 per cent for each additional member, up to a maximum 10 per cent).

The competence to organise and supervise the elections belongs to the Permanent Electoral Authority and, strictly during the electoral period, to the Central Electoral Commission and the other territorial electoral commissions. The Permanent Electoral Authority[21] is an autonomous administrative institution created by the electoral law, whereas the electoral offices are temporary bodies, composed of judges and representatives of political parties, with competences limited to the election period.

Despite legislative inconsistency and the failure of the uninominal system, parliamentary elections have ensured the functioning of democracy in Romania. The system was, and still is, weakened by factors such as the ideological shallowness of the political parties (which were mainly driven by group interests rather than by coherent political ideology) and their failure to 'energise' the voters' political views. However, an important improvement and evolution, from the point of view of the free exercise of the right to vote, of transparency and accountability, can be witnessed, compared with the inter-war period. The electoral process did not entail any notable fraud or manipulation (internal and international observers have supervised the process ever since 1990), but practices like 'bribing' the voters, and even attempts to 'buy' votes or to facilitate multiple voting, were still present, especially because of the immaturity and poverty of the electorate itself (the majority of whom, especially in the rural parts of the country, were more easily 'convinced' by minor material gifts and promises than by a sound analysis of the candidates' profiles).

C. The Structure and Internal Organisation of Parliament

i. Bicameralism

The Romanian Parliament has a bicameral structure: the Chamber of Deputies and the Senate, both elected for a four-year term, by direct and universal suffrage. Direct election was a natural choice after years of communism, when the people were not free to elect their

---

[21] Created in 2003 by successive amendments to the electoral laws and entrenched by the 2003 constitutional amendment.

representatives, while bicameralism was seen as a continuation of the pre-war 'democratic tradition'. At first, the 1991 Constitution provided for a perfectly equal bicameralism: apart from the minimum age for election, the number of members and the representation quota, the two chambers had the exact same competences and the law-making processes in each followed parallel procedures. It is well known that in countries that chose a bicameral parliament for reasons other than the federal structure of the state, a clear differentiation between the two chambers is a condition for the efficiency and flexibility of the parliament. In some countries, like Sweden and Denmark, bicameralism was eliminated precisely because of its egalitarian character.[22] Maintaining a bicameral Parliament just for the sake of the so-called 'balance' in the law-making process and tradition has become superfluous. Further reforms are necessary in Romania: a proper differentiation between the two chambers' functions, a difference in scrutiny, duration of term of office, legitimacy and/or representativeness, as none of these are features of the current Romanian bicameralism, even after the 2003 amendments.

The bicameral system is, as mentioned above, one of the few traditions of Romanian parliamentary democracy. The pre-2003 egalitarian bicameralism was highly criticised and the agenda for constitutional amendment included some corrections. These changes affected in particular the involvement of the chambers in the law-making process. An order of preference was established for the first reading of a bill, the main criterion being its subject matter (Article 75 CR). The Chamber of Deputies is the first chamber to be notified concerning bills for the ratification of international treaties and legislative measures deriving from the implementation of such treaties and agreements, as well as for most organic laws. Other bills are first submitted to the Senate. Whichever chamber is not first notified becomes the 'decisional chamber'. Each first notified chamber has 45 days to examine and adopt the bill (or 60 days for more complex laws, such as codes). Any inaction of the chamber during this period results in the tacit passing of the bill. After the bill is adopted, expressly or tacitly, in the first chamber, it must be sent to the other chamber, which will make a final decision. Therefore,

[22] The Constitution Unit, *Checks and Balances in Single-Chamber Parliaments: A Comparative Study* (London, UCL, 1998) 6 *et seq*. See also National Democratic Institute for International Affairs, 'One Chamber or Two? Deciding Between a Unicameral And Bicameral Legislature', Paper no 3, available at https://www.ndi.org/files/029_ww_onechamber.pdf.

laws can be the work of a single chamber, even without formal adoption. On the other hand, if there are divergences between the two chambers, the relevant provisions return to the first notified chamber, which makes the final decision. In the end, as academic circles commented after the constitutional amendment, this new, problematic legislative system claims to be bicameral but functions as a unicameral one, and is 'condemned to break, through some of its aspects, the most elementary principles of a parliamentary system',[23] including that of parliamentary debate.[24] The Venice Commission recently recommended that Romania should establish 'a more simple and effective parliamentary procedure', even a unicameral system.[25]

Other differences between the two chambers concern the members' minimum age (23 years for the Chamber of Deputies and 33 for the Senate) and the representation quota (a deputy for each 73,000 inhabitants and a senator for each 168,000 inhabitants of an electoral constituency).

ii. Internal Organisation: Groups, Committees, Speakers

The internal organisation of the chambers is set by Parliamentary Standing Orders, adopted by the chambers: the Standing Orders of the Chamber of Deputies, of the Senate and of Joint Sittings.

Parliament is organised politically in parliamentary groups and, as working structures, in parliamentary committees. Any bill, after its registration at the first-notified chamber, goes to the permanent specialised committee. Each Standing Order establishes the chamber's committees. Temporary special committees (such as the constitutional amendment committee) or inquiry committees may be created, the latter to investigate situations arising in relation to the executive or issues involving corruption. All committees are composed following the political structure of each chamber. Their main tasks are to examine bills or legislative proposals, to propose amendments and to give advisory opinions,

---

[23] T Drăganu, 'Câteva considerații critice asupra sistemului bicameral instituit de Legea de revizuire a Constituției' (2003) 4 *Revista de Drept Public* 55, 67.
[24] See also Venice Commission, *Opinion on the Draft Law on the Review of the Constitution of Romania*, Venice, 2014, §141: '[O]ne may understand that a single reading of the draft law in a Chamber could be enough to pass the legislation sometimes even without formal adoption by the Chamber.'
[25] ibid, §142.

before a bill is sent for debate to the plenary chamber. For more complex pieces of legislation, the committees may appoint expert groups to assist them in their work. Such groups, composed of academics and practitioners in different areas of law, were established for drafting the new codes (Civil Code, Criminal Code, etc) and for the amendment of the Constitution.

Committees also have other competencies, such as interviewing the candidates for ministerial positions. They are considered the most important working structures of the two chambers, the latter following, in most cases, the committee reports, although they are not binding. In practice, committees are the most important internal structures of Parliament, as most of the time they take the actual decisions on draft legislation, but also on other internal issues.

Political groups are composed of at least 10 MPs belonging to the same party. They are mostly active in parliamentary debates, but they can also act institutionally: a parliamentary group can complain to the Constitutional Court about the alleged unconstitutionality of a chamber's Standing Order. They have a central role in proposing candidates for presidents of the two chambers (speakers), the members of the committees and of other internal officials. Party discipline is very important within the parliamentary groups, and MPs who do not respect it in the voting process are usually excluded from their parties.

A frequent practice within Parliament is political migration or floor-crossing. This phenomenon entails the shift of elected MPs from one party to another, usually from the opposite side of the political spectrum. In the last legislature, the political composition that resulted from the elections was not stable until the end of the mandate. Political migration and new alliances within Parliament resulted in a shift in the majority in 2012, when the Government was dismissed by a motion of censure and a Government supported by the new majority was appointed.[26] The newly formed majority's primary goal was to acquire power at all levels of state, including the presidential function. Setting aside the unpopularity of President Băsescu and his Government, the hasty manner in which the new majority acted, although it respected the

---

[26] See B Iancu, 'Separation of Powers and the Rule of Law in Romania: The Crisis in Concepts and Contexts' in A von Bogdandy & P Sonnevend, *Constitutional Crisis in the European Constitutional Area* (Oxford, Hart Publishing, 2015) 154. See also Ch 3.

letter of the Constitution, was not entirely consistent with the principle of the rule of law.[27]

It is difficult to decide whether such 'political shifting' or 'floor-crossing' should lead to the loss of the parliamentary seat, as has been argued by some voices.[28] On the one hand, such a sanction could be justified by the fact that not only persons but also political parties were elected to Parliament, and that floor-crossing can change the entire political result of the elections, as actually happened. On the other hand, the Constitution says that 'deputies and senators are in the service of the people. Any imperative mandate is null'. This means that the mandate cannot be revoked by electors and cannot cease unless a serious offence is committed, or in case of incompatibility.[29] The 2013 constitutional amendment bill contained such a proposal—'[T]he mandate of deputy or senator ceases … on the day of resignation from the political party from which he/she was elected or on the day of his/her registration in another political party'—but was criticised by the Venice Commission[30] and declared unconstitutional by the Constitutional Court, on the ground that it would be contrary to the 'representative mandate' rule. This is a sensitive matter as it brings into consideration the actual representativeness of the parliamentarians: do they represent political parties rather than citizens, the electoral process being only a facade to legitimise any political representation? In this case, are the 'representative mandate' rule and the prohibition of the imperative mandate still legitimate?[31] A constitutional penalty for floor-crossing would not, in my view, breach the constitutional representative mandate rule, as it would not mean a revocation of the mandate by the electors but would be caused by the lack of representativeness according to the electoral result. Another possible solution would be the express and strict regulation of floor-crossing, with its limitations and consequences.[32]

---

[27] See Ch 3.

[28] The Constitution of Portugal contains such a provision.

[29] See below, D.i.

[30] Venice Commission (n 24), §130.

[31] V Ferreres Comella, *The Constitution of Spain. A Contextual Analysis* (Oxford, Hart Publishing, 2013) 101.

[32] For instance, the South-African legislation allows floor-crossing of elected representatives, but it is limited to a particular 15-day period in the second year following the election. Moreover, an elected member could only 'cross the floor' once without losing his or her seat (for further details, see H Klug, *The Constitution of South Africa. A Contextual Analysis* (Oxford, Hart Publishing, 2010) 161–62).

Each chamber has a bureaucratic apparatus, which consists of a Permanent Office/Bureau, composed of a president, vice-presidents, a secretary and other officials. The president/chairman of the chamber is elected at the beginning of the parliament and holds a representative position, playing an important role in the political and legal life of the chambers. For instance, the presidents of the chambers may refer to the Constitutional Court an objection regarding the unconstitutionality of a law, before promulgation. The presidents of the chambers may be dismissed from office, at the request of a percentage of the members, for 'serious' violations of the Constitution or the provisions of the Standing Orders. In July 2012, both presidents of chambers were dismissed following this procedure.[33] The presidents of the chambers also have a constitutional representative role: in the event of vacancy of the presidential office, the state will be represented, in order of preference, by the president of the Senate or by the president of the Chamber of Deputies. This situation has arisen twice so far, in 2007 and 2012, during the suspension from office of the President of Romania, when the acting presidents of the Senate took the position as interim heads of state.[34]

iii. Sessions and Sittings

Parliament meets in two ordinary sessions each year: the first lasts from September until the end of December, and the second from February until the end of June. Although there were no debates on a possible reform, with a view to increasing the working time of Parliament, such a measure will be necessary if the much-criticised high number of GOs decreases in future. If the Government's delegated legislative power is rationalised, Parliament will need more time to legislate. At present, a possible solution is that of organising more extraordinary sessions, which may be convened for urgent matters or whenever it is necessary to continue the legislative work outside an ordinary session.

---

[33] Chamber of Deputies, Resolution no 25/2012. The Resolution was referred to the Constitutional Court, which ruled that it was not competent to examine it as the Court may only review, according to its own jurisprudentially-established criteria, 'resolutions with a normative character, which affect constitutional values and principles' (RCC, Decision no 729/2012).

[34] See Ch 3.

The sittings of the plenary chambers of Parliament are usually separate. The Constitution sets forth those powers that the Parliament may only exercise in joint sittings: receiving the message of the President; declaring a state of war; appointing, based on the President's proposals, the directors of the intelligence services; appointing the Ombudsman; establishing the status of deputies and senators,[35] etc.

The deputies and senators have, besides the regular sittings and committee meetings, one day a week for work in the area where they have local parliamentary offices. All expenses relating to these activities are covered by the chambers' budgets.

D. Status of Members of Parliament

The status of the deputies and senators was established by the parliamentary Standing Orders until 2006, when an organic law[36] was enacted on this subject as a result of the constitutional reform in 2003. The new law prescribed the rights, duties, sanctions, incompatibilities, immunities and other rules on the mandate of MPs, implementing the rather concise constitutional provisions on the subject.

The parliamentary mandate of MPs usually ends on the day the newly elected chambers legally meet, but will also do so following exceptional events, such as resignation, loss of electoral rights (as a complementary criminal sanction by way of a judicial decision), incompatibility, or death. Resignation occurs most frequently in cases of incompatibility, but also for other reasons. In the event of a criminal conviction, resignation is not mandatory, except in those cases when the conviction includes the loss of electoral rights. However, it can be argued that a criminal conviction, especially for acts of corruption, would be ethically incompatible with the position of MP. Not all Romanian MPs share this concern. One of the latest examples is that of the Liberal Senator Tudor Chiuariu, former Minister of Justice, who was sentenced in January 2014 to three years' imprisonment, by a final decision of the High Court, with conditional remission of the sentence. He was, at the time of the sentence, the President of the Legal Committee of the Senate and Secretary of the Constitutional Amendment Committee.

---

[35] See below, D.
[36] Law no 96/2006 on the Status of the Deputies and Senators.

He resigned from these positions, but not from senatorial office. The president of the Senate's view was that 'as long as the sentence allows him to keep his mandate, we cannot take it from him'. This is a typical attitude of Romanian politicians in general and of MPs especially, the concept of 'resignation from honour'/*demission d'honneur* being almost inconceivable.[37]

i. Protection of Members of Parliament: Incompatibilities, Immunity

There are two main ways to protect the mandate of an MP: the setting of incompatibilities, to ensure the correct exercise of office, and of immunities, to reduce the risk of political or other kinds of pressure. The main incompatibilities with holding the position of MP are laid down by the Constitution, and the organic law introduced further incompatibilities with positions in the economy. Article 71 CR provides that the positions of deputies and senators are incompatible with each other. On the other hand, the position of MP is incompatible with any other office involving public authority, but MPs may be members of the Government. It is one of the characteristic features of the balance of powers: those MPs who are also members of Government should ensure the link between the two state powers and more effective work.

The incompatibilities established by the law of 2006 concern the economic milieu and the protection of MPs from potential influences or pressures from that direction. Thus, being a deputy and senator is incompatible with occupying a position such as top management in private and public companies or institutions, a state representative in the general assemblies of public companies, a company owner or a member of an economic interest group.

The existence of an incompatibility or a conflict of interest is determined by the chamber's permanent bureau, directly or after consulting the National Agency for Integrity (ANI).[38] Once an MP is found to be in an incompatible situation, he or she must resign from office. The decisions of the ANI may be challenged in court. So far, although most

---

[37] In January 2015, Chiuariu was involved in another criminal investigation, in a €3.5 million corruption case. He has never resigned from his senatorial seat.

[38] See Ch 3.

of its 'high-level integrity' decisions were challenged, in 80 per cent of cases the courts confirmed the ANI's conclusions.[39]

There have been several cases of incompatibility declared by the ANI against MPs. Some of the decisions were challenged before the High Court of Cassation and Justice (HCCJ), but the final judicial decisions were not actually executed in every case. In October 2012, the president of the Superior Council of Magistrates referred to the Constitutional Court a request to resolve a constitutional conflict between the judiciary and the Senate, because a final HCCJ decision, confirming an ANI incompatibility decision on a senator, had not been executed. More precisely, the Senate voted against executing the final judgment of the High Court regarding the incompatibility of a senator who had simultaneously been a theatre director and granted several contracts to his wife in this capacity. The Constitutional Court[40] held that 'the Senate has the obligation to take into account the existence of the incompatibility, as stated in the judicial decision ... and to determine the *de jure* cessation of Mr Mircea Diaconu's mandate as a Senator'. The Constitutional Court's ruling had not been applied when the term of office of the Senate came to an end, after which the senator in question finally resigned in December 2012. The situation was included as a negative point in the European Commission's CVM Interim Report from January 2013, which was reiterated in the Report of January 2014:

> Since July 2012, the judiciary has more than once had to refer to the Constitutional Court following unwillingness of the Parliament to terminate mandates as a result of final court decisions on incompatibility of a parliamentarian. The most recent ruling of the Constitutional Court on this issue dates from November 2013, however the Senate has as yet taken no action.[41]

The first version of the Constitution provided for stronger parliamentary immunity, there being no permission to even prosecute MPs. Currently, the situation has changed and the Constitution (Article 72) stipulates, under one generic term ('parliamentary immunity'), two kinds of immunity. The first type, which is that most usual in democratic parliaments, protects MPs against any responsibility for votes cast or political opinions expressed in the exercise of their office.

---

[39] According to the Institution's reports, available at https://www.integritate.eu.
[40] RCC, Decision no 972/2012.
[41] CVM Report, January 2014, at 4. Although progress was acknowledged, these concerns were reiterated in the January 2015 CVM Report.

The second type of immunity, which is more controversial, concerns the criminal responsibility of MPs. In 2003, due to the placing of the corruption issue on Romania's agenda for European integration, parliamentary immunity had to be curtailed. The new text stipulates that deputies and senators may be the subject of criminal investigations, or may be prosecuted for acts that are not connected with their votes or political opinions expressed in the exercise of their mandate. However, the second part of the article remained unchanged: MPs may only be searched, detained or arrested with the consent of the chamber to which they belong and after being heard. In case of flagrant offences, MPs may be detained and searched, but the Minister of Justice must promptly inform the president of the chamber. If the chamber finds that there are no grounds for an MP's detention, it may order the annulment of the measure. It is immediately noticeable that the curtailment of the generous immunity from criminal liability went only half way: the chamber as a political authority may substitute for the judicial authorities, even in the case of a flagrant offence.

In practice, however, especially in the first years after Romania's EU accession in 2007, lifting parliamentary immunity became easier, but not due to a sudden change in mentality: it was the consequence of the CVM monitoring by the European Commission and the further changes made to the legislation that were acknowledged by the Commission in its January 2013 Report. However, the Reports of 2013 and 2014, while acknowledging the further steps taken (introducing deadlines for parliamentary consideration of immunity-lifting requests), warned the Romanian authorities that the further steps envisaged 'will need to include ... that where the Parliament refuses to lift the immunity, it provides a full justification',[42] and expressed concerns that 'the effectiveness of the Statute will need to be assessed over time. Unfortunately, the practice during autumn 2013 did not always indicate that parliamentarians were looking to new rules to provide a new rigour in the proceedings'.[43]

Although the amended law entered into force in July 2013, it did not include any requirement to motivate the refusals to lift immunity. In January 2014, 28 Romanian MPs were investigated for corruption and

---

[42] Available at http://ec.europa.eu/cvm/docs/com_2013_47_en.pdf.
[43] Available at http://ec.europa.eu/cvm/docs/swd_2014_37_en.pdf, Technical report, at 27.

the number increased, some of them being investigated in more than one case. One of the European Commission's recommendations in order to speed up the progress of justice reform and the fight against corruption was the adoption of a parliamentary Code of Conduct, which should include 'clear provisions so that parliamentarians and the parliamentary process should respect the independence of the judiciary, and judicial decisions in particular'.

Despite the progress made in the area of immunity, there were also serious drawbacks that cast doubt on the actual commitment of the Romanian MPs and Parliament to transparency and anti-corruption strategies. In December 2013, in a chain of events now known as 'Black Tuesday', the Chamber of Deputies adopted two laws amending the Criminal Code, in which, amongst other things, the definition of 'conflict of interests' was changed so as not to include administrative acts (and therefore, mayors or ministers, for instance, could not be accused of such conflicts). Moreover, the President of Romania, MPs and liberal professionals were no longer to be considered 'public officials'. The direct consequence of the latter amendment, if ever applied, would have been that MPs could not be charged for the taking of bribes, trading in influence and abuse of office (offences specific to public officials). The judicial bodies, including the High Court and the Supreme Council of the Magistracy, promptly reacted and expressed serious concerns about these amendments, while the European Commission criticised them in its January 2014 CVM Report.[44] The Constitutional Court, in its turn, declared the amendments to be unconstitutional, on the ground of breaching the principles of equality before the law and of the rule of law, in the context of the need to intensify anti-corruption efforts.[45] The draft law was finally rejected by Parliament in November 2014, after the presidential elections. This was considered a typical reaction of the MPs to anti-corruption actions, and was allegedly motivated by the fear of future prosecutions.

As regards the refusal to lift parliamentary immunity, one of the most blatant cases took place in March 2014, when the Chamber of Deputies refused permission for the criminal investigation of an MP and former Minister of Finance suspected of corruption.[46] In November 2014,

---

[44] COM(2014) 37 Final, at 10.
[45] RCC, Decision no 2/2014.
[46] The request was renewed and denied again in February 2015.

following the presidential elections, an impressive number of five liftings of immunity for former ministers were decided in Parliament, at the request of the National Anti-corruption Directorate (DNA).[47] Another case that has shaken the political and judicial scenes was the Chamber of Deputies' refusal to lift the immunity of Prime Minister Ponta (who is also an MP), in order that he might be pursued and tried for alleged criminal offences of corruption (conflict of interests) committed during office. Ponta, a former prosecutor and lawyer, was accused of forging private documents and being an accomplice to tax evasion and money-laundering at the time he was a lawyer associated with the law firm of Dan Sova, a prominent member of his party, who was also accused in the same case. During this time, Ponta allegedly received legal assistance contracts for state-owned companies, as well as the use of luxury cars, benefits in exchange for which, when appointed Prime Minister, he nominated Sova as a member of his Government. The case is still pending, but the refusal to lift Ponta's immunity in the pursuit of criminal charges was harshly criticised by the press, in judicial circles and by Romania's foreign partners. An important drawback is also that the main reason publicly invoked by MPs when justifying the refusal was the alleged political partisanship of the DNA and of the judiciary.

E. The Opposition

In any healthy democracy, the opposition plays an important part within Parliament. The mechanisms to protect the political minority vary, but all have the same goal: to ensure that power is exercised fairly, in conformity with the principles of tolerance and mutual respect, specific to democracies.

The opposition does not have an 'institutional' role in the Romanian Parliament, all political groups having equal status. However, besides the political tools that result from the voting rights exercised according to the Parliamentary Standing Orders, the Constitution places in

---

[47] In January 2015, the DNA started criminal investigations of accusations of corruption against a Constitutional Court judge, appointed by the Senate in 2013 and formerly an MP. It was the first time a constitutional judge had been placed under criminal investigation. Following the arrest and a demand from the DNA, the judge resigned from office in February 2015.

the hands of the political minority a few legal tools that enable it to express its views and even hinder actions of the majority in the legislative process: the right to legislative initiative, and the right to contest the constitutionality of Parliamentary Standing Orders and of other parliamentary resolutions Another powerful tool is the right to challenge a law before the Constitutional Court, after adoption but before promulgation by the President. A group of at least 50 deputies or of 25 senators may refer such a complaint to the Constitutional Court, before a law is promulgated. If the law is considered unconstitutional, Parliament has the obligation to re-examine it and 'bring it in line with the Constitution'. The unconstitutionality card has been played frequently by the opposition, and many times successfully. For example, in 2012, two laws modifying the electoral legislation were declared unconstitutional, following complaints from the opposition.

The opposition may also act in the political legislature-executive balance of powers, by initiating a motion of censure against the Government, either directly or within the procedure of engagement of responsibility by the Government itself.[48]

F. The Legislative Process

Although the Romanian Parliament is defined by the Constitution as the sole legislative authority, its legislative power is split with the Government. On the one hand, over 90 per cent of draft laws come from the Government; on the other hand, acts of legislative delegation (including the laws that enable and endorse it) outnumber the laws adopted by the regular legislative procedure. Moreover, the cumbersome legislative procedure and the deficiencies of Romanian bicameralism, which enables a law actually to be adopted by only one chamber,[49] contribute to the inefficiency of Parliament as legislator.

i. Legislative Initiative

In Romania, unlike in France, no constitutional power has a monopoly over the legislative initiative. It is a shared competence, between the Government, MPs, the President (for constitutional amendments

---

[48] See Ch 3.
[49] See below, iii–v.

only) and the people. Those bills emanating from the Government are 'legislative projects', the others being 'legislative proposals' (a French-inspired classification).

The popular initiative has certain constitutional limits: it must be supported by at least 100,000 voters coming from at least a quarter of the country's territorial departments, with at least 5,000 signatures from each department. A popular initiative may not cover tax issues, international issues, amnesty or pardons. The conditions for and the procedure of the popular initiative are established by a special law.[50] The main difference between the popular initiative and the other types of legislative initiative is that the former must be published in the *Official Journal* once it has been positively advised by the Legislative Council. The law also expressly provides that such an initiative may not be promoted by elected officials, members of the Government and other public officials, or by persons who may not be members of political parties. The Constitutional Court can verify the constitutional and legal requirements of a popular legislative initiative. In practice very few initiatives come from MPs (around 10 per cent)[51] and the right to popular legislative initiative has never been exercised.

ii. The Legislative Council

The Legislative Council has existed, under various names but with similar competences, since the mid-nineteenth century; it was established under this name in 1925, following the 1923 Constitution. The Council ceased to exist in 1948, was re-established in 1971 and again ceased to function in December 1989. The present Council, although re-established by the 1991 Constitution, started to function only in 1996, because only then was its Regulation adopted. This is another example,

---

[50] Law no 189/1999.
[51] Even fewer actually became laws (around 20% of the total number of initiatives introduced by MPs). Among the reasons for such a low rate of parliamentary-originated legislation are the low resources and expertise of the parliamentary offices, mainly due to favouritism or nepotism (parliamentarians frequently employ relatives or friends as 'experts') and the high rate of absenteeism from the meetings of parliamentary committees. For further details, see A Ionaşcu, 'Searching for Representation. Romanian Parliamentary. Elites and their Political Roles' (2013) 2 *Studia Politica. Romanian Political Science Review* 247.

along with the Ombudsman,[52] of a transitional situation, where the functioning of a new institution was delayed much longer than necessary after the coming into force of the Constitution.

The Legislative Council is an expert advisory body of Parliament. The main task of the Council is to examine and advise on legislative proposals coming from MPs and citizens, but also to elaborate more complex legislative projects, at the request of the Government. The advisory opinion of the Council is a mandatory step in the legislative process regarding proposals coming from sources other than the Government. The Council's advisory opinion accompanies the bill through the further stages of the legislative process: they may not contain political remarks. The Legislative Council also keeps the official record of all legislation in Romania. The Council is run by a president and by presidents of sections (public law, private law, official record of legislation), elected by Parliament in a joint sitting.

iii. Introduction to the Competent Chamber

Depending upon its subject matter, a bill must be registered either in the Chamber of Deputies or in the Senate as first-notified chamber. It must be put on the draft agenda of the chamber by the permanent bureau within five days. Unlike legislative projects (which come from the Government), legislative proposals, in order to be included on the agenda, need the advisory opinion of the Legislative Council and the opinion of the Government. All bills must be accompanied by an explanatory report, stating the necessity for the bill and the issues it addresses.

iv. The Committee Stage

After meeting all due requirements, bills are sent to the specialised permanent committees for debate and advisory opinions. The relevant committee examines the bill and may propose amendments. The committee report may recommend the bill's adoption, with or without amendments, or its rejection. If the bill needs to pass through more committees (in the case of a more complex law), each report shall include the conclusions of the other committees involved. If the bill has an advisory opinion from the Legislative Council attached to it, the

---

[52] See Ch 6, section IV.B.

committee report will show whether and how the suggestions made by the Council were followed.

v. Plenary Debate and Adoption

Once a bill is included on the agenda of the plenary chamber, it will be presented by its author, accompanied by all advisory opinions and amendments adopted so far by the committees. After presentation of the conclusions of the committee's rapporteur, the representatives of the parliamentary groups can express their opinions on the bill in the plenary session. Before closing the debate, the author of the bill and the committee's representative have the right to speak. No amendments may be proposed at this stage. When the committee report proposes rejection of the bill, a vote is cast after the closing of the general debate. If the chamber disagrees with the committee's conclusion, the bill will follow procedure and will be debated at a future sitting.

The second reading (debate of the bill article-by-article) takes place only when there are proposed amendments in the committee report. New amendments may not be proposed at this stage. When the debate on amendments reveals important consequences for the bill, the president of the chamber may send the relevant texts back to the committee, requesting an opinion. All amendments are decided by separate votes. Once a final version is achieved, the chamber may give its final vote in a separate sitting.

Ordinary laws are adopted by a simple majority, organic laws by absolute majority and constitutional amendment laws must gather a qualified majority of two-thirds of the total number of members of each chamber.

After the vote, the law is sent to the other chamber (the 'decisional chamber'), which examines it using an identical procedure. In case of disagreement on one or more texts, these are sent back to the first chamber, which will make a final decision in an emergency procedure. Therefore, a law can be exclusively the work of one chamber.

The legislative process is therefore lengthy and 'exceedingly cumbersome'.[53] A delay of six months or more is usual before a bill becomes law. This is the reason why, especially in the economic field, the Government has frequently used delegated legislation, which is easier to adopt

---

[53] ibid, at 254.

although still submitted to parliamentary control, at least in theory. The massive number of GOs was common to all Romanian governments since 1992, and was one of the main points of concern for the European Commission during the CVM, after Romania joined the EU.[54] Using the 'emergency argument', the Government adopted an excessive number of ordinances (in some years, ordinances and laws of approval outnumbered all other laws) and the Romanian Parliament became an instrument for endorsing delegated legislation. After the European criticisms of 2012, the balance reversed in 2013, when the number of ordinances dropped dramatically.

G. Parliamentary Resolutions

In its current activity, Parliament adopts, besides laws, resolutions and motions. Parliamentary resolutions regulate the internal activity of the two chambers. Standing Orders ('the rules of Parliament') are the most important normative resolutions. 'Individual' resolutions lack normative character and apply to individual situations, for example nominations to various positions, elections, lifting civil immunity from arrest, other internal decisions. These acts have a primarily political character, although by nature they are legal acts. The resolutions concerning the Standing Orders of the chambers must be adopted by an absolute majority, whereas the other resolutions need a relative majority (half plus one of the members present in each chamber). Since 2010, all resolutions may be submitted to the review of the Constitutional Court, although the Constitution itself only gives the Court the power to review Standing Orders. A change in the Court's law, in 2010, introduced this new power, as the Constitution leaves open the list of the Court's powers.[55] The Court curtailed its own jurisdiction by adding to the legislative provisions, and laid down that it is only competent to review resolutions that 'affect constitutional principles and values'[56] and have a normative character, and that individual resolutions that have a political character may not be reviewed. For example, the Court stated

---

[54] See Ch 3.
[55] See Ch 5.
[56] RCC, Decision no 53/2011.

that 'the replacement of a person with another, respecting the Standing Orders' procedures, cannot represent a matter of constitutionality'.[57]

H. Other Functions: Control and Supervision

The Romanian Parliament has the constitutional function of supervising the executive by all classic parliamentary means of control: questions, interpellations and motions addressed to the Government, as well as investigations by committees of inquiry, the power to adopt a motion of censure and dismiss the Government, as well as the power to suspend and impeach the President.

The role of Parliament in appointing the Government is the source of this political control. The Government draws its legitimacy from the vote of confidence given by Parliament. This determines the political accountability of the Government to Parliament, which may go as far as withdrawing its confidence by the adoption of a motion of censure.[58]

Deputies and senators have the right to address questions to members of the Government or to other leaders of the administration. These questions are employed to draw the attention of members of the executive to a great variety of issues: health, education, trade, infrastructure, etc. Questions may become a tool of the opposition to highlight sensitive issues, sometimes coming from the electoral constituency of the MPs. The question procedure is provided by the chambers' Standing Orders, and differs for oral and for written questions. Oral questions may be addressed, during Question Time at the Chamber of Deputies, every Monday between 6.30 and 7.30 pm, only to members of the Government.[59] The subject matter of the questions must be notified in writing during the previous week, at the office of the Secretary of the Chamber of Deputies, who informs the Minister for the Relations with Parliament about the oral questions that will be addressed. Written questions may be addressed to members of the Government and other leaders of the public institutions. These types of questions are registered with the secretary of the chamber and transmitted to the relevant recipient. All written questions and their answers are published on the chamber's website.

---

[57] RCC, Decision no 729/2012
[58] See Ch 3.
[59] Chamber of Deputies Standing Order, Arts 167–168.

Interpellations are written requests addressed to the Government by a parliamentary group or by the MPs, requesting explanations of important matters of internal or external governmental policy. The interpellations usually concern economic and social problems with a degree of importance or urgency. If the authors of the interpellations do not find the answers satisfactory, they may ask the chambers to adopt simple motions to express their position.

Questions, interpellations and motions are tools both in the relationship between the Parliament and Government, and between the majority and the opposition. They may help to render the Government more politically accountable before the representative assemblies and more eager to implement its policies. In a developed, mature constitutional culture, interpellations should be instruments of dialogue on difficult problems rather than political tools that hinder progress. The increasing number of questions and interpellations[60] is ongoing proof of the development of such a 'culture of control'.[61] The Government does not react in a significant way to these milder means of parliamentary control. The motion of censure remains the most important form of control that may be exercised over the Government, because a vote of no confidence entails its dismissal.[62]

Committees of inquiry may be created when an investigation is necessary 'to clarify the causes of events or actions with negative effects and the circumstances in which they were produced', as well as to establish the conclusions, responsibilities and necessary measures'.[63] For example, in November 2013, a joint inquiry committee was established to investigate the circumstances in which the eldest daughter of the former President of Romania was awarded a €1 million loan by a state-owned bank, to buy agricultural land on the outskirts of Bucharest.

Parliament makes appointments to various public offices, or confirms those made by other authorities. Each chamber of Parliament appoints three Constitutional Court judges.[64] Parliament appoints the

---

[60] The number of the questions increased from 1,075 in 2012 to 3,078 in 2013, while interpellations increased from 461 in 2012 to 1,014 in 2013.

[61] S Boyron, *The Constitution of France. A Contextual Analysis* (Oxford, Hart Publishing, 2013) 126.

[62] See Ch 3.

[63] Article 73 CD Standing Order.

[64] See Ch 5.

Ombudsman[65] (*Avocatul Poporului*) and the directors of the intelligence services in a joint sitting. Through the permanent committees, Parliament advises on the appointment of ministers and other public officials. In a joint sitting, it receives the message of the President of Romania, and the annual reports of the Court of Auditors and of the Ombudsman.

Parliament advises on or confirms executive decisions of the President of Romania. Before calling a consultative referendum, the President must consult Parliament. Parliament also backs up the President's decisions in matters of national defence: the partial or total mobilisation of the armed forces may only be decided with the prior or (in exceptional cases) subsequent approval of Parliament. Parliament must also be informed by the President by official message in the event of armed aggression against the country. If Parliament is not in session, it shall be convened within 24 hours. The President may also be held politically accountable before Parliament: in the event of a serious breach of the Constitution, the President may be suspended by Parliament, but may only be dismissed by popular vote, expressed within a binding referendum.[66]

I. Dissolution of Parliament

This classic feature of any parliamentary regime is established in a rationalised form by the Romanian Constitution. In the *checks and balances* equation, Parliament can be dissolved by the President of Romania. However, this power is extremely limited, and may only work if there is institutional consensus for anticipated elections. Thus, the President may only dissolve Parliament if it fails to give a vote of confidence, during a period of 60 days, to two Government proposals. This would be highly unlikely to happen unless all the parties involved were to agree. Parliament could not dissolve itself, therefore, if the political majority felt that it had the strong support of the electorate; the only way it could trigger anticipated elections would be with the support of the other powers. In this scenario, the Government would resign, the President would formally appoint a candidate who is rejected by Parliament, the situation would be repeated within the required period of 60 days and then the President would dissolve Parliament. It is clear that such a

---

[65] See Ch 6.
[66] See Ch 3.

situation is only likely to happen when the President supports the political majority. In this case, the dissolution would also bring him or her political benefits, perhaps resulting in his or her re-election. In periods of cohabitation (understood as 'the situation where the president from one party holds the power at the same time as a prime minister from an opposing party and where the president's party is not represented in the cabinet'),[67] when conflict between the President and Parliament is at its peak, paradoxically it is very unlikely to see a dissolved Parliament, unless there is a true interest in consolidating the political majority.

J. Budgetary and Financial Powers

i. Adoption of the Budget

The adoption of the state budget and of the state social security budget is the main financial power of the Parliament. The budgets are drafted annually by the Government and submitted separately to Parliament for approval, which usually involves the simple endorsement of the proposal. In order for the budget to apply for the next financial year, it must be approved at least three days before the expiry of the previous financial year (31 December), otherwise the previous year's state budget and state social security budget shall continue to apply. In December 2013, for the first time in 24 years, the law on the budget was on the verge of not being promulgated by the President. Following agreements with international financial organisations, the Government had introduced new gasoline taxes in order to increase tax revenues. The President opposed the new taxes on social grounds, also claiming that they were needed by the Government to 'pay off the local barons' for the upcoming election campaign. Therefore, the President threatened not to promulgate the budget until the Government withdrew the new taxes. Following an agreement between the Prime Minister and the President, the Government agreed to postpone the application of the tax by three months and the President agreed to promulgate the budget in time. This is a typical consequence of political 'cohabitation'

---

[67] R Elgie and I McMenamin 'Explaining the Onset of Cohabitation under Semipresidentialism' (2011) 59 *Political Studies* 618.

in Romania, based more on 'image exercises', last-minute threats and negotiations, with little care and attention to the public interest. A similar situation occurred in November 2014, when the Government did not submit the draft budget in time because of the presidential elections in which the Prime Minister was a candidate.

The Constitution also provides that taxes, duties and any other revenue of the state budget and state social security budget shall be established solely by law (or acts with equivalent legal force). Over the last few years the tax legislation (especially the Fiscal Code) was frequently changed through emergency ordinances issued by the Government, a practice that, although technically constitutional, is a reason for permanent criticism because it circumvents parliamentary debate.

ii. Financial Control Through the Court of Auditors

The Court of Auditors is an important body through which the Parliament exercises its financial powers. It is not an entirely novel institution:[68] the first Romanian 'High Court of Auditors' was created in 1864 as an organ entrusted with the task of verifying the public finances throughout the whole country. The Constitutions of 1866 and 1923 preserved the institution, which had jurisdictional functions. The Court of Auditors ceased to exist in 1948, but during the communist regime an organ of financial control was created (in 1973), with the task of 'following the observance of the party and state decisions in the financial field and the defence of the socialist property'.[69] In 1991, the Court of Auditors was re-established by the Constitution as the main organ enabled to exercise control over the formation, administration and use of the financial resources of the state and the public sector. In 2003, by constitutional amendment, it was deprived of jurisdictional powers, all litigation resulting from its activity being placed under the jurisdiction of the specialised judiciary courts. The organic law[70] stipulates that the Court of Auditors acts autonomously, according to the Constitution and the law, and represents Romania as a 'supreme audit

---

[68] See also B Murgescu et al, *Istoria Curții de Conturi a României (1864–2004)* (Bucharest, Orizonturi românești, 2005), available at http://www.curteadeconturi. ro/sites/ccr/RO/Documente%20publice/istoriaCCR.pdf.

[69] Law no 2/1973.

[70] Law no 94/1992, modified by Law no 217/2008.

institution' in international organisations. The Court of Auditors may initiate *ex officio* control procedures, which cannot be stopped unless so decided by the Parliament in the event of the Court's exceeding its lawful competences.

The Romanian Parliament may ask the Court of Auditors to check on the management of public resources and to report on its findings. The Court is obliged to present to Parliament its annual report on the management accounts of the previous budgetary year. No other public authority can request control over the Court of Auditors. The Court has local branches—the departmental chambers of auditors—that exercise the control of public funds at local level. Their acts and decisions can be challenged before the ordinary courts of law. In the field of European funds, the external audit is exercised by the Audit Authority, created in 2005 with this special competence.

K. Conclusion

The powers and functions of parliaments worldwide have undergone important changes in recent years. Their functions as legislators were curtailed by the extensive use of legislative delegation, as a result of the need for more speedy regulations in difficult economic and social contexts. This is true in Romania as well. Parliament was intended to be the sole legislative organ and the supreme representative forum, with strict control over the Government, but this role has never been accomplished in full: instead, Parliament became an 'endorsement' organ, often tacitly adopting pieces of legislation, submitted by the Government as bills, as regular or emergency ordinances or by responsibility engagement.[71] Although Parliament's constitutional role cannot be contested, the practices and mentalities of parliamentary life should be revised and reformed. The control and self-control function is also adversely influenced by the political migration phenomenon,[72] and by the constant theme of corruption.

Refusal to lift parliamentary immunity and to grant judicial organs the right to prosecute present or former members of the Government is another sensitive issue affecting the public image of Parliament.

---

[71] See Ch 3, section III.D.iv.
[72] See above, C.ii.

Repeated corruption issues, together with the tendency of parliamentarians to enact laws granting themselves material privileges (increased salaries, increased expenses, special pensions), have contributed to a very low level of representativeness and popularity of the institution. Parliament, 'the supreme representative organ of the people', consistently gains a maximum of 20 per cent in social polls on the public's trust in this institution. This is also the result of the phenomenon of the 'negative vote', which has characterised Romanian elections over the last decade: voters have tended to choose the lesser of two evils, rather than a party or an alliance that has actually gained the public trust.

Therefore, a more balanced legislative procedure, ensuring respect for the rule of law by not shielding MPs from judicial investigation, rationalised recourse to legislative delegation, all these are problems that must be tackled by the Romanian Parliament.

FURTHER READING

M Dogan, 'Romania, 1919–1938' in M Weiner & E Ozbudun (eds), *Competitive Elections in Developing Countries* (Durham, Duke University Press, 1987) 369–89 (for the parliamentary elections in the inter-war period).

A Ionaşcu, 'Territorial Dimensions of the Romanian Parties. Elections, Party Rules and Organisation' (2012) 2 *Studia Politica. Romanian Political Science Review* 185.

——, 'Searching for Representation. Romanian Parliamentary Elites and their Political Roles' (2013) 2 *Studia Politica. Romanian Political Science Review* 22.

C Preda, 'The Romanian Political System: after the Parliamentary Elections of November 30, 2008' (2009) 1 *Studia Politica. Romanian Political Science Review* 9.

——, 'Partide, voturi şi mandate la alegerile din România (1990–2012)' (2013) 1 *Studia Politica. Romanian Political Science Review* 27.

ES Tănăsescu & G Vrabie, 'Un bicaméralisme unicaméral: le Parlement de la Roumanie postdécembriste' in E Montigny & F Gelineau (eds), *Parlementarisme et francophonie* (Quebec, Presses de l'Université de Laval, 2013) 205.

R Weber, 'Constitutionalism as a Vehicle for Democratic Consolidation in Romania' in J Zielonka (ed), *Democratic Consolidation in Eastern Europe* (Oxford, Oxford University Press, 2001) 226.

3

The Dual Executive and the Avatars of Romanian Semi-presidentialism

———◆———

Semi-presidentialism – The Republic – The President – The Government – Cohabitation – Corruption

I. INTRODUCTION

According to the classic division of powers principle, obsessively denied during the totalitarian era as belonging to the 'bourgeois heritage', the 1991 Romanian Constitution establishes a clear distinction between the legislature and the executive. Article 1 §4 CR expressly emphasises that 'the State shall be organized based on the principle of the separation and balance of powers—legislative, executive and judicial—within the framework of constitutional democracy'.[1] This is the only place where the Constitution refers to the 'executive' as a 'power of the State'. In Title III—*The Public Authorities*, the executive power comes after the legislative power—the Parliament—and its structure is dual, specific to 'mixed' political systems (semi-presidential or semi-parliamentary): a President and a Government led by a Prime Minister. The Government draws its legitimacy from Parliament (through the vote of confidence) and the President from the people, being directly elected. Having chosen to fashion a semi-presidential regime, in the hope that this would solve the problem of a directly elected but less powerful President, the constitutional drafters of 1991 were forced to design the

---

[1] See Ch 1, section III.B.i.

executive's institutional construction within the dualist scheme, despite its imminent dangers. Thus, the written Constitution provides for a weak President alongside a Prime Minister and Government endowed with responsibility for the internal and external policy of the country.

Nevertheless, the living constitution confirmed the dangers of semi-presidentialism: on the one hand, the excessive personalisation of political power, due to the high political legitimacy of the President, and, on the other hand, the inner conflict between the two parts of the executive. The first tendency manifested itself when the parliamentary majority was congruent with the presidential one. The second tendency appeared when the parliamentary majority diverged from the presidential side (so-called 'cohabitation').[2]

II. THE PRESIDENT

A. The Origins of the Presidential Function in Romania

In order to better understand this 'aversive'[3]—to the point of being contradictory—attitude as regards the presidential function in Romania, brief insight is necessary into its origins and development before the constitutional moment in 1989–91. Although the Republic was proclaimed in December 1947, along with the installation of the communist political regime, the position of President was only created in 1974, by the dictator Nicolae Ceauşescu. Originally, the 1965 Constitution did not include the presidential function, the head of state being considered the President of the Council of State (the supreme executive organ). In 1965, on the death of the former communist leader Gheorghiu-Dej, Nicolae Ceauşescu took the first position in the political hierarchy, becoming Secretary-General of the Communist Party. He shared power with two other leaders, the President of the Council of State and the President of the Council of Ministers. In 1967, Ceauşescu took over the position of President of the Council of State and thus became the 'supreme leader' of the country. In March 1974, during a

---

[2]   R Elgie & I McMenamin, 'Explaining the Onset of Cohabitation under Semi-presidentialism' (2011) 59 *Political Studies* 618.

[3]   See Ch 2, section III.B.ii.

great plenary meeting of the Communist Party, important changes to the constitutional system were decided: the creation of the position of President of the Socialist Republic of Romania and the proposal, addressed to the Great National Assembly (Parliament) to elect Nicolae Ceauşescu to this position. The Assembly promptly rubberstamped the proposals, changed its regulation and the Constitution, and, following a sumptuous ceremony, 'elected and [unanimously] proclaimed' Nicolae Ceauşescu as the first President of the Republic on 28 March 1974. This final act meant, according to the Institute for the Research of Communist Crimes in Romania (IICCMER), 'officialising the personal dictatorship of Nicolae Ceauşescu and the first tangible sign of a dynastic scenario which violently ended 15 years later'.[4] The new President then acquired even more power, as one of the 'supreme organs of state power' according to the Constitution, in practice embodying the 'supreme' political and constitutional power in the country. His constitutionally conferred attributes were only a facade: being the supreme chief of the Communist Party enhanced the President's power exponentially and made him practically uncontrollable.

The amended 1965 Constitution defined the President as 'the head of state' and the representative of the state internally and externally, but also made him President of the Council of State and, when necessary, enabled him to 'establish measures of special importance which concerned the supreme interests of the country': he appointed ministers and the president of the supreme tribunal (when the Great National Assembly was not in session), and he granted citizenship. In time, Ceauşescu, his family and close entourage managed to control the entire political and constitutional mechanism. The fall of his regime, the last but the most tyrannical dictatorship in Central and Eastern Europe, through the violent revolution of December 1989, meant, for the people, the beginning of a journey of no return. Romania was the only country in the region, following the overthrow of the communist regime, to completely denounce its Constitution, the ad hoc revolutionary power abrogating it on the first day of the revolution. That is why the drafters and builders of the new regime had to be very careful in designing the new constitutional order.

---

[4] Available at http://www.iiccr.ro/ro/evenimente/pro_memoria/28_martie_1974_intronarea_unui_presedinte/.

B. The Design of the New Presidential Institution

Although, at the onset of the new Constitution's drafting process, it was, for various reasons, clear that the republican form of government must be maintained,[5] the new constitutional design of the presidential institution was a difficult task, as the function did not exist in the country's 'democratic tradition'. Therefore, the only available models were foreign.

Anxiety caused by Romania's totalitarian past was the dominant sentiment[6] in the process of drafting the Constitution in 1991, including the chapter on the President. Fear of past authoritarian regimes, which ended in tyranny, was the main concern of Romanian political society in 1990. The drafters of the new Constitution were in search of a solution to an apparent dilemma: how to enable the people to elect a President, without giving the latter too much power. In doing this, they eliminated from the start the presidential regime (with a too-powerful president) and the pure parliamentary regime (where the President is not directly elected, as the drafters were certain that a Constitution providing for an indirectly elected President would not be welcomed by the people). In this context, the French semi-presidential regime, established by the 1958 Constitution, seemed the perfect model. French law has been a source of inspiration for Romanian law ever since the nineteenth century,[7] therefore recourse to the French experience in this case seemed perfectly legitimate. However, in adopting this approach, the Constitution-makers neglected some important issues: on the one hand, legal transplant does not lead to automatic copying of the functioning of the model institutions, neither does it involve replication of the chosen society. On the other hand, fear or anxiety does not always suggest the best solution to a problem: in fact, a closer look at history would perhaps lead some less anxious drafters to discern that the real danger lay in the Romanian people's attraction to a strong, authoritarian leader. If their fear was justified, they had to eliminate any such possibility. But, as this anxiety was difficult to tackle, the result was a system the founding

---

[5] See Ch 1.

[6] For a theory of 'constitutional sentiments' that influence constitution-making, see A Sajo, *Constitutional Sentiments* (New Haven and London, Yale University Press, 2011).

[7] See Introduction and Historical Overview.

fathers truly thought provided for every eventuality, furnishing tools to resolve any problem. The decade 2004–14 proved them wrong.

The Constitution places the President first within the executive power structure. This arguably does not ensure the President's primacy within the executive, as in France[8] (ie as regards the Government and Prime Minister). The President appears first simply because of his or her greater legitimacy, being directly elected (see below), as well as being the representative of the state. The living constitution reveals the actual meaning of the constitutional design: a Romanian President inherently more powerful than as provided by the constitutional text, especially in a period of congruency between the presidential majority and the parliamentary majority. 'Presidentialisation' has undoubtedly been a general feature of the Romanian constitutional system. The impact of this reality over Romanian constitutionalism must be assessed in the context of Romanian anxiety about the head of state's authoritarianism.

C. The Election of the President

The Romanian President is elected by direct and universal suffrage, according to the Constitution and the Law on the election of the President.[9] Candidates must be Romanian citizens of at least 35 years of age, and their candidacy must be supported by at least 200,000 voters. The number of candidates, after increasing from six in 1992 to 16 in 1996, seemed to have remained steady at 12 for the 2000, 2004 and 2009 elections, but increased to 14 in 2014.

The election process usually consists of a two-round ballot. Theoretically, the President can be elected by obtaining the majority of votes of persons registered on the electoral lists in the first ballot, but in practice this has never happened. The second ballot, between the first two highest ranking candidates after the first ballot, is organised if none of the candidates has obtained a majority. In this round, the candidate who obtains the highest number of votes will be elected. The electoral campaign lasts 30 days and is usually organised by the political parties supporting the candidates. Independent candidates may also run for

---

[8] S Boyron, *The Constitution of France. A Contextual Analysis* (Oxford, Hart Publishing, 2013) 56.
[9] Law no 370/2004.

office. The Constitutional Court is competent to confirm the results of the presidential election, unlike parliamentary elections, where this competence belongs to the Central Electoral Commission.

D. The Presidential Term of Office

Since 2004, the President's mandate has been for five years. Initially, the Constitution provided for a four-year term, consistent with that of Parliament. Due to anxiety about potential authoritarianism, the duration of the mandate was changed in 2003 to five years, to avoid the simultaneity of parliamentary and presidential elections, and therefore identical presidential and parliamentary political majorities. This concern was generated by the fact that, between 1990 and 2003, the candidate who won the presidential elections acted as a 'power-engine' or 'trail-blazer'[10] for his party, transforming it into a 'presidential party' and favouring trends towards presidentialisation. However, cohabitation and its potential adverse effects were not expressly envisaged. This evolution of the Romanian system shows again the paradoxes of legal transplant. In France, after decades of *septennat* (the seven-year mandate of the President of the Republic), an amendment from 2000 shortened the President's term of office to five years, with the explicit purpose of making it equal to the mandate of the *Assemblée Nationale*, in order to avoid cohabitation, which 'was made possible by the difference between the lengths of the mandates of the President of the Republic and the members of the Assemblée Nationale'.[11] This change was the result of the lesson learned from long periods of cohabitation, which proved not only dangerous[12] but also dysfunctional. In Romania, otherwise known for its deference to French law, the opposite occurred: after 12 years of identical terms of office, it was decided to increase the President's mandate by one year, therefore making it more likely that cohabitation would occur. The events that followed a few years later in political and constitutional life proved that it was a mistake. After another decade and two periods of cohabitation, politicians were willing to change the

---

[10] ES Tănăsescu, 'The President of Romania or the Slippery Slope of a Political Regime' (2008) 4 *European Constitutional Law Review* 69.
[11] Boyron (n 8), at 62. See also Elgie & McMenamin (n 2), at 625.
[12] Boyron (n 8), at 63.

Constitution once more: the 2014 constitutional draft amendment provided a return to the President's four-year mandate.

After the experience of dictatorship, the Constitution set an absolute limit on multiple terms of office. Thus, according to Article 80 §4, no one may serve more than two terms of office, which can be consecutive. Ironically, the first 'exception' from this rule was the first elected President, Ion Iliescu. He had been elected President of Romania under the provisional act, Decree-Law no 92/1990, which regulated the state institutions and the first elections before the adoption of the Constitution. He was in office until 1992, when he was re-elected, under the new Constitution, ending his term in 1996. His candidacy for another term of office in 1996 was challenged at the Constitutional Court, which ruled that the 1990–92 office could not be counted as a 'first' term, because the President had not been elected under the new Constitution, which restricted the number of periods of office to two.[13] President Iliescu did not win a new mandate in 1996, but the situation was repeated in 2000, when he ran for office and eventually won his second and last term.

E. Role and Powers of the President

According to Article 80 CR (inspired by the French Constitution, with some subtle differences), the President represents the Romanian state and is the safeguard of national independence, unity and the territorial integrity of the country. Furthermore, the President shall guard the observance of the Constitution and the proper functioning of the public authorities, acting, to this effect, as a mediator between the state powers, as well as between state and society. The President is, therefore, the representative of the state, the guardian of state independence and integrity, the guardian of respect for the Constitution and the functioning of the state, and also a mediator within Romanian society. Moreover, he is commander of the armed forces and President of the Supreme Council for State Defence (CSAT), according to Article 92 §1 CR.

The drafters of the Constitution intended to keep the President in a neutral zone of the political scene, as a more representative and symbolic figure with few powers to intervene in practice. However, only

---

[13] RCC, Ruling no 2/1996.

President Emil Constantinescu came closest to this picture, acting more like a 'republican monarch'.[14] Both the other Presidents, Ion Iliescu and Traian Băsescu, exceeded this role, in a more or less obvious manner. Their situations were slightly different. In all his presidential mandates, Iliescu was supported by the parliamentary and governmental majority, which made his involvement in the political arena less obvious. In reality, the President was dominating the political scene, through obedient governments and a passive Parliament, which was content to watch the governments legislating by ordinance and to rubberstamp governmental policies. Traian Băsescu, on the other hand, a self-proclaimed 'player President', clearly intended to be more than a mere mediator, and to become actively involved in the political game and in all sectors of governance, even taking over the role of the Prime Minister. This cost him the first cohabitation[15] (2005–08), during which he was suspended from office, but paradoxically or not, it also gained him popularity. He was re-elected in 2009, after a controversial second ballot, and re-entered the zone of parliamentary and governmental domination, under the governments led by Prime Minister Emil Boc (2009–12). Thus, as was correctly noted in legal scholarship,

> despite the poor legislative and executive powers initially allocated, the Romanian President, especially during Băsescu's presidency, developed informal powers and strong political influence which brought the inevitable political conflict with the [Prime Ministers] to quite extreme and undesirable intensity.[16]

The President's influence within the executive power was enhanced by presidential interpretations of the Constitution, frequently confirmed by the Constitutional Court (especially during Traian Băsescu's term of office), as will be discussed below. This increase in powers did not, however, lead to an increase in the President's accountability,[17] as shown by the interpretations of the Constitutional Court in matters such as presidential immunity, political responsibility or other presidential obligations.

---

[14] M Guţan, 'Romanian Semi-Presidentialism in Historical Context' in (2012) 2 *Romanian Journal of Comparative Law* 275.

[15] For a detailed account of this first period and its effects, see L Stan & R Zaharia, 'Romania' (2008) 47(7–8) *European Journal of Political Research* 1115.

[16] Guţan (n 14), at 295.

[17] B Dima, *Conflictul dintre palate* (Bucharest, Hamangiu, 2014) 187.

i. Representative of the State

The President has a dual role: representative of the people and representative of the state. However, the function of people's representative is only the result of the direct election,[18] not of the presidential powers, which circumscribe the President's role as representative of the state. In this capacity, the President has the power to conclude international treaties and agreements and then submit them to Parliament for ratification. He or she can declare partial or general mobilisation, and declare a state of war, of siege or of emergency. All these powers are subject to the prior or subsequent approval of Parliament. Among the representative powers that are not subject to the Parliament's consent are the powers to confer orders and titles of honour, to promote members of the armed forces to the ranks of marshal, general and admiral, and to grant individual pardons. The President also nominates three judges to the Constitutional Court and appoints all magistrates by decree, at the proposal of the Superior Council of Magistracy (the Romanian high judicial council).[19]

In 2012, the Constitutional Court was called on to resolve a constitutional conflict between the President and the Government: the Prime Minister refused to acknowledge the rights of representation of the President at the European Council Summit of 28–29 June 2012.[20] The conflict arose in the context of cohabitation, and began with exchanges of letters between the Presidency and the Ministry of Foreign Affairs on the delegations that should participate in the Summit. Parliament adopted a political declaration (at the request of the Prime Minister, Victor Ponta), which stated that the Prime Minister was entitled to represent the country at the Summit. Finally, the Constitutional Court was called on to settle the matter. Upon a detailed analysis (in which, inter alia, the Romanian system was wrongfully equated with the French system of semi-presidentialism), the Court stated that the Government

---

[18] The Constitution says that the Parliament is the 'supreme representative organ of the people', which means that, although there are other representative organs (eg the President), their representative function is inferior to that of Parliament.

[19] See Ch 5.

[20] For a detailed account of and comment on the matter, see CM Banu, 'Comments on the representation of Romania in the European Council and on its consequences for democratic accountability' (2014) 14(1) *International and Comparative Law Review*, Palacki University of Olomouc 5 at 34.

and the Prime Minister have the constitutional power to assure the achievement of the country's foreign policy, but only the President may engage the state as a subject of international law, and that Parliament's declaration might not change the constitutional dispositions. The Court emphasised that other EU member states were represented by authorities having the power to engage the state in international agreements, and therefore concluded that 'the President not only has the right, but also the obligation assumed by the act of adhesion to participate in the meetings of the European Council; otherwise, Romania's engagements would be breached'.[21] This is one of the many instances where the Constitutional Court became involved in a political conflict between the President and another authority, clearly favouring the former.

ii. Mediator and Guarantor of the Constitution

The role of the President as mediator between all political and social actors should be enhanced by the fact that, after election, he is forbidden to be a member of a political party. This neutrality should begin right at the start of the presidential mandate, according to Article 84 §1 CR. He also may not engage in any other public or private office. Mediation is thus seen as a political function of the President, who should be neutral in his or her actions towards all political forces.

In reality, although they formally resigned from their parties, all previous Presidents were, to a greater or lesser extent, supporters of those parties that, in their turn, had promoted them into office. President Iliescu was the true head of his party during his mandate, when he was supported by an obedient parliamentary majority. President Constantinescu was the only one who attempted to maintain neutrality, whereas President Băsescu was an active promoter of the party he formerly led (PDL), especially during the term of office of Prime Minister Emil Boc. Therefore, the mediation role was almost non-existent. President Iohannis, elected in November 2014, was also the leader of the party that supported him in his campaign, but it is too early to say whether he will maintain political neutrality during his term of office.

The Constitutional Court's jurisprudence contributed to the dilution of the mediation function of the President. The Court rigidly interpreted the President's role as a mediator in a juridical key, which led to the

---

[21] RCC, Decision no 683/2012, §8.

enhancement of the possibility for the President to bypass his obligation of neutrality. In 2007, in an advisory opinion on the President's suspension from office for seriously breaching the Constitution, the Court stated that

> the attitude [injurious towards political opponents of his former party] and the opinions imputed to the President cannot be considered infringements of the Constitution, because Article 84 of the fundamental law provides that he/she cannot be a member of a political party, but is not forbidden to keep the links with the party that supported him/her in elections or with other political parties.[22]

The Court then referred to the President's immunity as regards his political opinions, disregarding the fact that, according to the Constitution, immunity only applies to the *legal* responsibility of the President, whereas the mediation function essentially entails *political* acts and therefore political accountability.

A similar interpretation was given by the Court in 2014, when the President was accused of actively taking part in the electoral campaign of a political party for local elections, by publicly transmitting messages of support (photos of the President wearing electoral t-shirts appeared on the party's banners, posters and other electoral materials, and he publicly expressed his choice to vote for that party). In this context, the Constitutional Court was called on to resolve a constitutional conflict between the President and the Government, on the ground that, by his actions, the President had affected the Government's competence to organise impartial elections and violated its obligation of neutrality under the Constitution. The Court refused to acknowledge the legal nature of the conflict and therefore declared the complaint inadmissible, but, in its analysis, it endorsed the actions of the President by stating that, 'the mediation function ... requires the President's neutrality, but it does not exclude the possibility to express his opinion on any [political] divergences and does not confer upon him the role of political competitor'.[23] The Court also refused to assess the implied linking of the President with the electoral campaign of a political party, by stating that this was not within its jurisdiction.

As for mediation between state and society, this was almost entirely absent, especially during the terms of office of President Băsescu.

[22] RCC, Advisory Opinion no 1/2007, §3.2.
[23] RCC, Decision no 284/2014.

In 2010, the President made himself the mouthpiece of the Government, announcing in a press conference the austerity measures taken by the latter to counteract the economic crisis (measures he had declared himself to be against only weeks before): cuts in salaries, pensions and other social benefits. When asked to explain the cuts to maternity benefits, the President declared that 'we are a country of mommies and babies', suggesting that there were too many beneficiaries, which generated strong protests from NGOs and society as a whole. The President was also twice found guilty of discrimination, by the National Council Against Discrimination (CNCD), for making racist remarks: in 2007, he used the expression 'stinky gypsy' against a journalist, after seizing her phone during a public encounter; and in 2014 he was censured for a remark made in November 2010 when, during an official visit to Slovenia, he stated that among the nomad Roma population, 'very few are willing to work' and 'many of them traditionally live on what they steal'.[24] Thus, instead of being a neutral mediator within society (especially as regards the social-economic and ethnic minorities) and a guarantor of constitutional principles, the President in question, on the one hand, took over the governmental function by getting involved in economic policies and, on the other hand, promoted, by his language, the discriminatory (and hence unconstitutional) conceptions that still dominate Romanian society as a whole.

As guarantor of respect for the Constitution, the President has the power to address a constitutional complaint to the Constitutional Court against a law, before promulgation, or to address a request to settle a legal conflict of a constitutional nature between authorities. Many times, President Băsescu in particular used this power to allow the Court to impose a 'presidential reading' of the Constitution, after orchestrating, in 2010, a favourable majority of judges within the Court.[25]

F. Relationship with the Government

The President's powers in his or her relationship with the Government are defined by the Constitution, but they have been increased through informal changes imposed by the Constitutional Court.

---

[24] Available at http://cncd.org.ro/noutati/Comunicate-de-presa/Comunicat-de-presa-referitor-la-hotararea-adoptata-de-Colegiul-director-al-C-N-C-D-in-sedinta-din-data-de-10-02-2014-193/.

[25] See Ch 5.

i. Appointment and Reshuffle

The President plays an important role in the formation of the Government. The Constitution meant to give the Government a stronger legitimacy by involving the two popularly elected authorities—the Parliament and the President—in its appointment.

Following elections or a Government dismissal, the President, after consulting the party or political alliance that holds the parliamentary majority, nominates a candidate for the office of Prime Minister, who needs to obtain Parliament's vote of confidence for the Government's composition and programme. The President seems to have only a formal role. After the Prime Minister and the Government have obtained the vote of confidence, the President appoints the Government, which is also merely a formal power.

The nomination of the Prime Minister is a key element in the relationship between the two elected authorities: if Parliament does not approve the candidate nominated by the President twice in a period of 60 days, it may be dissolved. There is a small loophole in the mechanism: the Constitution does not say whether the President, after Parliament has refused to give a vote of confidence, may or may not nominate the same person a second time. A clear example of presidentialisation in this matter, even against the parliamentary majority, occurred in October 2009. The majority coalition broke down and the opposition managed to dismiss the Government by motion of censure, right before the presidential elections.[26] President Băsescu, who was just starting his re-election campaign, refused to nominate the candidate proposed by the 'new majority' and made another choice. The presidential candidate was rejected by Parliament. Ironically, the refusal of a second candidate would not have exposed the Parliament to dissolution, which cannot occur in the last six months of the President's term of office. In December 2009, the President was re-elected and the former Prime Minister was acting as interim head of the dismissed Government. Meanwhile, a great number of parliamentarians from the majority resigned from their parties and became 'independent', while joining a new coalition orchestrated by the newly re-elected President. The newly formed majority gave the President's candidate, the formerly dismissed Prime Minister, Emil Boc, a vote of confidence.

---

[26] This was the first motion of censure adopted after 1991.

The group of 'independent' parliamentarians eventually formed a new party (National Union for the Progress of Romania—UNPR), which became a parliamentary party without having participated in elections.[27]

Another issue in the President's relationship with the Government concerns the reshuffle procedure. The Constitution seems clear when it says, in Article 85 §2, that in the event of a Government reshuffle or vacancy of office, the President shall dismiss and appoint, at the proposal of the Prime Minister, some members of the Government. If the reshuffle may lead to a change in the political structure of the Government, the President will need Parliament's approval in order to exercise this power, at the proposal of the Prime Minister. It is thus clear that the primary role in this procedure is played by the Prime Minister, who has the first voice in proposing candidates for vacant positions in the Government or in changing his ministers. However, with the help of the Constitutional Court, President Băsescu gave his own reading of this text, enhancing presidential powers in 2007–08, during the first cohabitation period with the Liberal majority and the Government of Calin Popescu-Tariceanu. In December 2007, following the resignation of the Minister of Justice, the Prime Minister nominated a new candidate. Previously, all Presidents who had been asked to confirm such nominations did so as a formal act, endorsing the Prime Minister's choice. In this case, because of tensions resulting from the cohabitation, the President refused the nomination, invoking the candidate's integrity in her professional capacity as a lawyer more than 20 years ago. Following a second refusal by the President of the same proposal, the Prime Minister addressed the Constitutional Court, with a request to resolve a legal conflict of a constitutional nature.[28] After admitting the existence of a conflict, the Court made a distinction between the obligation of the President as a result of the appointment procedure (a formal one, as the new Government is actually approved by resolution of Parliament) and that concerning the vacancy or reshuffle procedure: in the latter case, in the Court's view, the President would not be bound to accept the Prime Minister's proposal. The Court said that this procedure should function as a result of collaboration between the two authorities and that institutional blockages should be avoided. It also admitted that the Constitution does not provide for the right of the

---

[27] In 2014, this party was member of the governmental majority coalition.
[28] See Ch 5.

President to refuse the Prime Minister's proposal in such a case. Given the silence of the text and in the spirit of its 'obligation to resolve conflicts of constitutional nature', the Court claimed the right to create rules to fill perceived gaps in the Constitution, with the declared purpose of avoiding institutional malfunctioning. Despite its role as 'negative legislator', the Constitutional Court applied the principle of analogous interpretation and held that, since the President has the right to ask Parliament to re-examine a law *once*, this rule should apply, by analogy, to the reshuffle procedure: the President has the right to refuse a candidate for a vacant position in the Government *once*, with proper reasons, whereas the Prime Minister has *the obligation* to make another proposal. Besides being used with regard to totally different powers of the President, this analogy functions only unilaterally, as the President himself is not under the same obligation to propose another person if his candidate for the Prime Minister office is refused by Parliament. But this is a matter on which, it might be argued, the Constitutional Court was not called to rule.

In another decision, the Court indirectly endorsed the refusal of the President to take notice in due time of a vacant ministerial post and therefore to decide on a reshuffle, on the ground that 'the Constitution does not provide for a time within which the President must exercise this attribute'.[29] However, the Constitution provides for a maximum period of 45 days in which a ministerial post can be occupied *ad interim* (Article 107 §4), therefore a systematic interpretation would have been possible. The Court preferred to apply rigidly the article that sets forth the President's attributes (Article 85 §2), to the detriment of the proper functioning of the Government, as an indefinite delay by the President could create a serious institutional blockage.

The President–Government relationship should manifest itself regularly through the consultations between the two authorities. Thus, the Constitution provides that the President may consult the Government about urgent and extremely important matters. The President may also participate in meetings of the Government debating matters of national interest, with regard to foreign policy, the defence of the country, the assurance of public order and, at the request of the Prime Minister, in other cases. The President chairs those meetings of the Government in which he participates, but he cannot vote. It is relevant to note in this

---

[29] RCC, Decision no 356/2007.

context that, according to the Constitution, the President may not dismiss the Prime Minister (Article 107 §2). This provision was introduced in 2003, in order to clarify the relationship between the two heads of the executive. Previously, in 1999, President Emil Constantinescu, in the absence of a precise constitutional text, took a controversial decision to dismiss the Prime Minister.

ii. Cohabitation and its Effects

Unlike in France, in Romania the cohabitation phenomenon was not simply the result of elections and of the difference in the length of the President's and Parliament's terms of office. This difference surely contributed to the phenomenon, but did not determine it. Both periods of cohabitation (2005–08 and 2012–14) began principally as a result of another phenomenon, which is more specific to Romanian post-communist constitutional life: political migration, combined with the regrouping of the political alliances within Parliament. In its turn, cohabitation encouraged political migration, as a political weapon against the President.[30]

Cohabitation produced important tensions between President and Parliament, as well as between President and Prime Minister. Thus, in both periods of cohabitation, the President was suspended from office: in May 2007 and in July 2012. In both cases, the President was reinstated following compulsory referendums: by a majority of votes in 2007 and by invalidation of an overwhelmingly opposing referendum in 2012.[31] In 2012, the new 'ad hoc' parliamentary majority formed in May 'cohabited' with President Băsescu and decided his suspension from office during the constitutional crisis from July–August. In December 2012, the same majority was confirmed by the general elections, with over 66 per cent of the votes, a majority that had never been reached in Romania since 1990. The majority vote given in the invalidated referendum was thus confirmed, but this generated new political conflicts. Despite the outcome of the election, the President refused, at first, to acknowledge the political alliance that formed the majority as a partner in the consultations required by Article 103 CR in order to nominate

---

[30] See Ch 2.
[31] See section II.I.ii. below.

the candidate Prime Minister, on the ground that the Constitution only required him to consult with political parties and not with alliances. Eventually, President Băsescu gave up his radical view and nominated the candidate proposed by the majority, the acting Prime Minister Victor Ponta, who obtained the vote of confidence from the new Parliament. Nevertheless, this only happened after the two opponents— President and Prime Minister—had signed an informal *Agreement of cooperation and good governance between the President and the Government of Romania*, in other words, a 'cohabitation pact'. It seemed that after the events in the summer of 2012 and after the conclusions of the Venice Commission thereon, the main Romanian political actors were in need of a document to rely on in their mutual relationship, and in which to

> undertake to fulfil and refrain from engaging in political disputes on themes pertaining to Romania's commitments to international institutions. … avoid useless public confrontations, try to resolve differences behind closed doors; … refrain from encouraging divergent approaches in the institutions they each represent and [to] reprimand excessive public positions taken by party colleagues or members of staff trespassing on such rules of conduct, politeness, decency and courtesy.

This 'gentlemen's agreement' to lower the tension was supposedly the incentive the President used in order to start his new cohabitation with the quite overwhelmingly opposing parliamentary and governmental political majority.

Although some voices argued that cohabitation's effect of 'parliamentarisation' of the system can act as a counterweight to the presidency,[32] the majority of scholars agree that cohabitation 'can be harmful for the very survival of democracy',[33] which is also the case in Romania. Cohabitation was and remained a source of permanent tension in Romanian political and constitutional life. The tensions between the President and the Prime Minister had serious consequences on the quality of the governance (external representation, delays in the legislative process, delays in the process of a Government reshuffle), with serious but not irreversible effects on the overall quality of the democracy.

---

[32] See for details Elgie & McMenamin (n 2), at 618.
[33] ibid, at 619.

G. Relationship with the Parliament

The President has an ambivalent relationship with Parliament: although both authorities are directly elected, this does not place them on an equal footing. The President has some limited legislative powers, but the checks-and-balances mechanism gives precedence to Parliament. Although some voices have referred to the Romanian system as semi-parliamentary, the constitutional texts rather suggest a 'parliamentarised semi-presidential' system. In practice, as shown above,[34] there were also tendencies towards presidentialisation.

The President has the right and duty to promulgate all laws adopted by Parliament. This is not merely a formal sanctioning of the law, as the President has the right to veto a law by refusing its promulgation and returning it to the Parliament for re-examination. Normally, promulgation must be given effect within 20 days of the President's receiving the law. If the President refuses promulgation, Parliament has no time limit within which to re-examine or re-adopt the law. The President has the right to return a law to Parliament only once. After re-examination by Parliament and re-adoption of the law, the President is bound to promulgate it, even if it is in the same form.

Another tool to counterbalance Parliament as the legislature is complaint to the Constitutional Court. The President, upon receiving a law for promulgation, may challenge its constitutionality before the Constitutional Court. If the Court decides that the law is constitutional, the President is obliged to promulgate it. Therefore, if the President really opposes a law, the logical path to follow should be, first, to return it to Parliament and then, if he still does not agree with it, to challenge its constitutionality.

The parliamentarised character of Romanian semi-presidentialism also results from the absence of a legislative referendum. In France, the President has the power to convene a referendum by which to circumvent Parliament, submitting the adoption of a law to a popular vote. In Romania, this type of referendum does not exist, as it was considered too powerful a tool for a President intended to have weaker powers.

The President has a very limited power to dissolve Parliament,[35] as an expression of the mechanisms surrounding the separation of powers.

---

[34] See F above.
[35] See Ch 2.

The President's decision must be preceded by consultations with the presidents of the chambers and with the leaders of the parliamentary groups. Parliament cannot be dissolved more than once a year, and the President cannot exercise this power during the last six months of his mandate or during a state of mobilisation, war, siege or emergency. In terms of 'semi-presidentialism', this is another power granted only half-way: the 'model' French President may dissolve the French Parliament with no formal justification but with the same time restrictions. No dissolution of Parliament has occurred so far under the 1991 Constitution.

H. Foreign Policy and Defence Powers

As the representative of the state, the President has extensive powers in the field of foreign policy and defence, some of which are shared with the Government and most of which are subject to parliamentary consent.

The President concludes international treaties negotiated by the Government and then submits them to Parliament for ratification. Only after ratification do the treaties become part of domestic law. The diplomatic representatives of Romania are accredited and may be recalled by the President, on the Government's proposal. The President also approves the creation, closure or change of rank of Romania's diplomatic missions, and receives the accreditation of other states' ambassadors (Article 91 §3 CR).

The President is commander-in-chief of the armed forces and President of the Supreme Council of State Defence (CSAT). The Council is established by an organic law. The other members of the Council are the Prime Minister (who is also Vice-President of the Council), the Minister of Internal Affairs, the Minister of National Defence, the Minister of Foreign Affairs, the Minister of Justice, the Minister of the Economy, the Minister of Public Finances, the director of the Romanian intelligence service, the director of the foreign intelligence service, the chief of the general staff of the military and the presidential adviser for national security.

The President may declare, with the prior approval of Parliament, the general or partial mobilisation of the military. In exceptional cases, the President may take the measure and subsequently submit it for the approval of Parliament, during the five days following. He is also entitled to take measures against any armed aggression against the country and promptly bring them to the knowledge of the Parliament, through a message. No President has made use of these powers.

I. Accountability of the President

i. Incompatibilities and Immunity

The office of President is incompatible with holding any other public or private office, and the President may not be a member of a political party during his or her time in office. The constitutional text on presidential immunity (Article 84 §2 CR) does not expressly define it but only refers to the provision on parliamentary immunity. However, reference is made only to the first paragraph of Article 72 CR, according to which the deputies and senators cannot be held legally accountable for votes cast or political opinions expressed during their mandate. No mention is made of the following paragraphs, which allow parliamentarians to be prosecuted for acts done outside the exercise of their office but protect them from being searched, detained or arrested without the consent of the chamber to which they belong. Therefore, apparently, the President does not benefit from this kind of immunity. However, the Constitutional Court, by interpreting the Constitution, concluded that the only exception to the President's immunity would be his or her prosecution for high treason, as in all other cases there is no constitutional authority that can lift the President's immunity.[36]

The immunity clause does not mean that the President lacks all legal responsibility. According to the Code of Criminal Procedure, in the event of an accusation against the President for any offence other than high treason, presidential immunity entails a stay of proceedings until the end of the presidential mandate, and also the suspension of the limitation period for the offence, both of which then resume after the President comes to the end of his or her term of office.

ii. Suspension from Office

The partial immunity from legal responsibility does not exclude the political responsibility of the President, which, in cases of serious

[36] RCC, Decision no 678/2014.

breaches of the Constitution, can result in his or her suspension from office. Suspension from office is a sanction for 'serious offences violating the Constitution' and may be decided by Parliament, in a joint sitting, with a majority vote. The Constitutional Court must give its prior advisory opinion, which is not binding on Parliament. The President may present his or her position before Parliament regarding the allegations brought against him.

The Constitution does not define the notion of 'serious offences violating the Constitution'. In its second advisory opinion on the subject,[37] the Constitutional Court gave a definition of the term, which is essential to establish the political responsibility of the President. The Constitutional Court first said that any act by which the constitutional provisions are infringed is 'serious', by reference to the object of infringement. As the Constitution expressly provides that only 'serious' breaches may lead to the suspension of the President, a *summa divisio* must be made. According to the Court, 'not any act of infringement of the Constitution may justify the President's suspension from office, but only "serious acts", with a complex meaning'. The Court used four criteria to indicate the seriousness of offences: the constitutional value damaged; the consequences of the wrongful act; the means used; the person of the perpetrator and his intention with respect to the purpose of the act. 'Serious offences' were defined as meaning the following:

> decision-making acts or the avoidance of compulsory decision-making acts, by which the President of Romania would hinder the functioning of public authorities, suppress or limit rights and freedoms of the citizens, would trouble the constitutional order or pursue change to the constitutional order, or acts of a similar nature and effect.

Following this analysis, the Court said, in 2007, that President Băsescu had not committed such serious offences as to justify a suspension. Among the alleged violations were: political bias in favour of the Democrat-Liberal Party; an attempt to exercise the legislative initiative, although the Constitution did not allow him to do so; unauthorised interference in the economy (he asked the Minister of Economy to act in favour of a private company); attempts to influence the prosecutors

---

[37] Advisory Opinion no 1/2007. The first advisory opinion of the Constitutional Court on the suspension from office of the President was given in 1994, on a request to suspend President Iliescu, but it was not followed by a vote in Parliament.

in re-opening closed cases for political reasons; exercising his influence over the election of the President of the Superior Council of Magistracy; and several declarations made by the President against the Government and Parliament ('the Parliament is just an old shack in clinical death'), or on the foreign policy of the country. All these were considered by the Constitutional Court as being mostly political opinions or declarations, covered by presidential immunity (despite the fact that that immunity only covers legal responsibility). Nevertheless, as the Constitutional Court's opinion is not binding, on 19 April 2007 Parliament agreed to suspend the President from office. On 23 April, Parliament changed the law on referendums, removing the requirement for a quorum to validate the ballot. The Constitutional Court endorsed the new law, which was highly criticised for changing the rules during the game.[38] The referendum took place on 19 May 2007.[39] With a turnout of 44.4 per cent of the electors, the referendum was validated, and with a vote in favour of 74.5 per cent, the President was reinstated in office.

The second suspension from office of President Băsescu occurred in 2012, following the establishment of a new majority in Parliament as a result of 'political migration' or floor-crossing.[40] Many parliamentarians from the governing party crossed the floor to the opposition coalition and formed a new majority, which adopted a motion of censure and appointed a new Government. The intention of the new Government was from the beginning to dismiss the President and to impose anticipated presidential elections. The suspension proposal contained more serious accusations than in 2007. Allegedly, the President had substituted himself for the Government as decision-maker, especially as regards economic decisions in the context of the financial crisis, which was clear from his own statements. The Constitutional Court partly supported the allegations, stating that the acts of the President exceeded the expression of mere political opinions, and directly and accordingly determined the decisions of the Government: 'the fact that the President publicly assumed the initiative of adopting social and economic measures, before their adoption by the Government, can be interpreted as an attempt at diminishing the role and powers of the Prime

---

[38] For a totally opposite decision of the Court, see Ch 1, section B.

[39] See II.F.i. above and Ch 1.

[40] See Ch 2, section II.C.ii.

Minister'.[41] The other allegations were rejected by the Constitutional Court, but at the end of its advisory opinion the Court admitted that the President 'did not exercise with maximum efficiency and diligence the role of mediator between the state powers and between the state and the society'. Unlike in 2007, the Court did not give an overall 'positive' or 'negative' opinion, preferring to deal with all points separately and to leave the final decision to Parliament. On 6 July 2012, the parliamentary majority decided to implement the President's suspension from office.[42]

This rush by the new political majority to change all the leaders of the institutions (the presidents of the two chambers of Parliament had previously been dismissed, as well as the Ombudsman) generated an unprecedented political and constitutional crisis in July–August 2012. Following a series of errors and inconsistencies on both sides of the battle, including the Constitutional Court, which openly sided with the President,[43] the crisis ended with the President's reinstatement. Although the referendum turnout was 46.24 per cent, it was invalidated for lack of a quorum under the new law[44] and the 87.52 per cent of votes in favour of the dismissal were set aside. Table 1 offers an overview of the two suspension cases.

Table 1: Two suspension cases

Year of referendum	Turnout quorum	Result	RCC decision	Outcome
2007	44.45% of voters	74.48% against dismissal	validation	President's return to office
2012	46.24% of voters	87.52% in favour of dismissal	invalidation for lack of turnout quorum (imposed by another RCC decision)	President's return to office

[41] RCC, Advisory Opinion no 1/2012.

[42] For a very detailed analysis, see B Iancu, 'Separation of Powers and the Rule of Law in Romania: The Crisis in Concepts and Contexts' in A von Bogdandy & P Sonnevend (eds), *Constitutional Crisis in the European Constitutional Area* (Oxford, Hart Publishing, 2015) 153–69.

[43] See Ch 1, section II.B.iv.

[44] ibid.

The 2012 suspension was used, in the context of cohabitation, as a tool for political revenge against the President, by invoking his previous unconstitutional actions, against a background of widespread social protests against the President and his majority, which started in January 2012. The crisis that emerged had adverse effects on the external image of the country, as well as on the principle of the rule of law in general, because all the actors involved, including the Constitutional Court, used the Constitution to promote their own interests. Although, formally, the constitutional and legal procedures had been duly observed, the context in which and purpose for which they were used diminished their democratic character. On the other hand, the manner in which the President, with the support of the Constitutional Court, contributed to the annihilation of the popular vote, affected the idea of democracy and led to increased popular mistrust in the state institutions.

In the event of a dismissal following suspension, the Constitution does not forbid the former President from running for office again, provided he or she has not already exhausted two mandates. Nevertheless, for a dismissed President to run again would present a moral problem, although, given the silence of the text, the people as sovereign may overcome it by electing him or her to office once again.

iii. Impeachment for High Treason

The impeachment or prosecution of the President may be decided only by Parliament and only for the extremely serious offence of high treason. This is a special case entailing the legal (criminal) accountability of the President, unlike suspension, which entails political responsibility. Until 2014, the crime of high treason was not defined by law. The new Criminal Code, in Article 398, included high treason amongst the crimes against national security: the crime of treason in any of its forms is proscribed by law, as is any crime of action against the constitutional order, if perpetrated by the President of Romania or by any member of the Supreme Council for National Defence.

Prosecution for high treason is the only occasion on which presidential immunity is lifted. The procedure is established by Article 96 CR: the impeachment proposal (which must include the alleged facts suggesting high treason) may be initiated by Parliament (the majority of deputies and senators), and it must immediately be notified to the President so that he can give explanations of the alleged facts.

The Parliament makes its decision in joint session, with a qualified majority of at least two-thirds of its members. The President is suspended *de jure* from the impeachment date until the final judgment of the HCCJ, which has jurisdiction to investigate and judge the President. On the date of any final judgment stating the guilt of the President, he or she will be dismissed *de jure*. In the event of acquittal, the President returns to office. This procedure has never been applied.

J. Vacancy of Office

The vacancy of the presidential office may be due to resignation, dismissal, its being impossible to exercise the presidential duties or death. Elections must be organised within three months from the date of the vacancy. During this period, as well as when the President is suspended from office or temporarily unable to exercise his or her powers, the function is exercised by the President of the Senate, as interim President. If the President of the Senate is unable to exercise that the function, the President of the Chamber of Deputies will become the interim President of Romania.

The interim President is not entitled to exercise all presidential powers and duties. The Constitution prohibits him or her from addressing messages to Parliament on the main political issues, dissolving Parliament or convening a referendum. Since 1991, Romania has had two interim Presidents: Nicolae Văcăroiu (20 April–23 May 2007) and Crin Antonescu (9 July–27 August 2012).

K. Acts of the President

The President may issue presidential decrees by which he exercises his powers and duties. Most of the decrees have an individual character (appointments to office, awarding decorations, granting individual pardons, etc). The only decrees with a normative character are those declaring a state of siege or a state of emergency. In order to be effective, presidential decrees must be countersigned by the Prime Minister, with the exception of those decrees enacted within the discretionary powers of the President: nominating a candidate for the office of Prime Minister, the dissolution of Parliament, the appointment of Constitutional

Court judges, appointing judges on proposals by the Superior Council of Magistracy.

L. Conclusion

The ambiguity surrounding Romanian semi-presidentialism has been confirmed in practice, especially by the cohabitation periods and their adverse effects. Although it was envisaged as a system with a weaker President, there were clear tendencies towards presidentialisation (especially in the period 2004–14). These alterations of the constitutional spirit did not amount to authoritarianism, but they were incentives to constitutional and political crises. All these issues have been discussed at length in civil society and in academic circles, but the constitutional changes initiated in 2013 do not include any orientation towards a parliamentary regime. Instead, the intention was to reduce the term of office of the President to four years to avoid a greater risk of cohabitation, but as cohabitation in Romania has often been the result of floor-crossing within the elected Parliament rather than of regular elections, this risk has not been completely removed.

III. THE GOVERNMENT

The Government is the second element forming the executive power, entrusted with the accomplishment of the internal and external policies of the country and with general command of the public administration. Nevertheless, the living constitution reveals that the Prime Minister and the Government may become politically subordinated to the President (although the Constitution does not provide for it) during periods of intense presidentialisation of the political regime. At the same time, the last two decades have witnessed an increasing tendency by the Government to take over the legislative process through use of the instruments known as Emergency Government Ordinances (EGOs).

The Constitution distinguishes between, on the one hand, the President and the Government and, on the other hand, the public administration. This does not suggest that the President or the Government stands outside the administration. On the contrary, the President has clear administrative competences and the Government exercises the general management of the public administration. The intention, however, was to make a clear distinction between the political zone of the executive and the technical-administrative zone. Thus, those authorities with competences in the political dimension of the executive are the 'executive in the narrow sense' (the President and the Government) and the administration (or the 'executive in the wider sense') comprises the technical-administrative authorities—ministries and other public services—referred to as the 'public administration'. Obviously, the President, and especially the Government, to which the administration is expressly subordinated by the Constitution, transmits 'political impulses' to the administration, but, by their purely administrative competences, the President and Government are also a part of the public administration in the wider sense.

A. Appointment of the Government

The Government is appointed by the President, after obtaining a vote of confidence from Parliament. The President is also involved in the pre-appointment phase in his capacity as mediator; but as the 'representative' part of the executive, he must also nominate a candidate for the office of Prime Minister, after consulting the party that won the elections or the parties that form the majority in Parliament, or, if such a majority was not formed, all parties represented in Parliament. If the President is supported by the parliamentary majority, he or she will either nominate the candidate of his or her choice, or respect the choice of the majority. In periods of cohabitation, if the Government is dismissed, or if the result of new elections put the President in opposition with the Parliament, clashes may occur.[45]

In the next phase of the appointment procedure, the nominated Prime Ministerial candidate submits to Parliament the draft list of members and programme of the new Government, in order to seek a vote of confidence. The programme and the list are debated in a joint sitting of the two chambers, and Parliament bestows its confidence by a majority vote. After receiving the vote of confidence from Parliament, the actual appointment of the Government takes place before the President, when all the members take an oath. The day on which the oath is taken is considered the start of the Government's term of office.

[45] See II.F.i. above.

B. Structure, Competences, Functioning

i. Structure

The Government is composed of the Prime Minister, ministers and other members. An organic law set out the organisation and functioning of the Government.[46] The ministers head the ministries, which function as separate organs of the public administration. As most Romanian governments are formed by coalition rather than through a one-party majority, the members of the Government are usually the most prominent members of the coalition.

In periods of political instability, especially in the 1990s, 'technocratic' governments were appointed, in order to make the actual management of public policy less dependent on the political clashes. In this kind of government, the Prime Minister and most of the ministers were not politicians but specialists in various fields. However, this may not always be an adequate solution, as it could affect the public perception of governmental accountability: the political parties that participate in elections should assume responsibility for the governing rather than hiding behind a technocratic group. Technocratic governments are not, in their turn, immune from corruption and conflicts of interests, as their members usually come from the economic and financial milieu, where they may be subject to pressure.

Membership of the Government is incompatible with the exercise of any other public office of authority, with the exception of the mandate of deputy or senator. The Constitution also forbids members of the Government from exercising 'any office of professional representation paid by a trade company'. The same incompatibilities relating to the private sector, applied to MPs by the law on transparency in exercising public office, apply to members of the Government.

ii. Functions and Competences

The Government acts as a collegial organ, and it takes decisions during weekly ordinary meetings or, as the case may be, during extraordinary meetings. The decisions are adopted by consensus. When there is no consensus, the Prime Minister takes the final decision. The President

---

[46] Law no 90/2001.

of Romania may participate in the Government's meetings, and chairs those meetings in which he participates. Although Article 87 §1 CR apparently limits the situations in which the President may participate in the Government's meetings to 'problems of national interest regarding foreign policy, the country's defence and the assurance of public order', in the event that there is strong political support and compatibility with the Prime Minister, the latter may invite the President to participate in any Government meeting.

According to its organic law, the Government has the following functions:

1. the strategic function (which elaborates the strategy to implement the Government's programme);
2. the regulatory function (it adopts rules with a view to achieving its strategic aims);
3. the administration of state property and the management of state services;
4. the representation function (internally and externally); and
5. the state authority function (control over the application of legal rules in all fields under its supervision).

The Government exercises the general management of the public administration and is also the main initiator of legislation. In this capacity, the Government may be consulted by other holders of the right to legislative initiative for its opinions on legislative proposals. As head of the administration, the Government exercises a hierarchical control over ministries and other subordinated central administrative organs.

As an executive organ, the Government is responsible for elaboration of the development strategies of the country, and is required to implement the governmental programme approved by Parliament. The Government is also responsible for achieving foreign policy, and negotiates all international treaties and agreements. In its relations with other authorities, the Government leads the activity of the ministries and of other central public authorities, but also cooperates with the autonomous administrative authorities.

In fulfilling these functions and competences, the Government adopts resolutions and ordinances. Resolutions are the regular acts of government, with a secondary legal power, and are adopted in the execution of laws. Ordinances are acts of delegated legislation, having the same power as laws and being submitted for the subsequent approval of Parliament.

The mandate of the members of the Government will cease in the event of resignation, dismissal, incompatibility, loss of electoral rights or death. In such a situation, the Prime Minister appoints another member of the Government to fill the vacant seat temporarily, for a maximum period of 45 days.

C. The Prime Minister

The Prime Minister is the head of the Government: as provided by Article 107 CR, he or she directs the actions of the Government and coordinates the activities of its members. He or she represents the Government in its relationships with Parliament, the President, the HCCJ, the Constitutional Court and other authorities, with the political parties and other NGOs, as well as in international relations. The Prime Minister also holds the position of Vice-President of the Supreme Council for National Defence.

The Prime Minister's powers within the Government are considerable, but may be limited by political constraints. Although, theoretically, the Prime Minister is entitled to nominate ministers for vacant government seats, in a coalition government this power is restricted, as it depends on the agreement of all the coalition partners. Usually, each member of the coalition is assigned a few ministerial seats, and any replacement must respect this political structure. This may be the source of disagreement and conflict. For example, in January 2014, the Minister of Home Affairs resigned, due to his bad management of a rescue mission after a tragic plane crash. His replacement was delayed by a few weeks, because the leaders of the political coalition could not reach an agreement on the nominees.

The Prime Minister submits to Parliament reports and statements regarding governmental policy, and must answer the questions or interpellations addressed by MPs.

The Prime Minister cannot be dismissed by the President of Romania (Article 107 §2 CR). Only Parliament, adopting a motion of censure, may dismiss the Prime Minister and the whole Government. However, the Prime Minister's mandate will be terminated by resignation, loss of electoral rights, incompatibility, inability to exercise Prime Ministerial powers or death. In this case, the President will designate another member of the Government to be Acting Prime Minister, until a new Government is formed (Article 107 §3 CR).

D. The Relationship Between the Government and the Parliament

i. *Legislative Delegation*

Under Article 115 CR, the Government has the power to adopt acts having force equal to that of a law. However, although legislative delegation was 'reformed' in 2003, feeble parliamentary control and the actual political support of an oscillating parliamentary majority gives this power a variable geometry, not always respecting the principle of legal certainty. Originally, legislative delegation was intended to be an exceptional power, by which the Government would be able to stand in for Parliament when the latter was not in session. Parliament, expressly defined by the Constitution as 'the sole legislative authority of the country', may delegate its legislative power, in a temporary and substantively limited manner, to the executive. Nevertheless, the way in which legislative delegation was used in Romania, especially since 2000, proved that, on the contrary, Parliament was frequently willing to let the Government legislate.

Parliament may directly delegate power to the Government to adopt 'regular' ordinances, through an enabling law stating the field within which and the period during which ordinances may be adopted. The enabling law may also require the ordinance to be approved by Parliament before the enabling period ends.

Delegation may also be the effect of the direct application of the Constitution in the case of emergency ordinances, in which case no enabling law is needed. Such emergency ordinances must be motivated by an 'extraordinary situation, the regulation of which cannot be delayed', as required by Article 115 §4 CR. However, an emergency ordinance may only enter into force after its publication in the Official Journal *(Monitorul Oficial)*, and only if submitted for approval in an 'emergency procedure' at the competent chamber. This means that the ordinance has already produced effects when it is discussed by the Parliament. The Constitution requires that, if not in session, the chambers must be convened within five days of the submission. Nevertheless, this is only a formal requirement, as the constitutional text leaves an important loophole, used, in practice, by Parliament to let the Government legislate: if, in a 30-day period, the first chamber does not render its decision on it, the ordinance is considered adopted and will be sent to the other chamber, which will adopt it by means of an 'emergency procedure'. Many emergency ordinances have actually passed through this tacit adoption procedure.

The Constitution expressly prohibits the adoption of 'regular' ordinances in the reserved fields of organic laws. This provision was introduced in 2003, as a result of previous controversies on the subject. The Government had frequently used its power of delegation and had intervened in the field of organic laws, modifying or even adopting legislation. The Constitutional Court ruled, in 1998, that the constitutional prohibition on the adoption of ordinances in matters reserved to organic laws applied only to Parliament's power to adopt enabling laws in this respect (regular ordinances) and not to emergency ordinances which are, according to the Court, 'constitutional measures which allow the Government, under the strict control of the Parliament, to cope with an exceptional situation'.[47] In 2003, the express prohibition on adopting regular ordinances in the field of organic laws was introduced into the Constitution (Article 115 §1 CR).

Emergency ordinances can be adopted in the field of organic laws, but not in the field of constitutional laws (ie they cannot change the Constitution). 'Emergency ordinances cannot be adopted in the field of constitutional laws, or affect the status of fundamental institutions of the State, the rights, freedoms and duties stipulated in the Constitution, the electoral rights, and cannot establish steps for transferring assets to public property forcibly'.[48] The Parliament may approve or reject an ordinance by law, which will include the text of the ordinance and any amendments made by the legislator.

What is the status of ordinances in Romanian governmental practice? All Governments have used and abused the concept of legislative delegation, with the tacit consent of Parliament. The situation was repeatedly and strongly criticised, both by national legal scholarship

---

[47]   RCC, Decision no 34/1998.
[48]   Article 115 §6.

and by international bodies. Curiously, the use of ordinances was often criticised by the political opposition, which, once it come to power, did exactly the same thing. Therefore, adopting ordinances became a truly parallel legislative process. The obligation of the Government to duly explain the emergency situation, imposed by the Constitution, was not a barrier to this practice. After the EU accession in 2007, the practice of issuing emergency ordinances became a subject of concern for the European Commission, reflected in its CVM reports, as a potential source of legal uncertainty. The 2014 Report says, in its technical part, that 'The Government adopts many laws through Emergency Ordinances (a consistent trend of some 100 instruments per year, according to the Constitutional Court), thereby bypassing the normal parliamentary process.'[49]

In October 2013, the Constitutional Court adopted an important decision for the general regime of the ordinances. The case concerned the unconstitutionality of an emergency ordinance by which the Government tried to adopt the insolvency procedure. The Court reiterated that emergency ordinances must provide a detailed explanation of the nature of the 'extraordinary situation' and also of its 'urgent nature', and stated that, in order to justify an emergency ordinance, a situation must present a 'high degree of deviation from the common or regular', which was not the case here. The advice given by the Court in the end of its decision is significant in the general context of legislative delegation:

> [T]he rule of law requires that the mechanisms provided by the fundamental law be used according to the purpose for which they were established. This is the way to consolidate a true constitutional democracy.[50]

ii. Political Accountability of the Government

The political responsibility of the Government to Parliament, a feature of the classic parliamentary system, is the consequence of the political and legal legitimacy drawn by the Government from Parliament's vote of confidence. The political responsibility of the Government was

---

[49] COM(2014) 37 final, 22 January 2014, at 13.
[50] RCC, Decision no 447/2013.

customary under the 1866 and 1923 Constitutions (not expressly provided for by the Constitutions themselves), and it became a part of the 'democratic traditions'. However, this mechanism, seen as an expression of Parliament's constitutional power to control the Government, was significantly distorted by the mentality towards politics. By combining the power to dissolve Parliament with a vote of no confidence, the King used to dissolve Parliament first and then appoint as head of the Government the leader of the opposition, entrusted with the organisation of elections. By an elaborate mechanism using local administrative organs, the Government would manipulate the electoral process and win the majority in the new Parliament. Therefore, paradoxically, Parliament was legitimised by the Government and not vice versa.

In the troubled political context of the post-communist period, more precision was required in the rules on governmental responsibility. Therefore, the 1991 Constitution introduced a comprehensive mechanism, in order to avoid any abuse of power.

The Government is politically responsible for its entire activity only before Parliament. Each member of the Government is politically and jointly accountable with the other members for the activity and acts of the Government. The members of the Government individually are politically accountable only to the Prime Minister, but may also be held criminally accountable[51] according to Article 109 §2 CR.

iii. Motion of Censure

The motion of censure is the most important expression of the political accountability of the Government. The Chamber of Deputies and the Senate, in joint session, can withdraw their vote of confidence by adopting a motion of censure. The motion can be initiated by at least a quarter of the total number of deputies and senators. The Government is notified of the initiative. The joint session of the chambers in which the motion is presented must take place within five days of submission of the initiative. The actual debate on the motion takes place three days after its presentation in joint session. The Prime Minister and the Government are invited to participate. After the debate, the motion is submitted to the vote. If the motion is adopted, the Government is dismissed. In case of rejection of the motion, the vote of confidence is

---

[51] See below, E.

maintained and the initiators may not submit a new motion of censure during the same session of Parliament, except when the Government engages its responsibility by virtue of Article 114 CR.

Since 1992, 29 motions of censure have been initiated, but until 2009 none had been adopted. The 2008–12 legislature presented a record number of motions of censure: 11 motions were submitted, out of which two were withdrawn and two were adopted. This clearly showed changes in the majority within Parliament during the mandate, with the effect of the loss of the Government's political support. In practice, motions of censure were initiated even if they were not supported by a strong majority: they 'became important vehicles of the public discourse, constantly used by the opposition to criticise the Government's activity'.[52]

iv. Engagement of Responsibility

A more complicated and complex procedure by which the Government may become accountable before Parliament is the engagement of responsibility. The Constitution allows the Government to submit itself to the risk of being dismissed by Parliament, with the potential benefit of gaining confidence and imposing a law, a programme or a general policy statement. This procedure entails political and legislative stakes, as, by triggering it, the Government seeks two objectives: to obtain a vote of confidence; and to have a law adopted quickly, bypassing parliamentary debates. In practice, the Government tended to use this procedure when it was very sure of parliamentary political support and when the adoption of an emergency ordinance on the matter in question was not possible due to constitutional limitations.

The Constitution provides that the Government may engage its responsibility before Parliament, in a joint sitting, on a programme, on a general policy statement or on a legislative bill. The engagement of responsibility declaration allows Parliament to initiate and adopt a motion of censure. If such a motion is neither initiated nor adopted, the programme or statement the object of the engagement procedure become binding and the legislative bill is considered adopted. Theoretically, MPs may propose amendments to the bill, but the Government has complete discretion to reject or accept such amendments.

---

[52] Dima (n 17), at 89.

In practice, the procedure was not often used for programmes or political declarations, but successive Governments did use it to circumvent parliamentary debates on very important laws, such as: privatisation, economic reforms, laws on property, laws on public policies like health, education, etc. With the support of a comfortable parliamentary majority, the Government used it to transform Parliament from a genuine deliberative organ into an authority called on merely to rubberstamp governmental policies, as the procedure does not allow true debates on the content of a legislative project.

Problems and even 'constitutional legal conflicts between authorities' arose when the Government engaged its responsibility for legislative initiatives that were still on Parliament's agenda. The most interesting case in this respect was that of the Law on National Education, which, while still pending on the Senate's legislative agenda, was adopted by the engagement of responsibility procedure. The Constitutional Court agreed that there was a constitutional conflict, but it neither resolved it nor decided on the constitutionality of the engagement of responsibility, stating that this must be invoked separately as an element of 'external unconstitutionality' of the law in question.[53] In a later decision, the Court established a set of criteria in order to evaluate the constitutionality of an engagement of responsibility procedure on a legislative project: an emergency must exist that necessitates the adoption of the measures included in the proposed law; the importance of the field of the proposed law; the immediate applicability of the proposed law.

When a law has been adopted by the engagement of responsibility procedure, it may be challenged at the Constitutional Court, or the President of Romania may refuse its promulgation. In the latter case, the law is returned to Parliament, and the Constitution requires that it is examined in joint session. The majority required to adopt the final version is that prescribed by the Constitution for ordinary or organic laws, respectively.

In 2012, being called to examine the constitutionality of the law amending the electoral legislation, adopted through the engagement of responsibility procedure, the Constitutional Court declared it unconstitutional on the grounds that, amongst other things, 'electoral laws should be adopted after debate in Parliament and not through an exceptional procedure that bypasses the Parliament but compels it to give a

---

[53] RCC, Decision no 1431/2010.

tacit vote'.[54] The Court admitted, in this context, that the mechanism of the motion of censure, associated with the engagement of responsibility procedure, may have an illusory character when the Government is supported by a majority in Parliament, the adoption of a law in these circumstances being a pure formality.

Legislative delegation and the engagement of responsibility procedure are governmental tools for bypassing parliamentary debates on legislation, in both cases with the consent of the legislature to some extent. Although their excessive use was considered dangerous for the rule of law and the separation of powers, the two procedures became, far from exceptional, somewhat commonplace for Romanian Governments. In 2012 the Constitutional Court started a more serious trend of examining the constitutionality of the two procedures, but future constitutional amendments should impose more limitations on their use by the Government.

E. Criminal Accountability of the Members of the Government

The criminal accountability of members of the Government, usually associated with acts of corruption, may be engaged individually, following a special procedure prescribed by the Constitution and by the law on ministerial responsibility. The request for the legal institution of criminal proceedings against members of the Government for offences committed during the exercise of their office may be made, according to the Constitution,[55] only by the Chamber of Deputies, the Senate and the President of Romania. The member of Government against whom such a request has been made may be suspended from office by the President. If the member of the Government is tried in court, the suspension from office is compulsory. The HCCJ has jurisdiction in the case. In corruption cases, the investigation is pursued by the National Anti-corruption Directorate.

The criminal responsibility of ministers has been regulated in Romania since the 1866 Constitution, and such regulation is commonly found in other European constitutions. Currently, in Romania, the special

---

[54] RCC, Decision no 51/2012.
[55] Article 109 §2.

procedure only applies to investigations for offences allegedly committed by members of Government during their term of office. However, the involvement of political authorities in this procedure may be problematic. If the involvement of Parliament as the source of governmental legitimacy is unquestionable, presidential intervention, especially in periods of cohabitation, may pose serious problems regarding objectivity. Theoretically, the President can exercise this power within his role as mediator under the Constitution,[56] on condition that he is politically neutral. However, when the President's actions may be suspected as being influenced by political bias, the procedure is flawed from the start.

The rules on ministerial criminal accountability should be applied only to ministers who acted in the exercise of their office, and only for acts provided for by the special law (for example, '(a) the preclusion, by threats, violence or by using fraudulent means, of the exercise in good faith of the rights and freedoms of an individual; (b) the presentation, intentionally, of inaccurate information to the Parliament or the President, regarding the activity of the Government or of a ministry, in order to hide the perpetration of offences against the interest of the state').[57] For acts committed outside their term of office or for other offences, the ministers are held responsible according to ordinary criminal procedure.

The criminal accountability of members of the Government has been triggered mostly by acts of corruption. Some ministers were forced to resign after being found guilty of acts of corruption committed before their terms of office. Recently, a former Minister of Justice was sentenced to three years' imprisonment, suspended, for acts committed during his term of office. The minister is currently a senator and, despite the conviction, did not resign from Parliament. Other former ministers have been convicted for treason (divulging classified economic information to foreign powers), but most prosecutions have been for bribery and trafficking of influence. Although the accused politicians and party leaders often claimed that such requests for prosecution were politicised (used as political weapons by influencing the prosecutors), such allegations were not proven. In 2015, for the first time, the Acting Prime Minister was prosecuted for offences committed before his ministerial terms of office, but a request to prosecute him for

---

[56] See section II.E.ii.
[57] Article 8 of Law no 115/1999.

a conflict of interest during his mandate was rejected by the Chamber of Deputies.

IV. THE PUBLIC ADMINISTRATION

In Romania, the term 'public administration' (civil service) covers both the central administration and local government authorities. The central administration is composed of the ministries, other organs subordinated to the Government and autonomous administrative authorities (such as the ANI, the CSAT, the intelligence services, the public broadcasting services, the National Council of Broadcasting, the National Bank, etc). Civil servants have a special status,[58] but not all employees of the public administration are considered civil servants (for example, personal advisers of ministers, or other types of personal staff).

A. Public Office and Lustration

One of the most difficult problems with which the post-communist countries had to deal after the fall of the communist regimes was lustration, ie disclosure and/or the banning from public office of former collaborators with the regime. Lustration took various forms: in some countries, it was applied to all former members of the communist leadership and comprised a permanent or long-term ban on being able to occupy any public office; in other countries, it only covered disclosure of collaboration with the political police. Some countries enacted lustration laws almost immediately after their new democratic regimes were installed; others, like Romania, introduced them later on. In 1999, a decade after the fall of the dictatorship, a *Law on the access to personal files and the disclosure of the 'Securitate'* (communist political police) was adopted.[59] It belongs to the category of 'disclosure laws'. The actual enforcement of the law is made by the National Council for Studying the Former *Securitate* Archives (CNSAS), an agency placed under the control of Parliament, which, in its initial incarnation, verified and could disclose only collaborations with the former political police, and

---

[58] Law no 188/1999.
[59] Law no 187/1999.

only in those situations when fundamental rights and freedoms of other persons were affected by such activities. Lustration in its most radical form—the prohibition on former communist activists holding public office—was a demand formulated during the Revolution, in one of its most important acts, the *Timişoara Proclamation*. However, after things settled, it did not become an important matter of public debate until the creation of the CNSAS. Even then, in the absence of clear and substantial prohibitions on access to public office, it lacked any significance in public and constitutional life.[60]

In 2006, the law was changed, adding more punitive consequences. Any finding of 'collaboration' with the former intelligence services (not only with the 'political police') would lead to a prohibition on holding positions in the judiciary and prosecution offices. 'Collaborator' means any person who 'supplied information, in any form, as well as notes and written reports or recorded verbal accounts, by which were denounced activities or attitudes contrary to the communist totalitarian regime and which aimed at restricting fundamental human rights and freedoms'. The law was challenged at the Constitutional Court in January 2008, and the Court declared it entirely unconstitutional on the ground that the CNSAS was performing a jurisdictional activity contrary to the constitutional prohibition on extraordinary jurisdictions. As a result, a new regulation was enacted,[61] in order to maintain the activity of the Council, but with a more limited scope. A new law was adopted in 2008 and the CNSAS continued its activity. Recently, several findings of collaboration, concerning former parliamentarians and a former Minister of Justice were confirmed by final judgments of the High Court.[62]

A special law on lustration has never been enacted. A draft law was adopted in 2010, but it was rejected twice by the Constitutional Court, in 2010 and 2012, following an *ex ante* constitutional review. The Court considered, inter alia, that the law was excessive because the references to the categories of persons to be banned from public office were too general and therefore infringed the fundamental right to be elected.

---

[60] See, for details, B Iancu, 'Post-Accession Constitutionalism with a Human Face: Judicial Reform and Lustration in Romania' (2010) 6 *European Constitutional Law Review* 28.

[61] EGO no 25/2008.

[62] See, for example, HCCJ, Decision no 4211/2012 of 18 October 2012.

Another ground of unconstitutionality was the infringement of the non-retroactivity of laws. Last but not least, the Court considered, outside the scope of the constitutionality issues, that

> the lustration law was adopted 21 years after the collapse of communism. Thus, its belated character … is deemed relevant by the Court in assessing the disproportionate character of the restrictive measures, although they were pursuing a legitimate aim.[63]

B. Ministerial Administration

Ministerial administration, or the 'central public administration', is organised hierarchically: ministries are subordinated to the Government, politically and administratively. Each minister is politically nominated, and cases when the appointed person is a true specialist in the field overseen by the ministry are rare. The politicisation phenomenon is also a feature of the ministerial apparatus. Most nominations to leading posts at the ministries are political. Ministers may appoint Secretaries of State to assist or replace them in their current work. There are also political advisers, who are not part of the Government's civil service but are employed directly by the ministers. General civil servants are recruited by competition, subject to a special statute and enjoy stability in post. Specialised agencies can be created that are subordinate to the ministries. For example, the Council for Academic Diplomas and Degrees subordinate to the Ministry of Education, and it deals with the confirmation of higher academic diplomas and degrees (doctoral degrees, habilitations).

C. Autonomous Administrative Agencies

Within the wider range of the 'administration', the Constitution permits the establishment of autonomous administrative authorities or agencies. These are either directly created by the Constitution (like the CSAT), or established by organic laws, for a variety of purposes. Out of the wide range of agencies, one of the most interesting in the

---

[63] RCC, Decision no 820/2010.

context of the peculiarities of Romanian society is the National Integrity Agency (ANI).

The Agency was created in 2007, following the Romanian accession to the EU and at the direct request of the European Commission,[64] as an institutional guarantor of the fight against corruption. It represents an institutional construction clearly imposed from the outside, an interesting example of European 'cultural engineering', if not of cultural imperialism. The ANI was thus created with its competence partially predetermined by the European Commission and with a supervisory body appointed by the Senate (the National Council of Integrity, which proposes nominations to the Senate for the Agency's leadership, receives reports from the Agency on its activity and, in its turn, presents reports to the Senate). According to the principle of operational independence, although the Agency is placed under the supervision of a political organ—the Senate—its staff may not request or receive orders referring to their activity from any other authority, institution or person.

The creation of an 'operationally' independent body to tackle cases of corruption, conflicts of interests and issues of incompatibility within the Romanian political and public sector may seem an innovative and courageous idea, but it was not the consequence of a rational and conscious approach to the rule of law, and the evolution of the ANI's legislative framework and perception among the Romanian political class is relevant to this assertion. Thus, in 2010, only three years after its establishment, the Constitutional Court declared most of the ANI's activities to be unconstitutional. The decision was given following a referral of unconstitutionality raised in a case concerning the confiscation of the plaintiff's assets as a result of an ANI decision. The main grounds of unconstitutionality were that the pursuit of investigations by the ANI is similar to the pursuit of criminal inquiries, and that the finding of acts of corruption is equivalent to a judicial criminal indictment, because it ends with direct referral to a court of law, which is contrary to the Constitution. The Court also considered that the law infringed the constitutional principles of the presumption of innocence and of the presumption of legal ownership of property. Another ground of unconstitutionality was the legal obligation on some public servants to

---

[64] Decision 2006/928/CE establishing a mechanism for cooperation and verification of progress in Romania, [2006] OJ L354/56.

publish online the statements of assets, which was found contrary to the right to private life. Therefore, said the Constitutional Court, the ANI's activity was jurisdictional, exceeding the administrative nature of the authority and infringing the Constitution, which stipulates that justice is to be achieved through the courts of law and that the creation of extraordinary jurisdictions is prohibited.[65] As a result of the RCC's decision,[66] the law was changed, removing the 'jurisdictional' character of the ANI. At the same time, in a parallel regulation, the Law on the statement and control of the assets of public officials, introduced, as an intermediate step between the ANI and the court of appeals, the 'Assets Investigation Commissions', composed of two judges and a prosecutor, which screen ANI referrals to the courts.

This was seen as a regression by the European Commission, which, in its Report from July 2010, noted that the Agency 'was able to demonstrate a further consolidation of its capacity and track record regarding the identification of unjustified wealth, incompatibilities and conflicts of interest', and that it could be considered fully operational and had a promising track record of cases. However, the Commission expressed its discontent that

> these achievements are threatened by detrimental changes to the law on ANI which were adopted … as a reaction to a decision by the Romanian Constitutional Court. … The amendments to the law on ANI adopted by Parliament in response to the decision of the Constitutional Court remove the possibilities to sanction discrepancies between assets and income identified and therefore eliminate the control of dignitaries' and officials' accumulation of assets whilst in public office.[67]

While admitting that the Romanian Parliament had to revise the law in accordance with the controversial decision of the Constitutional Court, the Commission firmly stated that Romania also had the obligation to respect the commitments made at the time of accession to the EU. The Commission considered the new ANI law a 'significant step back' in the fight against corruption, and therefore a breach of those commitments. Meanwhile, the Constitutional Court ruled on the changes to

---

[65] A similar situation occurred in 2008, when the Constitutional Court declared unconstitutional the 'lustration law' on the ground that the CNSAS was assuming an 'extraordinary jurisdiction' prohibited by the Constitution (Decision no 51/2008).

[66] RCC, Decision no 415/2010.

[67] COM(2010) 401 final, Report of 20 July 2010, at 5.

the law, which were referred to it before promulgation by the President of Romania, and declared them unconstitutional on the ground of procedural breaches of the legislative process provided for by the Constitution. Finally, the amended law was re-examined and entered into force on 2 September 2010. Nevertheless, the Commission persisted in voicing its concerns, stating, in its 2011 Report, that 'there is a need for a further amendment to the law to allow ANI to appeal decisions of the Assets Investigation Commission'.[68]

The ANI is an institution that embodies a complex range of constitutional feelings in the present Romanian political context: the EU's lack of confidence in the national capacity to fight corruption, the imposition of this 'cultural engineering', and the continuous supervision of its functioning and development, combined with a permanent suspicion that the European requirement is undermined by national adaptations. On the other hand, reading between the lines, the atavistic fear of the Romanian political class regarding 'integrity imposing' authorities can be detected. The ANI has constantly been seen as a 'foreign body' within the Romanian system, and as an irritant by politicians and public officials at all levels. Most of its decisions have been contested in the courts. Its acceptance as an intrinsic part of the Romanian legal and political system depends on a radical change of mentality. Otherwise, its short existence will not have been sufficient to achieve its purpose on the long run. After the end of the CVM, it will be decided whether the ANI has fulfilled its initial goal and will remain unchanged, or whether it will become the 'victim' of national adaptation and therefore another 'form without substance'.

D. Conclusion

The phenomenon of corruption has had a significant impact on the entire Romanian constitutional context. High-level corruption cases continue to make the front page of newspapers and headlines of news threads. Although corruption cannot be considered a general phenomenon in Romanian society as a whole, the culture of accountability is very weak in the Romanian public sphere. The rules must be very detailed

---

[68] COM(2011) 460 final, Report of 20 July 2011, at 6.

and buttressed by legal sanctions in order to be enforced. In many cases, ministers resigned only after being convicted. Only in the last few years have public officials started to acknowledge this culture of accountability, resigning from office on mere suspicion of their activities, or those of close relatives or spouses.

Although it is strongly expressed in the media and through various NGOs, public opinion is often disregarded by the political sphere, even in cases of evident suspicion of corruption. Civil society receives little concrete response from governmental circles. Politicians, including ministers, or even the Prime Minister, have frequently expressed sympathy for convicted political colleagues, in some cases even questioning the 'objectivity' of judicial decisions. As the European Commission put it, 'corruption is not always treated as a serious crime'.[69] In the conclusions of the CVM January 2014 Report, the Commission stated that

> the resolution with which the law has been applied to high-level corruption needs to be maintained and extended to small-scale corruption. In this area Romania should: ensure that corruption laws apply equally to all on an equal basis; improve the consistency and dissuasiveness of penalties applied in corruption cases in all courts cross Romania; step up efforts in the prosecution of petty corruption; develop the National Anti-Corruption Strategy to introduce more consistent benchmarks and obligations for public administration, with results to be made publicly available.[70]

V. CONCLUSION

The Romanian executive is, after 25 years of 'new' democracy, still in search of solutions to certain normative and functional difficulties: the constitutional status of the President, the fluctuating relationship between the two branches of the executive (President and Government), which has resulted in dysfunctional cohabitations, and, last but not least, corruption. Some of these issues can be addressed by constitutional amendment, but all of these difficulties can also be addressed by changing the political and legal behaviour of the actors involved. The future will show which path will actually be followed.

---

[69] EU Commission CVM Report, January 2014, at 10.
[70] ibid, at 14.

FURTHER READING

B Dima, 'Shaping the Role of the President: The Influence of the Romanian Constitutional Court's Jurisprudence' in M Guțan & B Selejan-Guțan (eds), *Europeanisation and Judicial Culture in Contemporary Democracies* (Bucharest, Hamangiu, 2014) 105.

——, 'The European Models of Semi-presidentialism: the Peculiarity of Romania's Post-communist System of Government' (2014) 1 *Romanian Journal of Comparative Law* 60.

M Guțan, 'Romanian Semi-Presidentialism in Historical Context' (2012) 2 *Romanian Journal of Comparative Law* 275.

B Iancu, '"Serenity in Overcoming Crises". A Parochial Gloss on the Transnational Shift in Constitutional Vocabularies' (2013) 1-XIII *Studia Politica. Romanian Political Science Review* 9.

——, 'Separation of Powers and the Rule of Law in Romania: The Crisis in Concepts and Contexts' in A von Bogdandy & P Sonnevend, *Constitutional Crisis in the European Constitutional Area* (Oxford, Hart Publishing, 2015) 153.

ES Tănăsescu, 'Conflicting Revisions to Romanian Constitution Give Rise to Questions about Semi-presidentialism' (2014) 1 *Romanian Journal of Comparative Law* 35.

——, 'The President of Romania or the Slippery Slope of a Political Regime' (2008) 4 *European Constitutional Law Review* 64.

R Weber, 'Constitutionalism as a Vehicle for Democratic Consolidation in Romania' in J Zielonka (ed), *Democratic Consolidation in Eastern Europe* (Oxford, Oxford University Press, 2001) 222.

4

Local Government

―――――――

Administrative Organisation – Local Autonomy – Decentralisation

I. BRIEF HISTORICAL OVERVIEW

THE PRESENT CONSTITUTIONAL organisation of local government in Romania (with all its anxieties regarding decentralisation and regionalisation) is deeply indebted to the nineteenth-century institutions, principles and concepts imported from or inspired by the French and Belgian administrative systems.

The first traces of a modern administration can be found in the administrative organisation created by the Russian power through the Organic Regulations in 1831–32. However, the first true administrative reform took place after the unification of the two Romanian Principalities,[1] by the laws for administrative organisation, adopted in 1864 during the reign of Prince Cuza. This involved a complete reorganisation of the system, based on massive legal import from French and Belgian law.[2] As a consequence, the new administration was highly centralised. Almost all the current institutions were introduced into the Romanian system in 1864, and they kept names borrowed from French law. It is important to emphasise that the principle of decentralisation was established under the influence of the French philosophy of local freedoms, and that it bore no resemblance to the English system of self-government: all local freedoms were granted by the central power,

―――――――

[1] See Introduction and Historical Overview, section II.A.iii.

[2] M Guțan, *Istoria administrației publice locale în statul român modern* (Bucharest, All Beck, 2004) 134.

instead of being allowed to 'naturally' develop in the local community. Another paradox of the new system was that, although the decentralisation was proclaimed, including at the constitutional level (see, for example, Article 132 of the 1866 Constitution), the administrative system was dominated by centralisation until the communist age, when it was replaced by the soviet-inspired 'democratic centralism': all local authorities became state authorities and were controlled by the state, and there was no principle of autonomy. Current legal scholarship has almost unanimously agreed that in Romania, 'in practice there never was true local autonomy and for the first time in the country's modern history, the principle of local autonomy was granted by the present [1991] Constitution'.[3]

This propensity for centralism, a constant feature of the pre- and inter-war Romanian administrative system, was justified, first, by the influence of French law and, secondly, especially after 1918, by the obsession with the integrity of the national unitary state. Thus there existed the fear of dismantling the newly created nation state, despite the generous constitutional and legal provisions establishing autonomy and decentralisation at local level. Until 1918, this centralism was reinforced in practice by the almost complete lack of a solid administrative culture. The previous local administrative organisation had been influenced by the Greek Phanariot system,[4] marked by corruption and instability. After the Great Union of 1918, the obsession surrounding the national state was added to the main background of the Romanian administrative system.

During the inter-war period, two phenomena—born in the nineteenth century—grew to prominence in the Romanian administrative culture: the unjustified increase of the number and role of public servants (*funcționarism*[5]—public service was seen in this context as a means of social-climbing and of material gain, mostly by acts of corruption); and the almost permanent and complete political control of local authorities (*politicianism*). Both trends were favoured by, and favoured in turn, the third main collateral phenomenon of the Romanian public administration: corruption. All three phenomena were present, in

---

[3] A Iorgovan, 'Article 122' in *Constituția României revizuită. Comentarii si explicații* (Bucharest, All Beck, 2004) 259.

[4] See Introduction and Historial Overview.

[5] M Guțan, *Istoria administrației publice românești* (Bucharest, Hamangiu, 2006) 199.

various forms and degrees, in all ages of development of the Romanian administration.

During the right-wing dictatorships (1938–44), in the context of the authoritarianism that dominated European political regimes, the decentralisation principle was put aside in favour of a centralism based on the supremacy of the executive organs over the deliberative ones at local level. This meant that the local councils had not been convened.[6]

The communist era (1948–89) recognised a typical party–state centralism, of soviet inspiration, characterised by the disappearance of any trace of decentralisation. Some forms of corruption-based *functionarism* and *politicianism* (applied mutatis mutandis) were preserved. Corruption remained a constant under communist rule, and it was made worse by the permanent shortage of goods and services for individual citizens, thus being a continual presence in the Romanian public culture.

Starting in 1990, the objective was to return to pre-communist principles and institutions, and, at the same time, align with European trends and standards. These objectives were reflected in the 1991 Constitution and in the legal provisions that followed, but their application was, as expected, much more difficult to achieve.

II. CONSTITUTIONAL PRINCIPLES OF THE CURRENT SYSTEM OF LOCAL GOVERNMENT

Romania is constitutionally proclaimed a national unitary and indivisible state, and all the relationships between central and local government should be assessed from this perspective. The country's ethnocentric constitutionalism and predominantly old-fashioned understanding of the nation state colour the actual meaning of the constitutional principles of local autonomy, decentralisation and 'deconcentration'. From the start, the principle of indivisibility was combined with the principles of local autonomy and 'decentralisation'. In 2003, the principle of 'deconcentration', although existing in practice, was expressly added to the constitutional text, in order to better delineate the scope of decentralisation at the local level. These principles created the basic framework for a local government system that continued to suffer many subsequent changes, from the methods of appointment of the local leaders to the recent attempts to create an intermediate 'regional' level.

---

[6] ibid, at 271.

From a structural point of view, the Constitution maintains a 'territorial' understanding of the basis of local government. This resulted from its heritage, and was also the majority view during the constitutional drafting process, as opposed to a more community-orientated view, also proposed in 1991 within the Constituent Assembly.[7] Thus, the basic entities of local government are named 'administrative-territorial units', rather than 'local/territorial communities' as in other countries. The word 'community', or even the phrase 'local government', is not used in the Constitution; only the law on local administration introduces the notion of 'local collectivity' (defined as the 'total number of inhabitants of a territorial unit').

The administrative-territorial entities are listed in Article 3 of the Constitution, which establishes the general regime of the state territory: the counties (*judeţe*), which are the largest units; the towns (*oraşe*); and the associations of villages with legal personality (*comune*, after the French *commune*). This territorial organisation is a two-tiered one, but within the framework of the local autonomy principle: there is no subordination between the tiers, only a relationship based on coordination. Romania does not have, so far, a regional organisation involving the region as an intermediate link between the state and the local communities. A debate on the introduction of a third level took place in the context of the 2012–14 constitutional amendment process, but it has had no effect so far.

Each territorial unit has its own corresponding set of authorities, divided into two main categories: authorities issuing from the local autonomy principle; and authorities achieving the decentralisation and deconcentration principles.

A. Decentralisation and Deconcentration

Decentralisation and deconcentration are the key principles in the relationship between local and central government. Decentralisation is established by Article 120 CR and by the law on decentralisation,[8] which defines it as 'the transfer of administrative and financial jurisdiction

---

[7] *Geneza Constituţiei României [travaux préparatoires* of the Constituent Assembly of 1991] (Bucharest, RA Monitorul Oficial, 1998) 556.

[8] Law no 195/2006.

from the central level to the local level or to the private sector'. According to the legal provisions, the principle of decentralisation is achieved through:

1. subsidiarity (jurisdiction in different matters belongs to the authority closest to the citizen, which is endowed with the necessary capacity), ensuring the necessary resources according to the transferred competences;
2. the responsibility of local authorities;
3. equity (the access of all persons to the public services).

However, decentralisation was not intended as the opposite of but only as a limit to centralisation.[9] Thus, decentralisation may not be interpreted as total independence from central government, because this would mean a breach of the state's unitary character. Therefore, central government exercises an 'administrative trusteeship' (*tutela administrativa*) over the decisions of the local authorities, through a special authority, the Prefect.[10] At the central level, the Ministry of Administration and Internal Affairs has general competence for supervising the implementation of the decentralisation principle.

By virtue of the constitutional principle of decentralisation, the law on decentralisation establishes that the local authorities exercise three categories of competence: exclusive competences, shared competences and delegated competences. The exclusive competences are those directly attributed by law to local and county authorities, such as: management of the public and private domain of the community; management of the infrastructure of local roads; management of local cultural and health institutions; the water supply; cleaning services; local territorial development; local public transport, etc. At the county level, the authorities have exclusive competences as regards the management of local airports, of county cultural and health institutions, etc.

Shared competences are exercised together with other levels of the administration (county or central), with the separation of financing and of the decision-making power. The fields in which competences can be shared are: the building of social housing; primary and secondary education; public order and safety; social aid to persons in difficulty;

---

[9] D Apostol-Tofan, *Drept administrativ*, 2nd edn (Bucharest, CH Beck, 2008) vol I, 219.
[10] See Ch 4, section III.A.

the prevention and management of emergency situations at the local level, etc.

Delegated competences are granted to the local authorities by the central authorities. Any such delegation should be accompanied by the transfer of the necessary financial resources. Delegated competences mostly concern the payment of certain social aids.

Deconcentration[11] is a specific feature of the relationship between central and local levels. Although the 1991 constitutional drafters originally considered that deconcentration was an implied consequence of decentralisation, in 2003 it was expressly introduced into the constitutional text and was defined by the law on decentralisation as 'the redistribution of administrative and financial jurisdiction from the ministries and other central administrative organs to their own territorial structures'.[12] Thus, in the case of decentralisation, the decision at the local level is made by an autonomous authority, whereas in the case of deconcentration, the decision-making body is appointed by the central administration. However, in the latter case, the governmental agents are not merely 'instruments' of the central power but are endowed with their own decision-making power, maintaining a subordinate relationship with the Government. This subordination does not exist in the case of decentralised organs.[13]

B. Local Autonomy

The principle of local autonomy is laid down by Article 120 CR, and is defined by the organic law on local administration[14] as 'the right and

---

[11] From the French *déconcentration* = the transfer of power from centralised authorities to the authorities that represent the central power at the local level in the territorial divisions (P Serrand, *Manuel d'institutions administratives françaises* (Paris, Presses Universitaires de France, 2002) 121).

[12] Deconcentration had existed from the 19th century, at least in substance and as recognised by the public law doctrine, but was not expressly mentioned in the Constitution. Deconcentration was expressly mentioned in a law for the first time in 1939. See M Guțan, *Istoria administrației publice locale in statul român modern* (Bucharest, All Beck, 2005) 125, 287, 358.

[13] See European Commission for Democracy through Law (Venice Commission), *Opinion on the Draft Revision of the Constitution of Romania*, adopted by the Venice Commission at its 54th Plenary Session, Venice, 14–15 March 2003, 7–8.

[14] Law no 215/2001, as amended and republished in 2007.

effective capacity of the authorities of local administration to solve and manage, in the name and interest of the local communities which they represent, the public matters, as prescribed by law'. It is worth mentioning that the national law applies and partly mirrors the language of the European Charter of Local Self-Government (Council of Europe, 1985).[15] Local autonomy therefore confers full powers on local authorities in deciding upon matters given by law to their competence.

However, true local autonomy is influenced by many factors such as: history, traditions, the geographic situation, the economy, the degree of civic and political education, as well as national and international law.[16] Local autonomy is also considered an essential component of democracy, as it counterbalances the central Government, which may be tempted to disregard a community's interests or needs.[17] In the current constitutional and legal design, local autonomy entails the following features: it has a purely administrative character, excluding autonomy on other grounds (ethnic, cultural, territorial, etc); it has a financial character (local authorities have their own decision-making power as regards their financial resources); local authorities are the result of the expression of the community's will, and have public legal personality and their own powers and budgets; local autonomy excludes any subordination of local authorities to other public authorities at a local, county or national level.

By virtue of their autonomy, local authorities are entitled to adopt specific legislation—norms regulating their fields of jurisdiction. These normative acts are considered secondary legislation, and they must be in accordance with state legislation (laws and government resolutions) and are subject to judicial review. Some of these acts can be suspended by the Government's representative (Prefect)[18] by virtue of the 'administrative trusteeship' exercised by this institution over the local authorities. Local council and county council acts cannot be suspended, however, as these authorities are elected by the community and represent the local legislative power. However, these acts may be challenged in court on grounds of legality.

---

[15] Ratified by Romania in 1997.

[16] V Vedinaş, 'Articolul 120' in I Muraru & ES Tănăsescu (eds), *Constituţia Romaniei. Comentariu pe articole* (Bucharest, CH Beck, 2008) 1163.

[17] Apostol-Tofan (n 9) 251.

[18] See III.A. below.

C. The Sensitive Issue of Linguistic Pluralism

In the process of constitutional drafting, several proposals were put forward by the representatives of the Hungarian minority, to introduce express constitutional provisions granting the right of persons belonging to national minorities to use their mother tongue in their relationship with the local administration.[19] The proposed amendments were not accepted at that time, because of the view that the principle of an official language (Romanian) meant that no other language was to be used in the relationships between citizens and any public authorities.[20]

In 2003, under internal and external pressure, the revised Constitution granted the right of persons belonging to national minorities to use their language in their relationships with the local administration, but only in those administrative-territorial entities in which the relevant minority has a 'significant weight'. This new constitutional provision in Article 120 §2 was the result of lobbying by representatives of the Hungarian minority. The notion of 'significant weight' is defined by the law on local administration as representing a minimum of 20 per cent of the total population of the respective local community. The text allows the use of the mother tongue in the relations of individuals with both local authorities and with the deconcentrated public services from those territorial entities. This right entails a corresponding duty on the authorities, namely, to ensure that at least the staff employed in the structures that have contact with the public can communicate in the language of the national minority. No such right is granted as regards relations with the central administration.

As Romanian is, constitutionally, the official language of the state, all meetings of the local bodies take place in Romanian and all documents are drafted in Romanian. There is one exception, namely, the situation when, in the local council, the representatives of a national minority form at least one-fifth of the total number of councillors: in that situation, that national minority's language can be used in the council's meeting. The law also prescribes the obligation to translate published or

---

[19] See *Geneza Constituţiei României* (n 7) 776–86.

[20] It is interesting to note that the senator who proposed the amendment, Kiraly Karoly, was the only parliamentarian who was absent from the final vote on the Constitution in the Constituent Assembly (see *Geneza Constituţiei României* (n 7), at 1050).

communicated documents into the language of any national minority accounting for more than 20 per cent of the local populace. In practice, the right to use the minority language in relations with the administration at a local level is mainly used by the Hungarian minority.

The struggle for linguistic freedom was backed and followed by a permanent struggle, on the part of the Hungarian minority's political groups, for cultural and even territorial autonomy of the regions inhabited by the Hungarian minority. Granting such autonomy would be contrary to the Constitution, but the individual minority rights already recognised,[21] including the use of minority languages in administration, are quite extensive.

III. THE RELATIONSHIP BETWEEN CENTRAL AND LOCAL GOVERNMENT: A TRUE AUTONOMY?

The largest territorial entities in Romania are the counties (*județe*). Each county comprises municipalities: towns (*orașe*) and *comune*. The *comune* are formed by two or more villages. At present, there are 41 counties and the Municipality of Bucharest, which has its own administration, similar to a county. Each territorial entity is run by a set of authorities, with particular features established by law (mayors and local councils for the towns and communes, and county councils for the counties). The relationship between central and local government is ensured by an intermediary—the Prefect.

A. The Prefect

Territorial representation of the central Government is achieved through the institution of the Prefect (from the French *préfet*). This institution, although included in the same chapter of the Constitution as local councils and the mayor, is not a local authority *per se*. Its inclusion is due to the fact that the Prefect exercises 'administrative trusteeship' over the local government, as the representative of the central Government. Administrative trusteeship involves exercising control over the legality of acts of the local authorities: local autonomy is not

---

[21] See Ch 6.

absolute and there must be a level of correspondence between local interests and central policy-making. The Prefect ensures the existence of this link.

The institution was first created in 1864. In spite of a terminological resemblance, the office of Romanian Prefect was different from its French counterpart,[22] borrowing many characteristics from Belgian legislation too. The Prefect was then the representative of the Government, but also acted as the executive authority of the county council, having the double function of representing both central and local interests. From the actual context and the functioning of the institution, the Prefect turned into a true master of local interests, simultaneously being the agent of the Government and, therefore, the exponent of actual centralism.

The present design of the office of Prefect does not maintain the pre- and inter-war features. The Prefect is now, according to Article 123 CR, the representative of the Government at the local level, and runs the 'deconcentrated public services' of the ministries and of other central organs, which function in the territorial entities. The Constitution expressly states, after its 2003 amendment, that there is no subordination relationship between the Prefect and the local elected authorities, that is, local councils, mayors, county councils and their presidents. At the same time, the Prefect exercises administrative trusteeship, by his or her right to challenge before the courts the acts of the county councils, of the local council and of the mayors, if he or she considers that they are illegal. If a challenge is made, such an act is suspended *ex officio*.

Prefects are appointed by the Government on the proposal of the Minister of Administration and Internal Affairs. Since 2003, Prefects have been granted the status of 'high public officials', thus being subject to the provisions of the Law on the status of public servants.[23] This was an attempt to 'professionalise' the Prefects, by turning them from politicians into public servants. Political criteria should no longer prevail: the persons proposed to be appointed as Prefects must fulfil the conditions prescribed by law for higher public officers and should be appointed following a competitive process. In the same spirit, the

---

[22] M Guțan, 'La réception de l'institution napoléonienne du préfet en Roumanie' in M-L Moquet-Anger (ed), *Les institutions napoléoniennes* (Paris, L'Harmattan, 2006) 67.
[23] Law no 188/1999.

Prefects and their deputies are forbidden to be members of political parties or similar organisations. Despite these legal provisions, meant to ensure the fairness and transparency of local government, politicisation still prevails, embodied in the recurring phenomenon of *politicianism*: although all public servants (including 'high public officers') must be recruited following a competitive process (in the latter case, a 'national competition'), in practice the overwhelming majority of key offices are still occupied, on political grounds, by persons faithful to the governing party.[24] In the same way, the Prefect has remained an obedient tool of the Government, mirroring, on a narrower scale, the inter-war Prefects, who were the main instruments used to manipulate elections. This phenomenon has led to the emergence of corrupt local interest groups or 'clans', headed by 'local barons' (influential local business-men supporting and supported by the central Government and often elected as presidents of the county councils), which 'make the law' at local level.

B. Financial Autonomy

Administrative decentralisation would normally imply a level of financial autonomy, in order to better function in the achievement of local projects and goals. In Romania, true financial autonomy is still wishful thinking, as the central power is extremely reluctant to grant it to local communities. According to the framework law on decentralisation, the transfer of competences takes place only after the transfer of the necessary financial resources by the central administration. In practice, this rarely happens on time, and sufficient funds are often lacking.

Formally, a budgetary autonomy exists and the territorial entities may adopt their own local budgets. However, the problem surrounding the funding of these budgets reveals the true character of this 'autonomy'. In order to meet expenses, these budgets depend to a great extent on the national state budget and, thus, on the will of the 'centre'. Local taxes are established by the national Fiscal Code, and local authorities have only limited power to set the amounts of certain taxes (property tax on buildings and land, vehicle tax, advertising tax, hotel tax, etc) within the boundaries fixed by the same law. The national budget

---

[24] See also Ch 3, section III.C.

allocates back to the local communities only a certain percentage from the general income tax collected locally, and this amount varies according to the will of the central Government (presently, the amount given back is around 71 per cent of the collected income tax). These transfers from the state budget, necessary in order to balance local budgets, are almost at the discretion of the central Government, on the basis of certain criteria which change frequently:

> [E]very time when, for some reason, the incomes of the national budget decrease, the legislator or the Government *via* ordinances, can change the law granting financing to territorial entities. This is one of the ways in which financial centralisation affects the structure and the amount of the local budgets' revenues and thus, the local financial autonomy.[25]

Ironically or not, successive central Governments were very generous as regards the decentralisation of expenses: they transferred large amounts to the charge of local communities, especially in connection with education and health care, with serious negative effects centrally on these already underfinanced fields.

This is proof that, at the political level, there is still a fear of losing control of public financial resources, combined with a will to preserve influence over and a relationship of dependence with the local power, which can be used during electoral periods. For various reasons, especially relating to poor economic development, the imbalance of the local budgets encourages this view and increases that dependence. Many times, funding from the central budget is allocated according to political interests and not the actual needs of the communities: it is well known that those counties and/or towns where the Government party has or expects more votes are granted privileged funding, to the detriment of others. More than once, mayors elected from certain political parties which later lost the general election were forced to resign and join the Government party in order to receive more money from the central budgets for local projects. This phenomenon is dangerous for local autonomy and for the rule of law in general.

The problem is enhanced by the fact that there is no authority competent to solve potential conflicts between the central Government and local authorities, the Constitutional Court having no jurisdiction in

---

[25] C Oneţ, 'Din nou despre criza financiară şi insolvenţa unităţilor administrativ-teritoriale' (2013) 1 *Acta Universitatis Lucian Blaga Seria Iurisprudentia* 202.

this respect. These issues should be addressed by future constitutional change.

IV. CONCLUSION

From the constitutional point of view (as the majority of local government-related issues are regulated by administrative law and not by the Constitution), there are a few important matters to be emphasised as a conclusion to this chapter.

First, a topical issue in the field of local government is regionalisation, ie the creation of an intermediate layer of territorial units—the regions—in order to better administrate certain matters at local level. Although inspired by European trends and practice, regionalisation is regarded with caution in Romania, as it is seen by certain political circles as a threat to the unitary character of the state. This is partially due to the fact that, every time regionalisation has been a topic for debate, the Hungarian minority has come up with firm requests for territorial ethnic-based autonomy, which is contrary to state unity as provided for in the current constitutional system. This is the reason why all previous drafts regarding this issue designed the regions in such a way as not to include the three counties inhabited by a Hungarian majority. Establishing regionalisation would require the Constitution to be amended, and it was in fact a recurring topic during the 2012–14 constitutional amendment process. The proposed texts were criticised for lack of clarity by the Constitutional Court in its decision on the draft amending law. In any case, the amendment process was not resumed after the break-up of the governing political coalition in March 2014, and therefore the problem of regionalisation has once more been put on hold.

Secondly, although things have significantly improved as a result of the anti-corruption mechanisms and of the CVM, some issues still need to be resolved. For example, in the electoral year 2014, the Government enacted an Emergency Ordinance allowing local elected officials (mayors and local councillors) to change their political party (the previous legislation providing that, in such a case, that person would lose his or her office). The measure, intended to 'recruit', using the above-mentioned financial pressures, more faithful supporters at the local level in order to help during the electoral campaign, was strongly criticised by civil society and by the political circles of the opposition, as it was an obvious (and successful, as its effects were immediately apparent) attempt to manipulate the presidential elections of November 2014. However, the result of the elections was not the one expected by the Government,[26] and on 17 December 2014 the Constitutional Court rendered the Emergency Ordinance unconstitutional,[27] depriving it of all effect. It still remains to be seen what will happen as regards those local elected officials who changed parties: normally, they would have to be deposed from office following the publication of the Constitutional Court decision.

Politicisation[28] and corruption[29] remain strong features of Romanian local government. Romania is among the least developed EU member states from the point of view of professionalisation and overall quality of local and central administration, and is a state where the 'merits and competences of the applicants for public positions still are in the shadow of political loyalties and favouritism'.[30]

FURTHER READING

European Commission for Democracy Through Law (Venice Commission), *Opinion on the Draft Revision of the Constitution of Romania*, adopted by the Venice Commission at its 54th Plenary Session, Venice, 14–15 March 2003.

M Guțan, 'La reception de l'institution napoléonienne du préfet en Roumanie' in M-L Moquet-Anger (ed), *Les institutions napoléoniennes* (Paris, L'Harmattan, 2006).

---

[26] See Ch 3.

[27] RCC, Decision no 761/2014.

[28] See also the statistics published in J Teorell et al, *The Quality of Government Basic Dataset*, version 15 May 2013. *University of Gothenburg: The Quality of Government Institute,* available at http://www.qog.pol.gu.se, where it is quoted that in Romania the political connections of the applicants are more important in employing public servants in Romania than any other European country.

[29] In 2014 alone, 17 out of 41 county council presidents were arrested, pursued for criminal activity by the National Anti-corruption Directorate, or judged and convicted by the courts for corruption.

[30] L Vlăsceanu & M-G Hâncean, *Modernitatea românească* (Bucharest, Paralela 45, 2014) 129.

RN Petrescu, 'Considérations concernant le régime d'autonomie locale en Roumanie' in C Calinoiu (ed), *La science du droit, réalités et perspectives. Collection d'études dediées au Professeur Victor Duculescu* (Bucharest, VIS Print, 2004).

Ş Deaconu, 'La réforme de l'administration publique—facteur nécessaire de l'adhésion de la Roumanie à l'Union Européenne' in C Calinoiu (ed), *La science du droit, réalités et perspectives. Collection d'études dediées au Professeur Victor Duculescu* (Bucharest, VIS Print, 2004).

5

The Constitutional Court. Constitutional Aspects of the Judicial System

———————

The Constitutional Court – The High Court of Cassation and Justice – The Judicial System Independence

R OMANIA HAS A classic Continental judicial system, with one range of jurisdictions. There is no separate system of administrative courts, judicial review of administrative acts being carried out by ordinary courts with special competence. The Constitutional Court, on the other hand, is designed to be separate from the judiciary, and has its own separate title in the Constitution. However, the links between the judicial system and the Constitutional Court are important, from the dialogue inherent in the concrete constitutional review established by the Constitution, to the 'clashes' or tensions that frequently arise. Due to its role and impact on the whole constitutional and legal system, in the first part of this chapter I analyse the Constitutional Court and then sketch in the constitutional foundations of the judicial system.

I. THE CONSTITUTIONAL COURT

A. The Foundations of the Romanian Constitutional Court

Judicial review was introduced in pre-World War I Romania, in a peculiar way: American-style judicial review emerged as a result of an acknowledgement, by the Romanian judiciary, of French public law ideas.[1] After the hesitant jurisprudence of the supreme court of the land from the 1870s, in 1912 a lower court asserted, in the American Marshall-court manner, and supported by two reputable French lawyers (Henri Berthélemy and Gaston Jèze), the right of tribunals to review the constitutionality of the laws applicable to the cases they are called on to resolve.

The 1923 Constitution 'rationalised' judicial review by expressly entrusting this power only to the supreme court of Romania—Court of Cassation/*Curtea de Casaţie*—with a view to avoiding jurisprudential conflicts. Apart from its concentrated character, the new procedure for judicial review of legislation retained the same features as the American model: it could only be invoked indirectly, by way of referral, and the final decision would produce only *inter partes* effects. In practice, due to the formal reluctance of Romanian judges—more comfortable applying the law than interpreting it—resort to judicial review was rare, and was exercised in a rather limited way. The system was maintained under the dictatorial regimes of 1938 and 1940, but in 1946 the Court of Cassation sang its own swan song, declaring unconstitutional a law establishing that decisions of special commissions which nationalised property were not to be submitted to judicial review. During the communist period, there was no constitutional-judicial review of legislation.

After the overturning of the communist regime, in the context of setting up a democratic regime based on the rule of law by adopting a new democratic Constitution endowed with supremacy, the need for constitutional review of legislation came into question. Despite the obvious preference for importing the so-called 'European' or Kelsenian model of constitutional review, there were voices that favoured the restoration of the 1923 Constitution's American-type system.[2]

---

[1]   See also H Schwartz, *The Struggle for Constitutional Justice in Post-Communist Europe* (Chicago, University of Chicago Press, 2000) 17; ES Tănăsescu, 'Constitutional Semantics and Legal Culture' in M Guţan & B Selejan-Guţan (eds), *Europeanisation and Judicial Culture in Contemporary Democracies* (Bucharest, Hamangiu, 2014); and G Conac, 'Une antériorité roumaine: le contrôle de la constitutionnalité des lois en Roumanie au début du XXème siècle jusqu'en 1938' in *Mélanges en l'honneur de Slobodan Milačić: démocratie et liberté: tension, dialogue, confrontation* (Bruxelles, Bruylant, 2007) 399.

[2]   For more details, see B Selejan-Guţan, 'La réception du modèle européen de la constitutionnalité des lois en Roumanie' in *Imperialism and Chauvinism in the Law* (Zurich, Schulthess, 2004) *passim*.

In the early post-communist and pre-constitutional transition (January 1990–December 1991), the supreme court in Romania attempted to introduce a judicial review procedure, on the basis of Decree-Law no 92/1991, which comprised provisions of a constitutional nature. By a 1991 Decision of the united sections (plenary), the supreme court declared itself competent, in this special composition, to examine issues of unconstitutionality, raised by means of an 'extraordinary appeal' by the general prosecutor. The procedure was slow and complicated, and it was never used, although the supreme court's decision was certainly valid and applicable until the creation and effective establishment of the new Constitutional Court (in June 1992).[3]

In the context of the enormous external interest in the constitutional changes in all post-communist countries, as well as with the help of the international forums, especially the Venice Commission, the European model was preferred and the Romanian Constitutional Court was established. This was not only a political decision made in a particular international context: the Kelsenian model eventually prevailed for a whole set of substantial reasons. Besides the classic arguments as to the alleged inadequacy of the American model in civil law legal systems[4] (mainly because of the peculiarities of the judicial systems and the lack of *stare decisis*), some other arguments, more specific to the social and political context of the newly established democracies, may be highlighted: fear of the past, lack of confidence in the old institutions (including the judiciary) and concern for the future, ie acceptance by European organisations. New institutions, like the Constitutional Court and the Ombudsman (*Avocatul Poporului/People's Advocate*), were seen as symbols of a permanent break with the past and of the coming of the 'European era' of the rule of law. The Constitutional Court was to be completely distinct from the classic state powers: it was not to be part of the judicial system, being expressly defined as 'independent from all state powers', and the Constitution dedicated an entirely separate title to it.

As the Constitutional Court was a novel institution in the Romanian constitutional system, legal import played an important role, and was

---

[3] For details, see C-L Popescu, 'Le contrôle judiciaire prétorien de la constitutionnalité des lois en Roumanie dans la période post-communiste et pré-constitutionnelle' in (2013) 1 *Est Europa, Revue d'études politiques et constitutionnelles* 87 at 104.

[4] See, for instance, M Cappelletti, *Le pouvoir des juges* (Paris, Economica-PUAM, 1990) 204.

used in an interesting manner in the process of its establishment. The constitutional drafters did not use a single model but looked for more sources of inspiration in their attempt to achieve the best result. Their efforts amounted to the creation of a 'hybrid' institution, with elements grafted from the French Constitutional Council as regards the Court's structure and from the Italian Constitutional Court as regards its powers and jurisdiction. Although it would have been a better choice in the long run, scarcely any elements were taken from the Austrian–German model. At the time of the 1991 'constitutional moment', the Constitution's drafters preferred a rather moderate solution, without granting individuals direct access to the Court's jurisdiction and with major emphasis on the political authorities' role in the Court's composition and functioning.

In its early years, the Court was composed mostly of academics, some of them former members of the constitutional drafting committee. Although this composition could imply a more daring jurisprudence, this was not the case. The early jurisprudence was prudent and rich in academic legal analysis. Political influence was not obvious, but it managed to reveal itself in difficult or sensitive political moments, like the second candidacy of President Iliescu in the presidential elections.[5]

The early Court had the delicate mission of dealing with some of the errors of Romania's totalitarian past. From a political standpoint this was not very difficult, as Romania was among the few post-communist countries not to enact lustration legislation immediately after the fall of the totalitarian regime. The Constitutional Court played an interesting role in the lustration issue, as in January 2008 it declared unconstitutional the entire law on access to files and disclosure of the former communist political police (almost 10 years after its enactment).[6]

In the field of criminal law, in 1994 the Court declared unconstitutional those provisions of the Criminal Code that punished sexual relations between same-sex persons,[7] and in 1996 it confirmed its position by declaring the constitutionality of the provisions that abrogated the Criminal Code text.[8]

---

[5] See Ch 3, section I.D.

[6] For more details, see B Iancu, 'Post-Accession Constitutionalism With a Human Face: Judicial Reform and Lustration in Romania' (2010) 6 *European Constitutional Law Review*, 29 and 47 et seq. See also Ch 3, section IV.A.

[7] RCC, Decision no 81/1994.

[8] RCC, Decision no 123/1996.

Another intervention of the Court in correcting errors of the past was in the field of property. The Criminal Code of the communist era made a distinction, with consequences as to applicable penalties, between private property and property of the state. Thus, reinforced criminal protection was conferred on 'common goods', ie state property, in contrast to private property. In the early 1990s, the ordinary courts continued to apply these provisions, despite their obvious discriminatory and therefore unconstitutional character, and despite the courts' ability to set them aside by directly applying Article 151 CR, which states that all prior legal provisions contrary to the constitutional text are to be considered abrogated *de iure*. The Constitutional Court, in its first interpretative decision of 1992, established the unconstitutionality of the unequal protection of property, but only in 1997 did the legislator effect changes to the Criminal Code, in line with the Constitutional Court's jurisprudence.[9]

Since 2000 the Court has been making more references to the case law of the ECtHR in its decisions. On the other hand, enhanced political influence can be detected in its decisions, especially in the period 2010–13, when it frequently endorsed presidential or governmental readings of the Constitution. In its most recent case law (2013–15), the Court has taken more controversial decisions, from declaring unconstitutional the laws on communications data surveillance,[10] to even assuming the position of 'positive legislator' by imposing imperative obligations on Parliament or by changing the meaning of legal provisions without declaring them unconstitutional.[11]

B. Composition of the Court: Appointment of Constitutional Judges, Independence and Impartiality

i. *Composition and Appointment*

The composition of the Court mirrors that of the French *Conseil Constitutionnel*: nine judges, three appointed by the Chamber of Deputies,

---

[9] For further details on the involvement of the Court in the field of criminal law, see ES Tănăsescu, 'Roumanie—un système judiciaire entre formalisme excessif et excès de pouvoir' in G Vrabie (ed), *Le pouvoir judiciaire* (Iasi, Institutul European, 2011) 89.

[10] RCC, Decision no 17/2015.

[11] RCC, Decisions nos 206/2013 and 418/2014.

three by the Senate and three by the President of Romania. The judges are appointed for a non-renewable term of nine years, and the Court is renewed with three new members every three years. All cases are heard by the plenary Court and most decisions are taken by a simple majority (with the exception of decisions regarding the constitutional amendment initiatives and of resolutions regarding the referendum procedure, which require a two-thirds majority). No procedure for appeal or reversal of decisions is currently provided.

The selection of the judges is subject to appointment criteria prescribed by the Constitution, which are quite loose: candidates must be jurists of high professional competence, with at least 18 years' seniority in legal practice or in legal education. No other criteria or selection procedures are provided for, and no guarantee of transparency is established. Practice to date shows that, besides legal academics, judges have been selected who were MPs, prosecutors, legal advisers/lawyers: only two career judges have been appointed to the Constitutional Court so far.[12] Over the last nine years, although the selection procedure might have seemed to be quite well balanced, in reality it has been dominated by the political factor. This is mainly due to the appointment procedure. Candidates are nominated by political groups in Parliament, and are subjected to hearings in the juridical parliamentary committees of the respective chamber. This step is usually a mere formality. The final step is the vote in plenary session of the chamber, where the decision is taken according to the majority of votes. The judges elect their chairman (or president) for a three-year term, which may be renewed. The chairman coordinates the activity of the Court and represents it in its relations with other authorities. He or she does not have direct budgetary powers, which belong to the Court's Secretary-General, appointed by the Plenum.

The second decade of the Court's existence was marked by the appointment of many former politicians or persons related to the

---

[12] Using approximate statistics (due to the double or even triple capacity of some judges): out of the 35 judges who have been in office during the first 22 years of the Court's existence, 14 were mainly law professors (combined with work in other fields, such as former lawyers, MPs), 10 were former MPs, 3 were former prosecutors (one also being a former MP), 3 were former legal advisers/lawyers (one being a former MP and one a law professor), 3 were members of the Government/executive (one being a professor) and 2 were career judges. The profession of law professor was the only one that could be maintained during a term of office as a constitutional judge.

political world or government circles. This was not directly reflected in the Court's decisions, but the practice did not go unnoticed by public opinion, and doubts started to be expressed about the Court's objectivity. The disputes surrounding the Court shifted from dealing with the past to involvement in current political crises. The peak was reached in 2010, when the appointment of three new judges became a public political scandal, and elections in the Chamber of Deputies were annulled and re-run for procedural reasons, because allegedly the 'wrong' candidate had won. At the Senate, a scandal broke out regarding the 'surveillance' of secret voting by the representatives of the majority. Since then, every time a new judge needs to be appointed, the talk in public is about which party managed to impose its candidate and less about the candidate's qualifications. This open struggle for control of the Court added to a reputation already shaken, and gave weight to the radical voices that contested its very existence in the constitutional system. After the constitutional crisis of 2012, these voices grew louder, but fortunately this radical change was not envisaged by the drafters of the constitutional amendments.

ii. Independence and Impartiality of the Court

The issue of the independence and impartiality of the constitutional judges is one of the most sensitive aspects of the present legislation, which recently has shown its shortcomings in times of crisis. The lack of accountability of the constitutional judges enhances this problem, but in this case, 'reconciling independence with accountability may be akin to squaring a circle'.[13]

The most controversial issue is the 'institutional' independence of the constitutional judges from political authorities. Theoretically, it is quite clear: although the Court is a dual-natured institution—political and jurisdictional, according to the Kelsenian model—one of its guarantees of independence is the 'duty of ingratitude' required from the judges towards the political authorities that appointed them—the two chambers of Parliament and the President of Romania. This is a salient argument in favour of constitutional courts in general, in answer to their detractors invoking the anti-majoritarian objection. Nevertheless,

---

[13] ML Volcansek, 'Appointing Judges the European Way' (2007) 34 *Fordham Urban Law Journal* 364, at 365.

legal and political reality may totally contradict theory. In several cases the independence and impartiality of Romanian Constitutional Court judges, as regards political parties and/or political authorities, have been doubted, especially when the Court has had to rule on political questions or give rulings with direct effects upon political life, such as advisory opinions on the President's suspension from office, the referendum law, cases of 'legal conflicts of a constitutional nature' etc. Moreover, some of the Constitutional Court's judges have been known to be former important members of political parties involved in such procedures or conflicts.

In 2006, a proposal to change the Court's law, in order to forbid candidates who have had links with a political party, was submitted to the Venice Commission for an opinion.[14] The Commission's rapporteur, M Cardoso da Costa, argued that although 'it would be completely undesirable that in the composition of the Constitutional Court appears a predominance, even a too large participation of judges having a formal relationship with a political party and coming directly from political life',[15] such a prohibition would be too harsh. Nevertheless, he noted that the limitation might be acceptable in 'totally exceptional cases or [for] reasons, *particular to Romania and to its experience with constitutional justice*' (emphasis added). The law has not been changed: political stakes are still high when it comes to appointing constitutional judges in Romania.

Formally, there are some constitutional and legal guarantees of the independence of Constitutional Court judges as regards political authorities: their irremovability, the impossibility of renewing their term of appointment, disciplinary autonomy, certain incompatibilities established by the Constitution and by laws. However, even if there were to be a suspicion of lack of impartiality, according to the law, constitutional judges cannot be recused and may not abstain from judging a case.

---

[14] 'Candidates should not have been members of a political party, have a family relation in first line directly, in second line collaterally and should not have been married or otherwise related with persons who are or were, in the last 5 years, members of the national steering organs of political parties'.

[15] JM Cardoso da Costa,'Observations sur des projets de lois pour la modification et le complement de la Loi no. 47/1992 relative a l'organisation et au fonctionnement de la Cour Constitutionnelle de la Roumanie', http://www.venice.coe.int/webforms/documents/default.aspx?pdffile=CDL(2006)009-f.

As regards the Constitutional Court's institutional independence from political factors, voices from civil society proposed integrating the Court into the judicial authority, by changing the Constitution, in order to 'emphasise its main role as a jurisdictional rather than political organ'.[16] Although it departs from the initial intention to place the Constitutional Court outside the power system, such a change could be beneficial in the Romanian context, where the system has proved its weakness, caused by overly-enhanced political involvement in the appointment of the constitutional judges.

Constitutional judges cannot be removed during their term of appointment. They benefit from jurisdictional immunity for criminal offences: they cannot be arrested or subjected to criminal trial unless the appointing authority gives its consent, at the request of the General Prosecutor. In 2015, for the first time a constitutional judge resigned after being the subject of a criminal investigation for corruption.

C. The Constitutional Court's Powers

Like most European constitutional courts, the RCC was given more powers than merely reviewing the constitutionality of legislation. New Kelsenian constitutional jurisdictions are also electoral jurisdictions and conflict-solvers. The Romanian Court did not yet play the role adopted by other European constitutional courts from the point of view of influence on legislation or on the protection of rights. This was partially due to the ordinary courts' reaction to its jurisprudence, but also to its own partial inconsistency and/or apparent political involvement.

The RCC has the following categories of powers:

1. *constitutional review powers*: these cover the abstract review of laws, review of international treaties, review of Parliament's regulations and resolutions, concrete review of laws and GOs, surveillance of the popular legislative initiative;

---

[16] 'UNJR. Curtea Constituţională să fie alcătuită exclusiv din judecători' [The Constitutional Court Should Comprise Only Judges], http://www.juridice.ro/stiri-juridice/flux-stiri/36603-unjr-judecatori-curtea-*constitutionala*.html; for some proposals regarding a reform of the Constitutional Court, see Societatea pentru Justiţie [Society for Justice], 'Curtea Constituţională şi Avocatul Poporului': http://www.sojust.ro/sistemul-juridic-din-romania-raport-independent/8-curtea-constitutionala-si-avocatul-poporului.html.

2. *electoral litigation*: covering surveillance of respect for the procedure for the election of the President of Romania, validation of the election's result, surveillance of respect for the referendum procedure and confirmation of the results;
3. *resolving political conflicts* and other political situations: resolving legal conflicts of a constitutional nature between public authorities; ascertaining the circumstances which justify the interim in the exercise of the office of President of Romania and to report its findings to the Parliament and the Government; giving an advisory opinion on the proposed suspension from office of the President; rendering decisions on complaints of unconstitutionality of a political party.

The most important and the most used powers are those involving constitutional review, which, in their turn, may be divided into 'classic' constitutional review powers and 'ancillary' constitutional review powers, such as the very controversial power to review parliamentary decisions, which places the Court on the borderline with politics.

i. Abstract Review

Abstract review is, at the same time, an *a priori* review: the Constitutional Court may examine the constitutionality of laws after their adoption by the Parliament and before their promulgation by the President. This review, known as 'objection of unconstitutionality', can only be initiated by public authorities from all branches of power: the President of Romania, one of the presidents of the chambers of Parliament, the HCCJ, at least 50 deputies or 25 senators, and by the Ombudsman. The only *ex officio* review is that of the constitutional amendment initiatives and laws. In this case, the Constitution only provides for the review of the 'amendment initiative', but the organic law of the Court added review of the adopted amendment law before being subjected to the referendum approval.

A particular form of abstract review is the constitutional review of international treaties. A treaty that is found to be unconstitutional may not be ratified by Parliament until the Constitution has been amended to eliminate the reasons for the treaty's unconstitutionality. In this case, the Court can be addressed by the presidents of the two chambers of Parliament, or by at least 50 deputies or 25 senators. This type of review has not been exercised to date.

All *a priori* constitutionality challenges are judged by the Plenary Court, and there is no form of appeal against the decision. The Constitution establishes a distinction between the effects of the Court's decisions in the abstract and in the concrete review. Following a decision of unconstitutionality of a law before its promulgation, Parliament is bound to re-examine the law in order to revise it in accordance with the Court's decision.

Abstract review is a quite powerful form of review, used especially by the political minority to challenge laws adopted by the majority, and has actually become an important tool of the parliamentary opposition.

ii. Concrete Review

Concrete review is the type most frequently used by the Romanian Constitutional Court. It is exercised *a posteriori*, after the law has entered into force. Modelled in a similar way to the Italian concrete review, but under a different name, the referral of unconstitutionality (*excepţie de neconstituţionalitate*) has proved to be successful in defending fundamental rights and contributed to the 'constitutionalisation' of the legal system.

A concrete review may be initiated on the occasion of a trial of any kind, before a court of any level or an arbitral tribunal, at any moment in the proceedings, at the request of one of the parties, of the prosecutor or of the court *sua sponte*. The organic law of the Constitutional Court prescribes a set of admissibility criteria: the challenge of unconstitutionality must refer only to a provision of a law or of a GO; it must be relevant to the ongoing case; and the challenged legal provision must be 'in force', or, according to a Decision of the Court of 2011,[17] still produce effects even when it is no longer in force.

Until October 2010, once a referral of unconstitutionality was found admissible, the court had to adjourn the proceedings and refer the case to the Constitutional Court. This was the logical solution, introduced in 1997 when the RCC organic law was amended for the second time, in lieu of the optional adjournment provided for by the initial version of the law. The change was made after numerous criticisms of the doctrine were expressed, as the continuation of the proceedings while the risk

---

[17] RCC, Decision no 766 /2011.

remained of a finding of unconstitutionality of the legal provisions applicable in the case, was contrary to the principle of legal certainty. In 2010, following complaints from the judiciary that the challenge of unconstitutionality was frequently being used only as an instrument to delay cases, Parliament simply removed the obligation to adjourn from the law. In choosing this radical solution, the legislator considered neither the requirement for legal certainty nor any alternative with a less negative impact, such as giving the ordinary court the possibility to reject the referral if the Constitutional Court had already given a decision on the constitutionality of the contested legal text.[18] This strange (and singular in comparative law) solution affects one of the main concrete features of this kind of review: the effect on the case in which it originated. The new law also included the solution for this situation: if the Constitutional Court declares unconstitutional a law on which the ordinary court's decision was based, the case can be reopened according to new provisions of the procedural codes. However, the reopening of the case is time- and resource-consuming for the parties, therefore the possibility to adjourn would have been more appropriate.

Despite these shortcomings, the referral of a claim of unconstitutionality remains an effective means of defence of fundamental rights. The Ombudsman may raise it directly before the Constitutional Court, against laws and ordinances. This can reinforce its impact upon legislation, especially as regards the GOs, which otherwise cannot be challenged directly. Unfortunately, the Ombudsman has been very reluctant so far to exercise this important power (only three referrals in 2014, at the request of civil society).[19]

The Constitutional Court considers referrals based on unconstitutionality following the jurisdictional procedure established by its organic law, based on general civil procedure. A rejected referral can be made again. If a finding of unconstitutionality is handed down, the effect shifts to the norm rather than to its author. Thus Parliament or the Government (in the case of GOs declared unconstitutional) is under no imperative obligation to re-establish conformity with the Constitution, but the unconstitutional text ceases to produce effects:

---

[18] See B Selejan-Guţan, 'L'exception d'inconstitutionnalité: instrument de protection des droits fondamentaux ou technique dilatoire?' (2012) 1 *Romanian Journal of Comparative Law* 65.

[19] Avocatul Poporului, *Raport anual 2014*, available at http://www.avp.ro/rapoarte-anuale/raport_2014_avp.pdf, at 3.

The provisions of laws, ordinances or parliamentary regulations, which are found to be unconstitutional, cease their legal effects within 45 days from the publication of the Constitutional Court's decision if, in the meantime, the Parliament or the Government, as the case may be, cannot bring the unconstitutional provision into line with the Constitution. During this time limit, the impugned provisions are suspended *de jure*.[20]

The passive attitude of Parliament in such a case may lead to the inapplicability of an unconstitutional legal provision, but after the 45-day time limit, the legislator may enact a new norm, as its legislative competence cannot be limited in time.

The constitutional wording of the binding effects of the Constitutional Court's decisions is rooted in the Kelsenian doctrine of the 'negative legislator': the Court may not bring about direct changes to existing laws. It cannot enact, change or abrogate any legal text but only declare its unconstitutionality, in which case special obligations may arise for the legislator, who keeps its full legislative competence.

Although quite reluctant at the beginning, ordinary courts finally came to terms with the existence of constitutional review and of the Court's decisions. Their main problem lay, in the early years of democracy, in accepting the supremacy of the Constitution. There were judges who would not apply the Constitution because 'judges are subject only to the law'; there were courts—the entire system, in fact—who would not respect the binding effects of a finding of unconstitutionality by the Court regarding sensitive matters like the right to defence of the accused; there were judges who did not know how to refer to the Constitutional Court, and which referrals were admissible or not, despite the express provisions of the law.

In 1999, the then Supreme Court of Justice expressed a widespread view of that moment, that

the provisions of the Constitution are not addressed directly to the ordinary courts, which apply the ordinary law, but only to the legislator, who must comply with the Constitution and bring changes to the ordinary laws. The Constitutional Court decisions have the same status ... The courts are bound to apply the present ordinary law and not directly the Constitution; the legislator only is bound to comply with the constitutional provisions and principles, bringing changes to the legislation in this respect'.[21]

---

[20] Art 147 §1 CR.
[21] SCJ, Decision no 1813/1999.

This 'national legal nonsense'[22] was a dominant attitude of judges towards constitutional principles, including the relationship of national law with international human rights law. This situation has changed dramatically in the last decade, although the relationship between ordinary judges and constitutional judges is far from being ideal, especially at the level of the HCCJ.[23] Nevertheless, concrete review was and remains the most important and effective means of constitutional review exercised by the Romanian Constitutional Court.

iii. Other Powers

The RCC's extensive powers include, besides constitutional review, 'ancillary' powers, which have grown in importance and became controversial issues in the debates over the Court's role and independence. In this context, the Constitutional Court may become an instrument for consolidating the democratic process, or, as the case may have proved to be in Romania, exactly the opposite. Crossing the line between the two roles is extremely easy, and is mostly due to the high politicisation of the Court's structure and activity. These ancillary powers may be the cause of distorting the role of the Constitutional Court from negative to positive legislator.

a. Review of Parliamentary Resolutions

This new power was introduced in 2010 by amending the organic law of the Court.[24] It allows the Court to review the constitutionality of virtually all resolutions adopted by the two chambers of Parliament (other than parliamentary regulations, which were already submitted to the Court's competence). The new power has been highly criticised by the majority of commentators, especially because of its political consequence: submitting the political activity of Parliament to the scrutiny of the Court.

---

[22] C-L Popescu, 'L'exception d'inconstitutionnalité en tant que recours interne avant une requête individuelle devant la Cour européenne des droits de l'homme' in ES Tănăsescu & Şt Deaconu (eds), *Liber Amicorum Ioan Muraru. Despre constituţie şi constituţionalism* (Bucharest, Hamangiu, 2006) 197.

[23] See II.E. below.

[24] As Art 146 l) CR allows the introduction of new powers by merely amending the law of the Court.

This power has been characterised as excessive and even 'dangerous for the parliamentary life'.[25] Not long before the changes, the appointment of new constitutional judges had been the object of a real 'battle' between the political parties, with the aim of creating a 'new majority' within the Court to support the governing party.[26] The traditional role of a constitutional court, despite having other ancillary powers, must remain to review of the constitutionality of normative acts of primary regulation, ie laws or delegated legislation, and it should not have the power to review acts with political stakes, such as parliamentary resolutions.[27]

In June 2012, the legislator attempted to remove the new power of the Court, by re-amending the organic law. The amending law's constitutionality was challenged before its promulgation. In its decision,[28] the Court showed a manifest tendency to transform itself into an untouchable organ, situated above Parliament and any other authority, arguing that no other authority might express an opinion on the Court's activity.[29] The Court exceeded its constitutional limits as negative legislator: it substituted itself for the legislator—even the constitutional legislator—by giving a 'constitutional rank' to organic law provisions; it expressly limited the competence of Parliament by stating that 'the ability to limit, eliminate or reduce these powers [of the Court, introduced by the same legislator] ... would mean to distort the goal of perfecting the constitutional democracy'. Nevertheless, in an earlier decision from 2011,[30] while examining a constitutional amendment initiative, the Court admitted that the powers introduced by virtue of Article 146 l) CR had a 'legal rank' and not a 'constitutional rank', and proposed

---

[25] ES Tănăsescu, 'Chronique. Roumanie' (2011) XVII *Annuaire International de Justice Constitutionnelle* 987.

[26] As a supportive comparative law argument, such a power does not exist in other democratic constitutional review systems, a rare exception being Latvia. See A Mavcic, *Powers of Constitutional Courts and Equivalent Bodies*, European Commission for Democracy Through Law, CDL-JU(1998)10, at 3.

[27] For example, the US Supreme Court imposed the condition that the cases brought before it should lack a political character.

[28] RCC, Decision no 727/2012, adopted in record time: 27 June (day of the application)–9 July (day when the decision was pronounced).

[29] Decision no 727/2012: 'to assess and decide on the activity of the Constitutional Court ... means its incorrect reception and, moreover, to ignore the substance of its fundamental role'.

[30] Decision no 799/2011.

eliminating this constitutional provision altogether. It is interesting to note in this context that, in the reasons for its decision, the Court used no solid legal or constitutional argument to justify the need for such a power of review, and only repeated that such a review was 'important for the functioning of the rule of law and for the respect of the balance of powers'. Indirectly, the Court claims to be the sole guardian of democracy by means of checking any act of Parliament, thus becoming a 'universal reviewer', placed 'beyond the political conflicts which are inherent to the relationships between the majority and the opposition' and risking becoming a weapon to be used by the parties to political conflicts.

The Court substituted itself for the legislator once more when, despite the provisions of the modified law, it established a distinction between those resolutions that can and cannot be submitted to review: '[There] may be submitted to constitutional review only the resolutions … which affect constitutional values, rules and principles or, as the case may be, the organisation and functioning of authorities and institutions of a constitutional rank'.[31] The practice shows that, in exercising this power, the Court examined resolutions involving purely political stakes: appointments to and dismissals from office, the vote of confidence procedure and requests to lift parliamentary immunity.[32]

In this context, the warning given by Tom Ginsburg and Zachary Elkins on the ancillary powers of constitutional courts is applicable to the Romanian Constitutional Court:

> [P]aradoxically, the involvement of courts in ancillary tasks has the potential to undermine their ability to conduct effective constitutional review, precisely because it pulls them into political conflicts. … There is, however, a risk that constitutional courts will be drawn into inherently unwinnable zero-sum conflicts, which require deft maneuvering and skillful action. In new

---

[31]   RCC, Decisions nos 53 and 54/2011.

[32]   During his second term of suspension from office, President Traian Băsescu made the following statement, '[T]he whole institutional system must be reset by attacking before the Constitutional Court the abusive resolutions of the Parliament'. He did not refer to laws but to political resolutions. Therefore, on the President's meaning, one authority must make decisions with regard to the activity of the elected Parliament not only in matters of constitutionality—as initially designed by the Constitution—but in all matters. The Court would then become not only the 'guardian of the Constitution', but also the 'guardian of the Parliament' and would thus make the vehemently opposed *gouvernement des juges* a reality. For further examples of decisions, see Tănăsescu (n 25), at 987.

democracies, at least, it is not obvious that the courts themselves will always be up to the task.[33]

b. Electoral and Political Parties Review

The Romanian Constitutional Court does not have extensive powers in electoral matters. The Court has attributes regarding only the presidential elections, and has no involvement in parliamentary elections. It also has the task of supervising respect for the Constitution in the course of any referendum procedure. The Court's competence to declare unconstitutional a political party is set forth by the Constitution, but it has never been exercised.

c. Resolving Conflicts Between Authorities

This power was introduced by the constitutional amendment of 2003. In exercising it, the Court is limited to 'legal conflicts of a constitutional nature', therefore a preliminary control is necessary to establish the court's competence. Over the last decade, the Court has examined a wide range of requests, from conflicts between Parliament and the Government, and between the President and the Prime Minister, to more particular types of conflict, such as between the HCCJ and Parliament or between the CSM and the Government (the latter with the object of establishing competence to elect the candidates for the position of judge at the ECtHR).[34] Only some authorities have *locus standi* to address the Court with such requests: the President of Romania, the presidents of the chambers, the Prime Minister and the President of the CSM. The Court has no jurisdiction over conflicts between local and central authorities.

From 2003 to 2013, relatively few conflicts (18) were referred to the Court, which was addressed on almost equal numbers of occasions by the following holders of *locus standi*: the President of Romania (five requests), the presidents of the chambers (five requests), the Prime Minister (four requests) and the President of the CSM (four requests). The Court did not manage to create a coherent doctrine on 'legal

---

[33] T Ginsburg & Z Elkins, 'Ancillary Powers of Constitutional Courts' (2009) 87 *Texas Law Review* 1432, at 1461.

[34] RCC, Decision no 231/2013.

conflicts of a constitutional nature' which it may be called to resolve. It should be the Court's task to choose its methods and ways of reasoning in sometimes difficult cases of conflict. Despite a quite clear constitutional text, which compels the Court to resolve a conflict once it finds that there is one, sometimes it has avoided giving a solution.

One of the most famous cases brought before the Romanian Constitutional Court proved that the Court could not, or would not, cope with the mission it was expected to accomplish. The origin of the conflict was the adoption of the national education law. The long-awaited reform of national education started with some controversial salary increases in 2008 and continued with successive attempts to adopt an entirely new law replacing the existing one. The Government attempted to engage its responsibility, according to Article 114 CR, on a package of laws, including a draft of the national education law. The opposition, after failing to impose a vote of no confidence following the engagement of responsibility procedure, challenged the new law at the Constitutional Court before its promulgation. Quite predictably, in the way of reasoning, the Court declared the law unconstitutional for absence of the emergency required for an engagement of responsibility.[35] The Court also noted that such an approach would seek to avoid democratic debate in Parliament, in order to impose the unilateral view of the Government.[36] The draft law was returned to Parliament to be submitted to the ordinary legislative procedure. However, the referred chamber—the Senate—did not debate the bill for almost a year. This passive attitude once again drew the Government to engage its responsibility on the same law, in October 2010. In this tense political context, the president of the Senate addressed to the Constitutional Court a request to resolve a legal conflict of a constitutional nature between Parliament and the Government. Meanwhile, without waiting for the Court's answer, the Government engaged its responsibility on 28 October 2010, and the next day the opposition filed a motion of censure. However, Parliament blocked all proceedings, including the motion, until the Constitutional Court's decision on the constitutional conflict.

The decision came out rather promptly, on 3 November 2010,[37] but it was far from clarifying the situation: the Court established that there

---

[35] See Ch 3, section III.D.iv.
[36] RCC, Decision no 1557/2009.
[37] RCC, Decision no 1431/2010.

was indeed a conflict between the Government and Parliament, and that the engagement of responsibility, which started this conflict, was unconstitutional. The Court said nothing about the resolution of the conflict, and thus avoided fulfilling its constitutional role. Immediately, the question raised by all parties to the conflict was: What happens next? The parliamentary proceedings for the vote of no confidence were still blocked and, apparently, the Constitutional Court's decision on the unconstitutionality of the procedure would mean stopping them definitively. The Government addressed the Court once more with another request on resolving a constitutional conflict with Parliament. On 21 November 2010, the Court handed down a new decision,[38] in which it stated that the previous one only produced effects for the future, therefore it could not affect the pending engagement of responsibility procedure, Parliament thus being bound to continue the procedure and hold a vote on the motion of censure against the Government.[39]

II. THE JUDICIAL SYSTEM AND ITS CONSTITUTIONAL ROLE

A. General Remarks on the Romanian Judicial System

The modern Romanian judicial system, created in the nineteenth century and inspired by the French system, enjoyed its golden years in the first quarter of the twentieth century. It was and remained a classic Continental system, with courts composed of career judges, recruited and appointed immediately after graduating from their legal studies, and trained mostly to apply the law rather than to creatively interpret and/or create legal rules.

During the communist era, the judicial system was perceived as a repressive instrument of the political regime. There were 'subsidiary' criteria for recruiting judges: only those with 'clean' personal political

---

[38] RCC, Decision no 1525/2010.

[39] A few days later, one of the opposition parties withdrew the signatures of its members from the motion of censure, with the effect that the motion itself was withdrawn and the draft law was adopted. Following two more decisions of the Constitutional Court declaring it constitutional, it entered into force in February 2011, 'without the main political actors concerned and the direct beneficiaries of this important law being able to understand exactly why and how' (see Tănăsescu (n 25), at 1003–04).

files could accede to judicial functions. In the first two decades of the communist era—1945–65—a soviet-style judicial system was imported into Romania, with 'people's tribunals' or 'judges' who had not completed legal studies but who had an active political background. The last two decades of the dictatorship saw a compliant judicial system and a very powerful prosecuting system—the soviet-inspired *procuratura*, which very often acted on political command. The mechanism of repression established by the system, especially as regards political offences, and the weakness of the system in more ordinary cases (determined by the weak property law and by the lack of fundamental rights protection) dramatically affected the population's trust in the judicial system, seen as a cast of the privileged who faithfully served the regime. It was therefore a very difficult task to restore this trust after the fall of the communist regime—a trust that is only natural in traditional liberal democracies.

It is now commonplace to say that one of the main conquests of the 1989 Romanian Revolution was the restoration of the independence of justice. However, this is still a work in progress, and the trust in the judiciary has never been more controversial and difficult to restore.

B. Constitutional Principles of the Judiciary

The constitutional provisions on the judiciary are not always clear, especially because of the presence, in the same title, alongside the classic court system, of the 'Public Ministry', the former *Procuratura*, with a special status and organisation, and closer to the executive power. In the absence of clear constitutional provisions, the organic law on the judicial system[40] tries to shine more light on the issue, defining 'judicial power' as being 'exercised by the High Court of Cassation and Justice and by the other legally established courts of law'.

The paramount principle of a judicial system in a rule-of-law state, independence of justice, was given a privileged place and at the same time a guarantee, in one major constitutional provision, Article 152, which includes independence of justice among the substantive limits to amendment, alongside territorial integrity, political pluralism, the national, independent and unitary character of the state, etc. In other

[40] Law no 304/2004.

words, the Constitution may not be amended in such a way as to affect the principle of independence of justice. The principle is also proclaimed in a special chapter dedicated to the judiciary, among the salient constitutional principles set out in Article 124, 'Realisation of Justice': justice is done in the name of the law; justice is unique, impartial and equal for all; judges are independent and subject only to the law. 'Independence' is here an attribute of 'judges' and not of 'justice' as a whole, while 'justice' is never defined as such in the Constitution (it may include the whole 'judicial authority' or not).

In addition to the general principle of independence of justice, the Constitution sets forth other principles specific to the judiciary. Article 126 §5 prohibits the creation of extraordinary tribunals, as they may be an incentive for arbitrary justice. Secondly, the principle of the official language is established by Article 128 §1, with special guarantees for foreign or minority-language citizens. Thus, persons belonging to national minorities have the right to use their mother tongue in official court hearings, as prescribed by the organic law; on the other hand, persons who do not understand the official language are entitled to an interpreter, free of charge in criminal cases. Lastly, the Constitution sets forth the right of appeal, granting the right of all the parties to challenge judicial decisions, according to the law.

C. Organisation of the System and the Status of Magistrates

i. How the Judicial System is Organised

Article 126 §1 CR is dedicated to courts of law: 'Justice shall be administered by the High Court of Cassation and Justice, and the other courts established by law'. Subsequent organic legislation prescribes the rules of jurisdiction and procedure.[41]

The system features a territorial and hierarchical organisation. At the apex is the HCCJ. The lowest courts—courts of first instance or *judecătorii*—are found in some urban communities and deal with the most basic cases; the secondary courts—*tribunale*—have a larger territorial jurisdiction (each county has a *tribunal*) and may overrule the courts of first instance; while the superior courts—courts of appeal—have

---

[41] The law on judicial organisation, by the Code of Civil Procedure and by the Code of Criminal Procedure (new codes, in force since 2013 and 2014 respectively).

appellate jurisdiction over the secondary courts and territorial jurisdiction covering more counties. The secondary courts/*tribunale* also have jurisdiction in administrative litigation, as do the administrative sections of the courts of appeal and of the HCCJ. Romania does not have a separate administrative jurisdiction system, like France or Germany. Ordinary courts have general jurisdiction in civil and criminal cases. As for the specialised courts mentioned by the Constitution ('an organic law may create specialized courts in certain matters', Article 126 §5), thus far they are represented by a special court for family and children, with jurisdiction in matters involving minors and family issues, by three courts specialising in commercial cases and by military courts, which have jurisdiction, in criminal cases, determined by the defendant's status within the military.

ii. Recruitment, Appointment and Status of Judges: Guarantees of Independence

Romanian judges are career judges, as in most Continental legal systems. The law degree, obtained after four years of legal studies, is not sufficient for entering the profession. Upon passing a highly difficult examination, law school graduates enter the National Institute of Magistrates (INM), where they become auditors of justice and prepare for the 'magistracy' professions: judges or prosecutors. Judges are appointed to their function by the President of Romania and thereafter become irremovable (see further below), according to the Constitution and the organic law. Although it may seem a merely formal act, the law allows the President to refuse an appointment once, with proper reasons addressed to the Superior Council of Magistracy (*Consiliul Superior al Magistraturii*, CSM). There are no official gender-based statistics, but women have seemed to dominate the structure of the courts over the last few years. For instance, out of the 115 judges in the High Court, only 19 are men, meaning that women account for over 84 per cent of the total.

The independence of judges (subjective independence) and the independence of justice (objective independence) benefit from several constitutional safeguards: irremovability, incompatibility with other functions, regulation at the level of organic legislation, which is more difficult to change, and the supervision of the high judicial council (CSM), created after the French model but transformed in a very particular way.

Romanian judges are irremovable, which means, according to Article 125 §1 CR and Article 2 of the law, that they cannot be transferred, delegated, moved or promoted without their agreement, and that they can be suspended or fired only subject to the conditions set forth by the law. Moreover, the promotion, transfer or disciplinary sanctioning of judges fall within the jurisdiction of the CSM, ie are decided in the profession's own realm, not by a distinct authority. As a supplementary guarantee of independence, appointment as a judge is incompatible with any other public or private function, with the exception of teaching positions in higher legal education.

The accountability of judges is a rather sensitive issue. The Status of Magistrates Law[42] provides that judges are subject to civil, criminal and disciplinary responsibility. The statute sets out the reasons for disciplinary responsibility, to which have recently (2012) been added 'non-compliance with Constitutional Court decisions and with decisions in the interest of the law of the High Court'. This new provision might put judges at loggerheads with the two high jurisdictions, as judges are also entitled, according to the Constitution, to set aside legislation that is contrary to human rights treaties. If such a ruling were to contradict a decision of the Constitutional Court (which is not always consistent with human rights standards) but be in line with the judge's constitutional obligation as fundamental rights protector, should he or she be held responsible and face disciplinary sanction? In practice there has been no instance of such accountability so far. In disciplinary matters, the only competent jurisdiction is the CSM. However, a significant number of judges have been tried or convicted for corruption offences in the recent years, especially as regards the illegal restitution of property in land, but also for bribery, trafficking of influence and obstruction of criminal justice.

D. The Particular Situation of the Prosecution. The National Anti-corruption Directorate

The inclusion of the prosecution (*Ministerul Public*) in the constitutional chapter on 'Judicial Authority' generated many controversies—at the legal, doctrinal and even international level. It was not clear whether the

---

[42] Law no 303/2004.

intention of the constitutional drafters was to include the prosecution within the judicial power, or what the actual status of the prosecutors was meant to be. 'The Public Ministry' is functionally defined as 'representing the general interests of society and defending the legal order and the rights and freedoms of the citizens' within the judicial activity' (Art 131 §1). The Public Ministry comprises prosecutors, organised in prosecuting offices (*Parchete*) according to the organic law. Following the French model once again, the prosecuting offices are organised territorially alongside the judicial courts.

The most vivid controversies have concerned the constitutional and legal status of the prosecutors. The Constitution is unclear on this point, but sets out distinct principles for the prosecuting activity, including legality, impartiality and, above all, hierarchical control under the authority of the Minister of Justice. Therefore, the prosecuting authority is not governed by the independence of justice principle. The authority of the executive over the Public Ministry was enhanced in 2005, when the CSM lost, in favour of the Minister of Justice, the competence to propose the chief prosecutors at national level.

The most important consequence of the Public Ministry's inclusion in the chapter on judicial authority was the prosecutors' status as 'magistrates', established by the first laws on judicial organisation and maintained in a more subtle manner by the current legislation. This had important consequences for the actual status of the prosecutors, which is strongly reminiscent of the former regime's position as regards the *Procuratura*. The first version of the Constitution granted them important rights, including that of deciding on pre-trial detention, while the Code of Criminal Procedure stated that certain acts of the prosecutors were not to be submitted to judicial review.

This peculiar situation—the prosecution becoming a real power within the judicial system—generated reactions from a society more and more conscious of the existence of fundamental rights. Romania's accession to the ECHR contributed to this process, and so did the jurisprudence of the Constitutional Court. The first issue that came into conflict with the standards of a fair trial and access to justice was the exemption from judicial review of certain acts of the prosecutors from the pre-trial part of criminal proceedings. In 1997, the Constitutional Court declared, in an interpretative decision, that the relevant provisions of the Code of Criminal Procedure were constitutional only in so far as, in the absence of express legal provisions, Article 21 CR was directly applicable, allowing those types of acts to be reviewed by courts. However, the absence of special texts meant the absence of procedural rules for such a review, including rules of jurisdiction, so the Constitutional Court invited the legislator to take the necessary steps to fill the gaps in the legislation. Only in 2003, and only following a strong judgment from the ECtHR,[43] was the Code of Criminal Procedure substantially modified. Until then, no ordinary court had assumed jurisdiction for such acts of the prosecutor, therefore the Constitutional Court's decision, although binding, remained inapplicable.

The second issue was, in fact, the structural problem that affected the very nature of the Romanian Public Ministry and its relationship with the judicial power: were the prosecutors to be considered 'magistrates'? The determining factor that finally decided the matter was not the awareness of national authorities, who had no problem considering the Public Ministry as situated on the same level as the courts, being used to its special super-power status awarded by the communist regime. The trigger was the same ECtHR judgment in the *Pantea* case, which found eight violations of the Convention.[44] One of the most important statements of the ECtHR with general effect concerned the prosecutor's 'magistrate' status, by reference to the requirement set out in Article 5(3) of the ECHR that an arrested person should be promptly brought before a 'judge or any other officer authorised by law'. Here, the Government stated that in Romanian law the prosecutor is a 'magistrate' or 'officer authorised by law to exercise judicial power', therefore he or she has the right to decide upon a deprivation of liberty. The ECtHR separately analysed the conditions to be fulfilled by a prosecutor in order to be considered a 'magistrate' within the meaning of the Convention. The main requirements had already been established by the existing case law: the magistrate 'must present guarantees against the arbitrariness and unjustified deprivations of liberty and must be independent from the executive power and from the other parties'. The Court recalled that it had already declared, in an older case against Romania from 1996, that prosecutors, acting as representatives of the Public Ministry and hierarchically subordinated to and under the authority of the Minister of Justice, do not meet the independence requirement and therefore were not 'magistrates' within the meaning of the Convention.

---

[43] *Pantea v Romania* App no 33343/96 (ECtHR, 3 June 2003).
[44] Two breaches of Art 3, five of Art 5(1), (3)–(6) and one of Art 6(1) ECHR.

The reaction of the authorities under such external pressure was prompt this time. The political context was certainly different from that in 1996. Romania had advanced in its negotiations to join the European Union and NATO, the political criteria being under close supervision. In the same context, the constitutional amendment procedure had already started, so it was imperative that it also reflected the standards of the ECtHR as proof of the country's willingness to improve its democratic commitment. The Constitution was therefore modified and Romanian prosecutors lost the right to issue arrest warrants.

The new law on the status of magistrates, adopted in 2004, still expressly included the prosecutors in this category, stating that judges and prosecutors are magistrates. In 2005, a slight change occurred, this direct reference being removed; instead, the law defined 'magistracy' as the judicial activity of judges and prosecutors. Therefore, in a more nuanced way, prosecutors were still to be considered magistrates in Romanian law, contrary to the position of the ECtHR, although they had lost some of the strong powers that affected fundamental rights.

Within the Public Ministry, due to enhanced European supervision of the main problems of the Romanian system—justice reform, corruption and organised crime—a special and independent structure, the National Anti-corruption Directorate (*Direcția Națională Anticorupție*, DNA), was created, with jurisdiction to investigate offences of corruption perpetrated by high officials, public officers, members of the army and police, etc. The Directorate has since gained more power, and especially after 2007, it started to investigate and refer important cases to the courts. However, the timing of some investigations, as well as the methods used (DNA uses telephone tapping and microphone surveillance, and the results are massively leaked to the press), has sometimes led to questions about its true independence from political influences (at different moments in time, political adversaries of the Government were placed under investigation, or such investigations were made public following certain political events). These matters were presented as risking the transformation of the DNA into a political police force. Despite these concerns, the activities of the DNA proved fruitful as regards achieving its goal. An activity report for the period 2005–12 listed investigations ending with definitive convictions for acts of corruption of 11 dignitaries (1 former Prime Minister, 1 former minister, 2 former senators, 6 former deputies and 1 Secretary of State), 32 local authority members (mayors, presidents of departmental councils, etc),

24 magistrates, 164 police officers and many others. In one of its latest progress report, dated January 2015, the European Commission, although it praised the DNA's activities as 'professional and impartial', and considered it as being among the most significant indicators of progress, expressed its disappointment that, despite a relatively high rate of success in the field of high-level corruption, little progress had been shown in the sensitive matter of public acquisitions. Moreover, political interference in the prosecutors' activity was still very visible.

The appointment of the General Prosecutor and of the Chief-Prosecutor of the DNA is an important matter, as it involves political actors (the President and the Minister of Justice) as well as the CSM. Although criticised by the European supervisors in their successive reports, the political motivation for appointments to these offices was not totally removed and it seriously affected the appointment process in 2012–13. The European Commission asked for more transparency in the appointment procedure.[45]

E. The High Court of Cassation and Justice

Historically, the HCCJ was intended to follow the old French-inspired Court of Cassation, which functioned between 1861 and 1948 and was replaced by a soviet-style Supreme Tribunal in the communist era. The 1991 Constitution created, in its initial version, a 'Supreme Court of Justice', which was renamed the 'High Court of Cassation and Justice' in 2003, the main justification being respect for tradition: the pre-war Constitutions used the name 'Court of Cassation' (1866–1923) and 'Court of Cassation and Justice' (1923–47).

The HCCJ's main task is to ensure the uniform interpretation and application of the law by the other judicial courts, according to its jurisdiction established by law. The High Court is one of the largest supreme courts in Europe: it comprises over 100 judges, organised in five sections—two civil sections, one criminal section, one administrative and fiscal litigation section, and the plenary section—as well as three special panels—the five-judges panels, the appeal on points of law panel and the preliminary rulings panel. The organic Statute of the organisation of the judicial system establishes the special jurisdiction

---

[45] European Commission, SWD(2014) 37 final, *Romania: technical report*, at 19.

of each section and panel. The Court's judges elect their president for a period of three years. The Court has financial independence, setting its own budget, which is included in the annual public budget.

From the contextual point of view, there are two main points of interest regarding the HCCJ: its role in unifying the national jurisprudence and, in this context, its peculiar dialogue/conflict relationship with the Constitutional Court.

i. Consistency of Jurisprudence

Romanian courts have a hard time accepting the precedential value of previous decisions, and that this should a part of Romanian legal culture. This was remarked upon by the European Commission, which, in its 2014 CVM Report, noted that

> experts consulted by the Commission noted a view prevalent in many Romanian courts that it is for the individual judge to interpret the Codes without reference to the jurisprudence, contrary to what is seen as standard practice in EU member states, not limited to common law systems.[46]

This has frequently led to jurisprudential inconsistency. As a legal culture is difficult to change, some tools were found to address this issue, within the system, by the HCCJ: the appeal on points of law, and the preliminary procedure of 'solving legal issues'.

The constitutional role of the HCCJ to ensure the uniform interpretation and application of the law is achieved mainly through the appeal on points of law (*recurs in interesul legii*). This procedure has suffered successive changes since its creation in 1993, and became an instrument 'to ensure a uniform jurisprudence', designed to contribute to the achievement of the main constitutional role of the High Court. An appeal on points of law may be initiated in special circumstances, only if it is proven that the legal issues to which it refers were treated differently by final judgments and only by specific subjects, that is, the General Prosecutor, *ex officio* or at the request of the Minister of Justice, the leading board of the HCCJ, the leading boards of the courts of appeal and the Ombudsman. Moreover, the new Code of Civil Procedure states that the abovementioned authorities have 'the duty' to request a decision on an appeal on points of law, 'in order to ensure

---

[46] ibid, at 13.

the uniform interpretation and application of the law by all courts'. A request for an appeal on points of law is examined by a special panel of the HCCJ, and the ruling is binding on all courts from the date of its publication in the *Official Journal*. The rulings have an objective character, as they have no effect upon any specific case or judgment. The HCCJ has handled over 50 such requests in the last five years.

The new Codes of Civil and Criminal Procedure, in force since 1 February 2013 and 1 February 2014 respectively, created another procedure aimed at ensuring jurisprudential consistency, the preliminary ruling procedure, by which panels of judges from the HCCJ, the courts of appeal or of tribunals, called on to decide a case at last instance, may ask the HCCJ's corresponding section to adopt a 'preliminary decision' aimed at 'solving a legal issue' on which depends the resolution of the case. The legal issue must be 'new and [one] on which the HCCJ has not already ruled', and it must not be the object of a pending appeal on points of law. The procedure, although new, has proved to be successful, but has also given rise to 'clashes' between the High Court and the Constitutional Court, in those instances when they gave diametrically opposing interpretations of certain legal texts.[47]

ii. HCCJ and RCC: Dialogue or Conflict?

Until 2013[48] the Constitutional Court consistently held that the procedural provisions giving the HCCJ the power to unify divergent jurisprudence 'contribute to the achievement of the rule of law', and repeatedly confirmed the constitutionality of the appeal on points of law and of the binding character of the High Court's rulings:

> [O]ne cannot consider that the decisions of the High Court in such appeals would represent a legislative competence and contravene Article 61 §1 CR … The legislator imposed the binding effect of the High Court's interpretation with a view to a uniform interpretation of the law by courts.

However, in 2013, the Constitutional Court reversed its jurisprudence, ruling this time on the alleged unconstitutionality of the article on the appeal on points of law from the Code of Criminal Procedure.

The context of this decision is important in explaining the ruling of the Constitutional Court. In 2007, Parliament decided to decriminalise

---

[47] RCC, Decision no 265/2014.
[48] RCC, Decision no 992/2007; Decision no 1560/2010.

insult and libel, and to change the Criminal Code, in line with judgments of the Strasbourg Court which found excessive the criminal sanctions applied to journalists for this type of offence. The Constitutional Court declared the initiative 'incompatible with human dignity', further stating that since the instrument of repeal was declared unconstitutional, 'the repealed legal provisions continue to produce effects'.[49] However, the Constitutional Court is not a positive legislator and may not adopt, repeal or put back into force legal norms, such competence belonging exclusively to the legislature. Under Article 147 CR, Parliament had 45 days to correct the unconstitutionality, and since the same text does not provide for any sanction for exceeding this time limit, the legislature is free to decide upon its legal policy in criminal matters. Therefore, by the abovementioned conclusion, the Constitutional Court had exceeded its power, expressly limited by the Constitution, namely, to check the conformity of certain norms with the Constitution.

Because the legislature did not take any express legislative measures and the various courts took different views in applying the law, the General Prosecutor addressed the HCCJ with a request for an appeal on a point of law. In 2010 the High Court argued that declaring the instruments of repeal unconstitutional did not lead to the automatic re-entering into force of the provisions of the Criminal Code, and concluded that

> as long as insult and libel ... were not re-criminalised by the legislative power, the only authority enabled, according to the rule of law, to do this, one may not consider that those are criminal offences and that the abrogated legal norms had re-entered into force. As a consequence, the non-exercise, by the Parliament, of the prerogative to re-examine the legal text considered unconstitutional, cannot unilaterally lead to the solution to replace the essential legislative power in a rule-of-law state by another authority.[50]

In 2011, the High Court suddenly reversed its binding interpretation and stated that the Constitutional Court's decision must be considered as reinstating the repealed legal provisions, and that the courts should act accordingly.

To complicate the issue, the Constitutional Court decided, on 29 April 2013, that 'the ruling given to the legal issue' by the 2010 Decision of the HCCJ was unconstitutional. Once again, the Constitutional

---

[49]   RCC, Decision no 62/2007.
[50]   HCCJ, Decision no 8/2010.

Court exceeded the constitutional limits of its competence, as the Constitution does not allow it to review judicial decisions.

The European Commission, in its CVM Reports, positively mentions the appeal on points of law procedure, and even expects it to be more efficient,[51] and in a judgment from 2011 the ECtHR praised the procedure as an instrument for unifying divergent jurisprudence:

> [T]he Court considers that the mechanism provided for by Article 329 of the Romanian Code of Civil Procedure, as designed to resolve, and not preclude, conflicting court decisions, has proven to be effective, since in a reasonably short period of time, it has put an end to the divergence in the case-law …[52]

Therefore, the attempts of the Constitutional Court to minimise the effects of the appeal on points of law can be seen as a part of a struggle between the two high jurisdictions regarding their supremacy over ordinary judicial courts.

F. The Superior Council of Magistracy

The CSM is the Romanian high judicial council, created by the 1991 Constitution following the French model. In 2003 the Council's position and role were reinforced by the amended version of the constitutional text, and an almost autonomous council was thus established. The new text set out the role of the Council as guardian of the independence of justice, and expressly established its composition, the length of its mandate and the procedure for election of its president. As much as independence of justice is praised and protected by the Constitution, the CSM is apparently the only express institutional guardian of this salient principle. Article 133 §6 CR expressly provides that the President of Romania chairs those meetings of the Council in which he or she participates, which can be seen as curtailing the Council's independence, especially as the President is not a member of the Council. In practice, since 2005 only President Băsescu exercised this right in many sensitive sessions of the Plenary Council, especially on the occasion of elections,

---

[51] See, for instance, COM(2010) 113 final, *Interim Report From the European Commission to the European Parliament and the Council on Progress in Romania under the Cooperation and Verification Mechanism*, Brussels, 23 March 2010, at 3.

[52] ECtHR, *Zelca v Romania*, admissibility decision, App no 65161/10 (ECtHR, 6 September 2011), § 15.

and his presence was often seen as an attempt to indirectly impose certain political views on the members.

Although at the beginning the CSM was not very influential within the judiciary, due to its constitutional framework and legal structure, the amendments from 2003–04 (allegedly under the influence of European requests for reinforcement of the independence of justice) transformed it into a powerful corporatist organ, fully independent, at least in theory, from the other powers.[53] However, even in its new, judicially-enhanced form, the CSM was not free from controversy, nor even from accusations of political interference.

The composition of the Council is under the supervision of Parliament, through the Senate, which validates and elects different categories of members. The Council is mostly composed of magistrates: out of its 19 members, 14 are magistrates validated by the Senate, 9 are judges and 5 are prosecutors. The other members include two representatives of the civil society, elected by the Senate, the Minister of Justice, the President of the HCCJ and the General Prosecutor of Romania. The Council elects its President, for a one-year term of office, only from the magistrate members. The latter are, in their turn, elected by the general assemblies of the magistrates, ie by all judges and prosecutors in the country. The legislative and executive powers are involved both in the composition and in the functioning of the Council: Parliament, through the Senate, the Minister of Justice and the President (who chairs the meetings in which he or she participates).

As for its constitutional jurisdiction, the CSM has the main task of proposing the appointment of judges and prosecutors to the President of Romania. Secondly, the Council acts as a disciplinary court for judges and prosecutors, in a special composition, excluding the Minister of Justice, the President of the High Court and the General Prosecutor from casting votes. In line with the access to justice principle, the Constitution expressly provides that the rulings of the Council in disciplinary matters may be challenged before the HCCJ. The organic law gives the Council very extensive competences relating to the careers of judges and prosecutors: the CSM 'defends' them against any act that might affect their independence, impartiality or even professional

---

[53] See also ES Tănăsescu & R Popescu, 'Romanian High Judicial Council— Between Analogy of Law and Ethical Trifles' (2012) 36E *Transylvanian Review of Administrative Sciences* 170.

reputation; it ensures respect for the law and for the competence and ethical criteria in the professional career of magistrates. As well as proposing the appointment of magistrates by the President of Romania, the Council may propose their promotion, and even the distinctions that the President can confer on magistrates. It has full responsibility for supervising entry into the judicial professions, through the National Institute of Magistracy, which is under its coordination.

It is noticeable that the CSM, in its new form, follows the trend pointed out by Garoupa and Ginsburg, 'insulating judicial selection from partisan politics',[54] in the name of ensuring the highest possible level of independence of justice, especially in the institutional sense. Despite these efforts, in practice it has been shown, on the one hand, that judicial councils in general cannot, by themselves, truly guarantee judicial independence and, on the other hand, that the Romanian CSM has failed to fulfil its mission for reasons of accountability. In its early CVM reports, the European Commission stated that the CSM had 'yet to succeed in taking responsibility for its own integrity and accountability'.[55] Over the years, this view has changed and in the report from 2015, the Commission has only appreciative remarks.[56]

The highly divided views within the judicial system were obvious on the occasion of the 2013 election of the CSM's President.[57] In a controversial procedure, beset by accusations of politicisation and lack of transparency, the former Vice-President, a prosecutor, was elected President for the year to come. The first election of a prosecutor to this position generated a very negative reaction amongst judges throughout the country, as they felt that judges had 'lost control' of the Council, and almost immediately a 'turf war' started: the general assemblies of judges (composed of all judges of a particular court) started the procedure of revocation of membership of the two Council members (judges) accused of decisively contributing to this unexpected result. After a few weeks, the membership of the two members concerned was actually revoked, but one of them challenged the decision by a

---

[54] N Garoupa & T Ginsburg, 'Guarding the Guardians: Judicial Councils and Judicial Independence' (2009 a) 57 *American Journal of Comparative Law* 104.

[55] COM(2008) 494 final 5. See also further reports of 2009, 2010, 2011, available at http://ec.europa.eu/cvm/progress_reports_en.htm.

[56] COM(2015) 35 final 8, available at ec.europa.eu/cvm/docs/com_2015_35_en.pdf.

[57] The 2010 elections were also contested before the courts.

referral of unconstitutionality of the legal provisions setting down the revocation procedure. The legal procedure for revoking membership of elected members lacks precision, in that revocation is subject to the condition that the respective members 'did not fulfil or fulfilled in a inappropriate manner their attributions as Council members'. This, alongside with the statement of the Constitutional Court[58] that Council members have a representative mandate and not an imperative one, as the electors do not establish their mandated actions *a priori*, led to the conclusion that the respective articles of the law were unconstitutional. As a consequence, the membership of the two members was reinstated. However, the whole scandal seriously affected the image of the CSM, in the eyes both of the public and of members of the judiciary.

It was also signalled by commentators that a highly corporatist CSM is not *per se* a guarantee of improved quality in the functioning of the judicial system:

> [O]n the contrary, it brought an entire system of internal battles specific to the political arena into an institutional system that should have been separated from the typical controversies of authorities that are legitimated by its very internal competition.[59]

In this context, reform proposals were made in the draft constitutional amendment of 2013, regarding the composition of the CSM (to increase of the number of civil society members from two to four), its internal organisation (the draft amendment inexplicably limiting the right to be elected members of the Council to judges alone, excluding prosecutors, despite the fact that the latter are still considered magistrates and come within the jurisdiction of the Council) and its functioning (here, it was proposed that the degree of accountability should be enhanced in order to improve the public image of the Council, identified with the public image of the judicial system as a whole).[60]

Last but not least, some changes in the attitude of the CSM towards the judicial system in general would be welcome. It suffices to cite a decision from 2008, where the Council's Plenum, becoming an *ad hoc* constitutional interpreter, stated that

> as regards the alignment of the supreme court to the judgments of the European Court of Human Rights in the case *Beian c. Romania*, where Romania

---

[58] RCC, Decision no 196/2013.
[59] Tănăsescu & Popescu (n 53), at 172.
[60] ibid, at 175.

was convicted for a divergent practice at the level of the supreme court, we must bear in mind the provisions of Article 124 of the Constitution, according to which the judge is independent and subject only to the law, and not to the judicial precedent; therefore the argument that a judge may be 'bound' by previous rulings is illegal and foreign to the Romanian legal system. It is therefore the problem of the state to find the adequate instruments to avoid divergent rulings in practice, as the ECtHR judgment is not, by itself, a reason to pronounce a solution accordingly.[61]

The CSM failed to understand here that precedent, even used as a judicial tool rather than as an expressly recognised source of law, serves to avoid lack of uniformity or 'anarchy'[62] in applying the law.[63] Hence, contradictory jurisprudence appeared in the same legal text and individual rights violations occurred.

III. CONCLUSION

The Constitutional Court and the Romanian judiciary are separate. Although, according to the Kelsenian model, the decisions of the Constitutional Court are binding *erga omnes*, they were not respected from the outset by all authorities, including ordinary courts. Only after the constitutional amendment of 2003 were the *erga omnes* effects fully acknowledged by the courts, and only then due to an express new provision within the Constitution.[64]

In 2010, a presidential committee for amending the Constitution proposed in its report that the Court should share its powers with

---

[61] CSM Plenum Ruling 981 of 2 October 2008.

[62] Z Kühn, 'Worlds Apart: Western and Central European Judicial Culture at the Onset of the European Enlargement' (2004) 52 *American Journal of Comparative Law* 560.

[63] This mindset is due, in almost all post-communist countries, to the so-called 'communist legacy' in training judges. See M Matzak, M Bencze & Z Kühn, 'Constitutions, EU Law and Judicial Strategies in the Czech Republic, Hungary and Poland' (2010) 30(1) *Journal of Public Policy* 82.

[64] Before 2003, the Constitution contained a controversial provision, which affected the effects of the Court's decisions. Following an unconstitutionality decision given in the *a priori* review, Parliament was obliged to re-examine the law. However, if Parliament re-adopted the law, in the same form, with a two-thirds majority, the constitutionality objection would be overruled and the law would have to be promulgated. This provision was never actually used by Parliament. However, due to heavy criticisms, the constitutional drafters of 2003 decided to remove it from the constitutional text.

the ordinary courts, retaining only the power of *a priori* review. However, such a shared competence would lead to the ineffectiveness of unconstitutionality decisions, due to the potential lack of consistent interpretation by the ordinary courts. The binding *erga omnes* effects of unconstitutionality decisions would become illusory, because of the absence of, and even contempt for, the idea of *stare decisis* in Romanian law. Therefore, the principle of legal certainty would be seriously affected.

A thorough reform of the Constitutional Court is still necessary, and should cover both the constitutional texts and the attitude of the Court as to its own powers and role. Otherwise, the Court risks becoming another failed constitutional import (as in countries like Venezuela or Colombia, where constitutional review was used as an instrument of the authoritarian regimes).[65] The most problematic aspect is that of the 'constitutional-political practices of society'.[66] In a conflictual political society like that in Romania, a change of mindset is not possible, unfortunately, without corresponding normative coercion: a constitutional amendment is necessary[67] (but also not entirely sufficient sometimes) in order to avoid the Constitutional Court's becoming a supra-political authority.

Despite many shortcomings in its reasoning and attitude towards politics, the Constitutional Court has managed to create an institutional pattern of stability, especially as regards the protection of fundamental rights. With further improvements, the Court may reinforce its erstwhile role as a landmark institution of the Romanian constitutional democracy. A consolidated dialogue with the judiciary, and especially with the HCCJ, would enhance this role.

As regards the Romanian judiciary, its Continental structure and features (positivistic approach, lack of precedent, formalist application of law, reluctance to engage in dialogue with other courts), grafted on the communist principles of popular justice and strict hierarchical obedience, rendered it particularly resistant to change during the transition period. If the legislature and the executive political authorities were forced to transform, in a drastic and spectacular way, by the process of popular elections and by media scrutiny, the judiciary maintained

---

[65] A Brewer-Carias, *Constitutional Courts as Positive Legislators. A Comparative Law Study* (Cambridge, Cambridge University Press, 2011) 16–18.

[66] M Guţan, 'Raporturile dintre Preşedinte, Guvern şi Parlament în perspectiva revizuirii Constituţiei României' (2013) 1 *Revista de Drept Public* 94.

[67] See Ch 7.

the rules and privileges of the 'judicial cast', almost up to the present day. Changes in the laws of judicial organisation were few and timid. Even the successive 'face-lifts' made in order to comply with EU requirements were not able to resolve the structural problem of the Romanian judiciary, its incapacity to adapt to the new realities. The same was true for some Eastern and Central European countries— Poland, Hungary—whereas in the Czech Republic, for instance, 'due to an active, coaching role of the constitutional court, some evidence for de-formalising adjudication can be detected'.[68] Of course, one might invoke the 'exceptional nature' of transition periods (political and economic instability and strains, social changes, social movements) as an excuse for the malfunctioning of the authorities, including the judiciary. But in these special times, courts should rather be beacons of stability and legal coherence, engines of transformation (as they come into close contact with the social reality and with the new legislation),[69] otherwise the trust of the citizens in the judicial system is likely to be shattered, as has been shown, in practice, by recent social polls.[70]

One of the major criticisms aimed at the Romanian judiciary during the transitional period was its jurisprudential lack of coherence, and its misunderstanding of its role and of its own guarantees:

> [M]isused or misunderstood, functional independence of judges combined with a more and more complex legal system, brought diversity and uneven case law, which was found to be counterproductive and against the very principles of a state governed by the rule of law.[71]

The influence of the economic factor in the transitional development period must not be ignored: economic development, social welfare, the capacity to cope with financial difficulties, all are factors that play a crucial role in the evolution of the other dimensions of a transitional society, including the legal and judicial response to social practice. Transitions in post-war Germany and Italy, for instance, had a more rapid

---

[68] Matzak, Bencze & Kühn (n 63), at 82.

[69] See also R Teitel, 'Transitional Jurisprudence: The Role of Law in Political Transformation' (1996–1997) 106 *Yale Law Journal* 2033; R Teitel, *Transitional Justice* (Oxford, Oxford University Press, 2000) 6.

[70] See also W Sadurski, *Rights Before Courts. A Study of Constitutional Courts in Postcommunist States of Central and Eastern Europe* (Heidelberg, Springer, 2004) 296–97.

[71] ES Tănăsescu & Ș Deaconu, 'Romania: Analogical Reasoning as a Dialectical Instrument' in T Groppi & M-C Ponthoreau (eds), *The Use of Foreign Precedents by Constitutional Judges* (Oxford, Hart Publishing, 2013) 326.

and positive result, sustained by the important economic aid supplied in the context of the reconstruction of these countries (which both were given new constitutions in 1948–49). The comparison can go further in showing the importance of the international factor in the same equation: the 'unified Europe' plan of the 1950s, promoted by Schuman, Monnet and Adenauer, had no equivalent in the 1990s, when the European Community (and then EU) quickly became divided as regards plans for eastwards enlargement.

Justice and the judiciary in Romania, alongside corruption and organised crime, remained one of the main concerns of the EU institutions even after the end of the transition period, and remained so up to the moment of accession in 2007. Although the phrase 'end of transition' should mean stability, both in establishing and in applying established legislation, coherence and true respect for the rule of law, by enhancing the independence of judiciary and the sense of accountability among judges and all the other authorities, this was not the case in Romania. Successive CVM[72] Reports since 2007 have addressed all the problems detected within the Romanian judicial system, as well as those in the fight against corruption. The first Report of 2007 was extremely critical. The efforts of the HCCJ to unify jurisprudence were mentioned in the 2008 and 2009 Reports, the need for the enhanced accountability of the CSM in the 2010 Report, and so on. The Reports from 2013, 2014 and 2015 seem to note better progress in achieving the established benchmarks, but also emphasised those matter that were and are still pending: the actual entry into force of the newly adopted codes, jurisprudential unification, updating the jurisprudential database and, no less important, 'significant progress in the handling of high level corruption cases'.[73] However, despite clear improvements, the preservation of CVM in 2015 proves that the problems are far from being resolved.

---

[72] See Ch 1.

[73] 'The High Court will be crucial to the success of legislative reforms in establishing efficient arrangements and mechanisms for unifying jurisprudence … Legislative reforms alone will not solve inconsistent jurisprudence. It also requires a recognition of the importance of this issue amongst the judiciary. … There appears a persistent reluctance in some quarters to follow the jurisprudence of superior courts. … Inconsistency and a lack of predictability in the jurisprudence of the courts has also been identified as a major concern for the business community and for the wider society.' (Commission Staff Working Document, 'Romania: Technical Report', accompanying the *Report from the Commission to the European Parliament and the Council on Progress in Romania under the Cooperation and Verification Mechanism* COM (2012) 410 final).

FURTHER READING

C Dupré, *Importing the Law in Post-Communist Transitions* (Oxford, Hart Publishing, 2003) .

M Guţan, 'The Romanian Judicial Culture and the Application of the European Court of Human Rights' Case-Law' in M Guţan & B Selejan-Guţan (eds), *Europeanization and Judicial Culture in Contemporary Democracies* (Bucharest, Hamangiu, 2014).

Z Kühn, *The Judiciary in Central and Eastern Europe. Mechanical Jurisprudence in Transformation?* (Leiden, Boston, Martinus Nijhoff Publishers, 2011).

B Iancu, 'Constitutional-Judicial Culture in Romania—Ambivalence and Possibility' in M Guţan & B Selejan-Guţan (eds), *Europeanization and Judicial Culture in Contemporary Democracies* (Bucharest, Hamangiu, 2014).

——, 'Constitutionalism in Perpetual Transition: the Case of Romania' in B Iancu (ed), *The Law/Politics Distinction in Contemporary Public Law Adjudication* (The Hague, Eleven International Publishing, 2009) 187.

C-L Popescu, 'Le contrôle judiciaire prétorien de la constitutionnalité des lois en Roumanie dans la période post-communiste et pré-constitutionnelle' (2013) 1 *Est Europa, Revue d'études politiques et constitutionnelles*, numéro spécial 87.

H Schwartz, *The Struggle for Constitutional Justice in Post-Communist Europe* (Chicago, University of Chicago Press, 2000).

B Selejan-Guţan, 'Constitution in Time of Crisis: the Constitutional Court and its Enemies' (2012) 2 *Romanian Journal of Comparative Law* 321.

——, 'Transitional Constitutionalism and Transitional Justice in Post-communist States—the Romanian Case' (2010) 2 *Romanian Journal of Comparative Law* 283.

——, 'La réception du modèle européen de la constitutionnalité des lois en Roumanie' in *Imperialism and Chauvinism in the Law* (Zurich, Schulthess, 2004).

—— & ES Tănăsescu, 'Roumanie' (2013) XXIX *Annuaire International de Justice Constitutionnelle* 411.

ES Tănăsescu, 'Chronique. Roumanie' (2011) XXVII *Annuaire International de Justice Constitutionnelle* 983.

—— & Ş Deaconu, 'Romania: Analogical Reasoning as a Dialectical Instrument' in T Groppi & M-C Ponthoreau (eds), *The Use of Foreign Precedents by Constitutional Judges* (Oxford, Hart Publishing, 2013), pp. 321.

—— & R Popescu, 'Romanian High Judicial Council—Between Analogy of Law and Ethical Trifles' (2012) 36E *Transylvanian Review of Administrative Sciences* 165.

R Weber, 'Constitutionalism as a Vehicle for Democratic Consolidation in Romania' J Zielonka (ed), *Democratic Consolidation in Eastern Europe* (Oxford, Oxford University Press, 2001) 229.

6

Constitutional Protection of Fundamental Rights

───►•◄───

Human Rights – European Court of Human Rights – Constitutional Rights – Equality – Minorities – Proportionality – Limits

THE CONSTITUTIONAL ENTRENCHMENT of fundamental rights and freedoms follows the classic 'bill of rights' model, comprising an extended list of civil and political rights and economic-social rights respectively. The international legal and political context of the Constitution drafting generated a strong orientation towards European values in the field of the fundamental rights protection. Thus, the Constitution sets the priority of international human rights law over domestic norms, as long as the latter do not offer more favourable protection. The priority applies at the interpretative level to constitutional texts too. The international instrument that most influenced fundamental rights protection in Romania—especially during the 2003 revision process—was the European Convention on Human Rights (ECHR). This chapter will also explain the constitutional guarantees of fundamental rights, among which the Ombudsman has a particular position.

I. NATIONAL AND INTERNATIONAL FOUNDATIONS OF THE SYSTEM OF FUNDAMENTAL RIGHTS

It is important to say from the beginning that if many of the constitutional provisions on the political institutions were a result of an 'aversive constitutionalism', in the field of human rights they were the expression of 'aspirational constitutionalism'.[1] The recent totalitarian past had a salient role in establishing the current human rights system in Romania. In 1989, Romania was living under the cruellest, North Korea-type dictatorship in Eastern Europe. Except for a few social rights, Romanians did not enjoy any of the rights and freedoms commonly guaranteed to citizens of democratic countries, not even at the 'controlled' level formally set forth by the 1965 Constitution. An elaborate system of repression was created by the communist regime, especially through the secret political police, *Securitate*, by which the most elementary rights of human beings were constantly violated. Freedom of expression did not exist, neither did freedoms of association, of assembly or information. The right to life was not guaranteed (the death penalty was provided for by the Criminal Code), the right to private life was constantly breached (especially through telephone tapping and the placement of microphones in public and private places), the right to family life was strictly controlled. The prohibition on abortions was a very serious issue, as, exacerbated by the total prohibition on and lack of contraception, it led to thousands of deaths of and permanent injuries to women, but also to thousands of criminal convictions of women and doctors for illegally performing terminations. The system was in constant breach of human dignity: food and elementary standards of living were deliberately scarce (electricity, heating and water were provided for just two to three hours a day), healthcare conditions and facilities fell below any decent standards, and the education system was almost completely subordinated to the political directives, indoctrination and 'cultural engineering' being two of the major goals of the communist power.

The people's outrage against all these realities, in the context of the 1989 revolutionary events across Eastern Europe, led to the overthrow of the communist regime, the last in the region, which resisted until December 1989. This chapter will discuss Romania's journey from totalitarianism to an incipient culture of human rights, and how this culture has developed over the last 25 years.

---

[1] KL Scheppele, 'Aspirational and aversive constitutionalism: The case for studying cross-constitutional influence through negative models' (2003) 1 *International Journal of Constitutional Law* 300.

A. National Foundations

The present establishment of fundamental rights in the Romanian Constitution is attributable to various historical, political and cultural factors, which led to a very comprehensive set of rights forming the second main title of the Constitution.

From the very beginning, it must be emphasised that there was virtually no 'culture of rights' in Romanian law (in the Western sense of the expression) before the 1991 Constitution. Leaving aside the feeble preoccupations of the pre- and inter-war periods (centred more on principles of justice acknowledged by the elite rather than on individual rights), the long years of totalitarianism (1940–89) somehow erased from legal and judicial conscience and practice the idea that the individual might have rights, that these rights could be enforced by courts and, moreover, that constitutional rights could prevail over other interests due to the supremacy of the Constitution.

Back in 1991, the choices of the Constitution drafters as regards fundamental rights were mostly made under external influences (Western experts, including members of the Venice Commission, assisted in the Constitution drafting process) and/or pressures, rather than emerging from within the organic constitutional need, not because such a need would not have been natural after 50 years of dictatorship, but because it was apprehended only as a formal requirement to be met. Judges, prosecutors and even lawyers were not prepared to adjust to fundamental rights requirements as natural elements of their day-to-day practice. They were forced to do this later on, especially as a result of the judgments of the ECtHR.

Hence, the main foundations of the present constitutional text on fundamental rights were nearly the same as for the rest of the Constitution: 'totalitarian anguish' (a response to the totalitarian past and the fear of its revival); a certain sense of tradition (there is a link with the pre-war constitutional texts, especially with the provisions in the 1923 Constitution); and the desire—extremely profound in the early 1990s—to be accepted by the 'high life' of European democracies. One can detect here an atavistic aspiration (characteristic to Romanian legal culture) to accede to something better and/or more powerful, in this case to the European legal order and culture, or to achieve access to the 'European club' (just as in the nineteenth century, when the Romanian legal system reflected almost every characteristic of the

French one; or as in 1945, when soviet rules and habits were quickly adopted into many legal branches). Thus, the originally artificial establishment of a fundamental rights system became a central point of the new constitutional text, being a structural principle of the new democratic system.

Although the fundamental rights are enshrined in Title II of the Constitution ('Fundamental Rights, Freedoms and Duties of the Citizen'), references to rights appear in the first articles of Title I. In Article 1 §3, the Constitution proclaims human dignity, free development of human personality, and fundamental rights and freedoms of the citizens as 'supreme values' of the Romanian state. However, none of these values as yet plays a central part in structuring a system of fundamental rights, by contrast with other constitutional systems. It is well known, for instance, that in the German constitutional system, human dignity constitutes the 'highest value of the Basic Law, the ultimate basis of the constitutional system and the foundation of all guaranteed rights'.[2] Certainly, the status accorded to human dignity did not come about only as a result of the constitutional text (Article 1, Basic Law); it also derives from the jurisprudence of the German Constitutional Court. In the Romanian system, neither human dignity, nor other 'supreme values' stated as such in the Constitution acquired a similar position in the Constitutional Court's case law.

Another relevant right is the 'right to identity' of persons belonging to national minorities (Article 6 CR). This article confirms the multiculturalism of Romanian society, although the general constitutional conception is apparently an ethnocentric one.

The second paragraph of Article 4, in an almost classic formula, defines Romania as 'the common and indivisible motherland' of all its citizens, and prohibits any discrimination based on race, nationality, sex, opinion, political views, wealth or social origin. Article 16 (*Principle of equality*) refers to equality as a fundamental right rather than as a general principle. This distinction between certain rights as principles and rights as specific norms is characteristic of the Romanian Constitution: almost same approach applies to the right to access to justice/right to a fair trial. By contrast, human dignity as a principle is often confused with human dignity as a right on its own.

---

[2] W Heun, *The Constitution of Germany. A Contextual Analysis* (Oxford, Hart Publishing, 2010) 201.

B. International Foundations

After the fall of the totalitarian regime in December 1989, Romania's international position was not very strong during the transition period, as the newly established political regime did not evince from the start a stable attachment to democracy, rule of law and respect for fundamental rights. The events that took place right after the December 1989 Revolution (especially the miners' riots in Bucharest in 1990–91, but also the attitude of the new power towards the political opposition) did not help to improve that situation.

International and foreign inspiration during the constitution-drafting process was of the utmost importance in the field of fundamental rights. The future Constitution would have twin aims, each equally difficult to fulfil: to become a foundation for new laws and new mentalities, and to eliminate old laws and old mentalities.

Looking back to the 'constitutional sentiments'[3] that drove the drafters of the Constitution, in the international and European context, in the field of human rights, it must be noted that there was a natural fear of the totalitarian past and its legacy. To overcome this, they tried to create a large catalogue of rights, along with a set of general and specific guarantees, all having the international instruments of human rights protection, and in particular the ECHR, as sources of inspiration. The influence of the ECHR was extremely important in the amendment process in 2003, when the Convention and the Strasbourg Court's case law played a leading role.

Another determinative constitutional sentiment at the time of the drafting was the ambition to achieve European integration. To that end, the Constitution-makers needed to demonstrate that Romania had turned its back on the influences of the past. The wish to embrace Western conceptions of fundamental rights was illustrated by the prioritisation of the international law of human rights over national law in Article 20 CR. This entails that Romanian courts can theoretically discard legislation that is contrary to international conventions ratified by Romania, in so far as the national law is less favourable to the individual's rights. However, for a long time, this power remained theoretical, as the courts made no use of it.

---

[3] A Sajo, *Constitutional Sentiments* (Yale, Yale University Press, 2011).

The first European organisation to accept Romania as a member was the Council of Europe, in October 1993, after a journey along a long and winding path. A major point in the final decision of the Committee of Ministers, which was based on a report published in January 1993—drafted by Judge Alphonse Spielmann and by Jochen Frowein, Vice-President of the European Commission—was that, despite some shortcomings, the new 1991 Constitution represented the main proof that Romania was prepared to accept the Council's values: 'both the letter and the spirit of the Constitution of Romania amply meet the requirements of the European Convention on Human Rights'.[4]

In context, it is interesting that the report considered Article 20 CR to be 'the most important item of the Constitution, as it expressly lays down the principle of international law's precedence over national law'.[5] Therefore, the Constitution, its Bill of Rights and the priority of international law were the salient factors that led the monitoring and decisional bodies to recommend and accept Romania's admission as a member state of the Council of Europe. Nevertheless, 'the point is not so much the letter of the Constitution as its application'.[6] This was thus only a first step, and not the solution to Romania's many democratic and human rights problems. As one of the Council of Europe rapporteurs put it:

> [M]uch remains to be done, especially in the implementation of fundamental rights and freedoms and the rule of law. This is nothing short of simple and may require a certain amount of time. It may be relatively easy to change the law but it is much more difficult to change traditions and mentalities at all levels of society, particularly administration and officials. … We must appreciate that, on the one hand, an enormous amount of work has been done and considerable progress was made in many ways. … Of course, one cannot expect from a country like Romania to redress in just a few years the damage inflicted on the country by a disastrous and ruinous regime over a period of more than forty years.[7]

The European inspiration in prescribing the rights and their guarantees was accentuated by European pressure as regards some aspects, from

---

[4]   A Spielmann & JA Frowein, 'Report on Human Rights in Romania', Parliamentary Assembly of the Council of Europe, Doc AS/Bur (44) 94 of 25 January 1993, (1993) 14 *Human Rights Law Journal*, vols 3–4, 136.

[5]   ibid, at 133.

[6]   ibid, at 136.

[7]   Parliamentary Assembly, Doc 6918 1403-16/9/93-1-E, *Opinion on the application by Romania for membership of the Council of Europe*, 20 September 1993.

the 1991 draft to the 2003 revision. For instance, public prosecutors' power to decide on pre-trial detention, despite their lack of impartiality, although noted by European forums as early as 1993 during the monitoring process for accession to the Council of Europe, was removed from the Constitution only in 2003, as a result of a strong judgment from the ECtHR (*Pantea v Romania*).[8] The same arguments applied to supplementary guarantees on property rights and to the right to a fair trial (annulment appeals).

International and European influences determined, in time, the creation of special bodies for the protection of certain categories of rights. One of the best examples of good practice is the National Council Against Discrimination, created in 2001, an institution that successfully cooperates with Romanian civil society.

II. CONSTITUTIONAL PRINCIPLES OF RIGHTS

A. Equality

Equality was present, as a principle, in the pre-war and inter-war Romanian Constitutions (1866, 1923, 1938), but with little impact on constitutional life in practice. The first constitutional provision on equality—Article 10 of the 1866 Constitution—was rather restrictive, as it limited the discrimination criteria to a 'class' distinction: '[T]here is no distinction of class in the State. All Romanians are equal before the law and compelled to contribute without distinction to public debts and tasks'. On the other hand, the well-known and controversial Article 7 of the same Constitution stated that Romanians were defined by civil law regulations, whereas foreigners could only become 'Romanians' (citizens) if they were of the Christian denomination. This text was changed under external pressure in October 1879, by amending the Constitution. The change was the result of Article 44 of the 1878 Berlin Peace Treaty, which guaranteed the country's independence. This is one example of the institutionalised inequalities present in the constitutional system, the second important one being the hierarchy of wealth of the voters in 'electoral colleges' (thus the majority of the population being excluded from suffrage).

---

[8] See also Ch 5, section II.D.

The 1923 Constitution established a revised and enhanced version of the equality principle, the criterion of non-discrimination being included in the constitutional text of Article 8:

(1)   There is no distinction within the State as to birth or social classes.
(2)   All Romanians, with no distinction as to ethnic origin, language or religion, are equal before the law ...

Article 5 of the 1938 Constitution maintained approximately the same content, with different wording, rooted in the authoritarian background of the constitutional text:

All Romanian citizens, with no distinction of ethnic origin and religion are equal before the law, owing it respect and submission ...

The principle set forth in successive constitutional texts did not address actual and important inequalities occurring in real life. The most significant of these were the absence of voting rights for women, and the gross inequality between men and women as regards civil and family relationships. Paradoxically,[9] equality in this respect was established under soviet influence, by the post-war Constitution of 1948.

The 1991 Constitution dedicates more provisions to the equality principle: the general non-discrimination clause (Article 4) and the 'equality of rights' clause (Article 16). Article 4 §2 contains the general principle of non-discrimination:

Romania is the common and indivisible motherland of all its citizens, without any discrimination on account of race, nationality, ethnic origin, language, religion, sex, opinion, political views, wealth or social origin.

Article 16 §1 states, in the context of the non-discrimination criteria set by Article 4, that all citizens are equal before the law and public authorities, without any privilege or discrimination. Specific application of the general principle of equality can be found in other constitutional provisions: equal protection of property (Article 44), the principle of equal pay for equal work (Article 41), equality between spouses and the equality of children born out of wedlock with children born within marriage (Article 48), equal opportunities for persons with disabilities (Article 50), and non-discriminatory right-restricting measures (Article 53).

---

[9] Because the pre- and inter-war periods are considered the only democratic Romanian constitutional regimes before 1989, while the 1948 Constitution meant the beginning of the totalitarian communist era.

It is interesting that a common feature of virtually all Romanian constitutional texts (including the present one) is the use of the word 'citizen' to define the holder of the rights. If this wording may have been appropriate in the nineteenth and early twentieth centuries, it is quite obsolete today, in the context of the international and European systems of human rights protection. The Venice Commission took note of this in its 2014 opinion on Romania (regarding the 2013 draft law on amending the Constitution):

> [A]t the same time, the Romanian Constitution, adopted rather quickly after the beginning of the democratic transformation ..., very often uses the term citizen instead of 'everyone' or 'all individuals' in relation to fundamental rights ... To be in line with the universal and European standards, guarantees of fundamental rights and freedoms should apply to everybody not just the citizens.[10]

In practice, equality became a matrix principle due to the jurisprudence of the Constitutional Court and to subsequent legislation. The legislation, however, was enacted rather late, only in the early 2000s (anti-discrimination legislation, law on equal opportunities, establishment of a National Council Against Discrimination, etc), which meant that there was a 10-year gap between the introduction of the constitutional text and its permeation into the legal system. During this time, the Constitutional Court's case law tried to ensure that equality fulfilled its role of 'vector of constitutionalisation' within the legal system.[11] The jurisprudence of the Constitutional Court was mostly useful for imposing the constitutional principle of equality in other branches of law, especially property law, tax law, criminal law, labour law and procedural law.

B. Priority of International Law

Although there is no formal division within Romanian constitutional law, fundamental rights form a distinctive part of the system, alongside the law of the institutions.

The attitude towards international law of human rights is important in the context of the wish to achieve European integration. Given

---

[10] CDL-AD(2014)01, *Opinion on the Draft Law on the Review of the Constitution of Romania*, adopted by the Venice Commission at its 98th plenary session (Venice, 21–22 March 2014), §49.

[11] ES Tănăsescu, *Principiul egalității în dreptul românesc* (Bucharest, All Beck, 1999), *passim*.

the inclusion of ratified international law of human rights within the domestic order (Article 11 CR), awarding precedence to provisions of such international law was somehow natural. Article 20 CR originally provided two precedence clauses, one regarding the constitutional provisions and the other regarding domestic legal provisions. The former must be interpreted and applied according to the Universal Declaration of Human Rights (UDHR), along with the covenants and other treaties to which Romania is a party, whereas the latter can be removed from application in the event of conflict with international human rights provisions. The 2003 revision added a maximisation clause: international law will be given priority only if the national legislation does not offer a more favourable situation. This application of the *lex mitior* principle is logical, as it avoids the artificial application of the priority of international law to the detriment of the protection of the individual. The secondary constitutional legislator preferred an express provision rather than trusting in a logical and teleological interpretation by the courts (the exception might very well be deduced from the spirit, meaning and purpose of the text itself), because of the excessive formalism of Romanian courts, which were thus presumed to be capable of giving priority to international law even to the detriment of the individual.

It is interesting to see how this constitutional principle was received and applied in practice. For a long time, 20 years after its enactment, it was virtually ignored by ordinary courts (the first authorities entrusted with its application). The Constitutional Court itself made few references to international law in its efforts to interpret and apply the Constitution in cases within its realm of competence. During the 1990s, in cases relating to individual rights, courts scarcely searched for any norm conflicts, and were reluctant to apply the constitutional provisions of Articles 11 and 20 directly. They rarely referred to the provisions of international treaties as domestic law, and, moreover, hardly gave them priority whenever there was a conflict with domestic legislation. The ECHR, in particular, was deprived of its direct effect, given by Article 11, although it had already been recognised as a 'constitution of the European public order' to which Romania was so keen to accede. This state of affairs generated an enormous number of complaints to the ECtHR,[12] which led to a very high proportion of judgments finding violations.

---

[12] The first Romanian case examined on the merits was *Vasilescu v Romania* (1996), in Reports 1998-III.

This situation, and some strong judgments of the Strasbourg Court, finally led to the acknowledgment of the priority principle and to an increase in the cases in which Romanian courts invoked the ECHR and Strasbourg case law in their decisions. However, this does not mean that the Convention is directly applied.[13] The initial resistance has become, in most cases, pure obedience, as the provisions of the ECHR, and especially the judgments of the ECtHR, are mentioned mechanically, sometimes without a clear link to the case, just to make a formal statement of them. Nevertheless, the fact that the courts have, albeit timidly, assumed their role, as reviewers of conventionality and constitutionality in the field of fundamental rights, indicates progress, and it will surely improve the quality of their judgments and of the rational application of international law of human rights. By these means, the ECHR will be fully incorporated into the Romanian legal order, with a view to consolidating the actual fundamental rights protection. However, paradoxically, recent statistics[14] show that more than 90 per cent of the cases against Romania, examined on the merits by the Strasbourg Court, have ended in violation decisions.

To conclude, the priority principle has achieved, in the end, the internationalisation of the fundamental rights system, by consolidating the so-called 'constitutional adjudication of rights and freedoms' as a system of constitutional and judicial guarantees. This long process has not yet come to an end, and it seems that its importance is still not fully understood by the judiciary.[15] Commentators have noted that 'the courts have mistaken the review of norms with the adjudication of rights in the context of a norm-conflict'.[16] Courts would rather compare rules instead of applying the most appropriate of the conflicting rules to the individual situation and deciding which is more favourable

---

[13] M Guțan, 'The Romanian Judicial Culture and the Application of the European Court of Human Rights' Case-Law. An Empirical Research' in M Guțan & B Selejan-Guțan (eds), *Europeanisation and Judicial Culture in Contemporary Democracies* (Bucharest, Hamangiu, 2014) 220.

[14] Available at http://www.echr.coe.int/NR/rdonlyres/519DA600-0C28-41C1-B644-A4285556F296/0/Romania.pdf.

[15] See B Selejan-Guțan, 'Human Rights in Romanian Courts: A European Perspective' in R Arnold (ed), *Convergence of Fundamental Rights in Europe* (Springer, 2016, forthcoming).

[16] DC Dănişor, 'Înţelegerea trunchiată a competenţei exclusive a Curţii Constituţionale în domeniul contenciosului constituţional (III)' (2011) 6 *Pandectele române* 52.

and takes precedence. When judges fully apprehend this important task, they will finally assume their long-denied role as 'secondary constitutional judges'[17] of fundamental rights, and of infra-legislative rules at the same time.

C. Proportionality and Limitation of Rights

Most of the rights set forth in the Constitution are not absolute. Restrictions on the benefit of these rights may only be exceptional, however, and must fulfil certain requirements laid down by the Constitution itself. The limitation clause was inspired by international documents, and was adapted in 2003 to reflect the specific language of the ECHR. Most European countries have adopted such rules of limitation following accession to the Convention. In some countries, like Finland, although there is no specific text in the Constitution, similar rules drafted by the Constitutional Committee of the Parliament apply as 'customary constitutional law'.[18] The main sources of inspiration for the Romanian constitutional text on restrictions were the general derogation clauses of the United Nations' International Covenant on Civil and Political Rights (ICCPR) (Article 4) and the ECHR (Article 15), but also the special derogation clauses of the ECHR's conditional rights, the final result being a combination of general and specific derogation clauses.

Article 53 CR allows limitation of the exercise of fundamental rights and freedoms provided that it is prescribed by law, that it has a legitimate purpose (defence of national security, of public order, health or morals, of citizens' rights and freedoms; the pursuit of a criminal investigation; preventing the consequences of a natural calamity, of a disaster or of an extremely serious catastrophe) and that it is proportional to the legitimate aims concerned. The measure must be necessary in a democratic society, applied in a non-discriminatory manner, and it must not affect the existence of the right.

The Constitutional Court has repeatedly ruled that the requirements of Article 53 are applicable only to fundamental rights, and not to all

---

[17] ibid, at 54.
[18] J Husa, *The Constitution of Finland. A Contextual Analysis* (Oxford, Hart Publishing, 2011) 199.

rights, although the text does not make such a distinction. Other rulings of the Constitutional Court have concerned the legal foundations of restrictive measures. Until 2003, the Constitutional Court held that 'law', within the meaning of Article 53, meant not only acts of Parliament but also delegated legislation (government regulations, including EGOs, adopted according to the constitutional requirements). However, this meant that too wide a margin of appreciation was given to the Government, which was considered as potentially dangerous to the security of fundamental rights and to legal certainty in general. Therefore, in 2003, legislative delegation by means of EGOs was restricted, in the sense of prohibiting the adoption of such ordinances affecting fundamental rights and freedoms. The regular GOs (allowed by a special enabling law of the Parliament) are not excluded from the general meaning of the term 'law' used by Article 53.

The requirement 'necessary in a democratic society', inspired by the ECHR, entails, besides the exceptional and temporary character of the encroachment measure, a lack of arbitrariness. Necessity in a democratic society goes hand in hand with the proportionality principle, which is mentioned as a separate requirement in Article 53 §2. Proportionality is essential in the process of balancing the different interests at stake, the conflict of which determines the restrictive measures. The most delicate aspect of conciliation is when it is required in a conflict of rights, rather than between rights and other values.

The Constitutional Court has been called on to clarify these issues in relation to different conflicts of interests and values: the right to respect for private life versus the pursuit of criminal investigations; the right to free movement versus public order in the case of illegal migration; the right to property versus public health (prohibiting animal slaughter in places other than those designated by law; this legislative measure was considered unconstitutional by the Court).

The most well-known application of Article 53 in the last decade has been in connection with social and economic rights: the right to a salary (as a corollary of the right to work) and the right to a pension. The Government and Parliament had justified harsh restrictive measures regarding these rights (salary cuts, social benefits cuts, pension cuts), taken in 2010, by claiming that they were protecting 'national security' according to Article 53. In its decision the Constitutional Court upheld the view of the Government, because the impugned measures were declared 'temporary', and this was essential, in the Court's opinion, to preserve the substance of the protected right. The Court also upheld the Government's argument that

> the unconstitutionality critique is ill-founded because, as of 1 January 2011 the original amount of salaries will be reinstated. ... Achieving this result is an obligation on the legislator, otherwise it would break the temporary character of restricting the benefit of fundamental rights.

In an earlier decision of 2009, in the same context of the economic recession as a reason to restrict rights, the Court had taken the opposite view:

> [I]n a democratic society, restriction of rights is an exceptional case, if there is no other solution to safeguard state values that are endangered. It is the state's task to find solutions in order to counteract the effects of the recession, by an adequate economic and social policy. Diminishing the revenues of the employees of public institutions cannot represent, on the long term, a measure proportionate with the situation ... The extension of such measures can determine effects contrary to the envisaged ones.

As in its earlier jurisprudence,[19] the Court hardly made any reference to the proportionality requirement. As long as a restrictive measure meets the requirement of a mere justification, the Court finds it constitutional. Therefore, it should not be a surprise that the legislator itself tends to ignore the proportionality criterion. In practice, few Constitutional Court decisions have found violations of the restrictions criteria in legislation.

III. CONTENT OF RIGHTS

The first question one might duly ask after reading the second title of the Romanian Constitution would be: Is there a *system* of fundamental rights and freedoms, or only a heterogeneous catalogue inspired by international sources? It is true that the constitutional text lacks a rigorous, systematic character. However, it comprises a certain division of matters: a chapter on principles, one on fundamental rights and freedoms, one on fundamental duties and a last chapter on the Ombudsman (*Avocatul Poporului*), a specific institutional guarantee of fundamental rights.

---

[19] RCC, Decision nos 76/1999 and 73/2000.

A. Access to Justice

The Romanian Constitution gives access to justice a double function: as a principle supporting all fundamental rights, and as a right on its own. Its importance to the exercise of and respect for other rights and interests explains why it was placed in the chapter on principles rather than in the list of rights. Another explanation for heightening the importance of access to justice is that the judiciary was one of the most mistrusted authorities during the communist era, as it failed to protect individual rights. In the new constitutional order, access to justice is given its rightful place as an essential element of the rule of law and a safeguard of legal certainty.

A peculiarity of the constitutional text on access to justice is its heterogeneous structure. Thus, Article 21 lays down the principle of access to justice ('Every person may have access justice to defend his rights, freedoms and legitimate interests' (§1)), but also its absolute character as a 'right' ('No law may restrict the exercise of this right' (§2)). The second paragraph was introduced by the 2003 revision, as a result of indirect international pressure. The reason for adding the third paragraph of Article 21 was that the Constitution, in its initial version, made no express reference to the right to a fair trial. As a consequence of the direct applicability and priority of the international law of human rights, the right to a fair trial existed in theory in the material Constitution. Nonetheless, this theoretical existence was not always acknowledged by Romanian courts, which had a hard enough time applying the express norms of the Constitution, let alone any 'implied' norms, including international ones, because of the mentality that 'the judge must only obey the law' (in its restrictive meaning, as an act of Parliament, because the judges trained under the communism regime excluded the Constitution).[20]

A direct consequence of this lack of correct understanding was a great number of complaints to and judgments from the Court in Strasbourg, declaring violations of Article 6 of the Convention. Mistrust of the national judiciary and exaggerated trust in international courts (features which are a part of the national legal culture)[21] were behind the high number of requests addressed to Strasbourg, but the outcome

---

[20] See below, IV.A.
[21] R Bercea, 'Dreptul judecătorului (este) cultură' (2011) 6 *Pandectele romane* 19.

of the cases and pressure from the EU (as Romania was, in 2003, undergoing the last phase of accession) led to the revision of Article 21 by the addition of the last two paragraphs. For the first time, a Romanian Constitution expressly referred to the right to a fair trial:

> (3)   All parties shall be entitled to a fair trial and to resolution of their cases within a. reasonable time.
>
> (4)   Administrative special jurisdiction is optional and free of charge.

The text uses the language of the international instruments, especially that of the ECHR (but also of Article 10 UDHR or Article 14 ICCPR), but only in expressing the right, not in defining it. The only fair trial guarantee set forth in Article 6 ECHR and mentioned by the new Article 21 is the requirement for resolution of a case within a reasonable time. Following the constitutional revision, the subsequent legislation was also changed, to include restrictions and even sanctions on magistrates who, 'by imputable reasons', disregard the speed of justice.

B. The Pillars of Democracy: Rights to Free Speech, Association and Assembly

Free speech was probably the most desired and unattainable right during the totalitarian years. That is why it was given a special constitutional position, and is one of the most detailed constitutional provisions on rights.

Freedom of expression of thoughts, opinions and beliefs, as well as freedom of any creation, by words, in writing, in pictures, by sounds or other means of communication in public are deemed 'inviolable' by Article 30 §1. The text also provides specific limitations: freedom of expression cannot prejudice other persons' dignity, honour, private life and the right to one's image. The horizontal effect of the Constitution is clearly set forth, but any restrictive measures must meet the requirements of Article 53.[22] Several aims and values of general interest may also lead to limitations on free speech: defamation of the country or nation, instigation to national, racial, class or religious hatred, incitement to discrimination, territorial secession or public violence, as well as obscene behaviour, are all forbidden.

---

[22]   See above, II.C.

On the protection side, the Constitution prohibits any kind of censorship. Censorship was one of the most serious and well-known instruments of repression during the communist regime. It functioned both ways, but usually it was used prior to any publication or public manifestation of any expression. On the one hand, texts or images that were contrary to official dogma were removed from any cultural or artistic work; on the other hand, most such works had to contain references to the achievements of the regime, especially glorifying the main leader and his wife. The most visible use of censorship was in the media, where it annihilated any freedom of the press. That is why this specific form of freedom of expression, considered an essential part of a democracy, is given a special place in the Romanian Constitution. Freedom of the press is guaranteed (also by expressly mentioning the freedom to create publications), and any suppression of publications is expressly forbidden. However, newspapers and broadcasting companies have the obligation to publish their source of financing.

Freedom of speech and freedom of the press are among the most praised rights in Romania. The only major problem that was solved by the legislator[23] was that of criminal sanctions applied to journalists, which were considered disproportionate interferences with this freedom by the ECtHR.[24] There still is no detailed law regulating freedom of expression. In 2013, the European Commission, in its CVM Report, drew special attention to the role of the media and suggested 'the need for a review of existing rules, to ensure that freedom of the press is accompanied by proper protection of institutions and of individuals' fundamental rights'.[25] This observation was made in the context of alleged 'pressure' by the media on the judiciary and anti-corruption institutions. Therefore, the media seems to be, in the view of European observers, not only the watchdog of democracy but also a threat to its institutions.[26]

---

[23] Slander and insult were decriminalised in 2007, by a law modifying the Criminal Code, and were not included in the New Criminal Code of 2014.

[24] *Cumpǎnǎ și Mazǎre v Romania* App no 33348/96 (ECtHR, 17 December 2004), *Stângu și Scutelnicu v Romania* App no 53899/00 (ECtHR, 31 January 2006).

[25] COM(2013) 47 final, at 4.

[26] For further details, see B Selejan-Guțan, 'Political and Economic Challenges of the Freedom of the Media' (2014) 1 *Percorsi costituzionali* 141, at 158.

The *right to information* is set out in a separate article (Article 31 CR), although it is a part of the freedom of expression. Its distinct regulation emphasises the obligation of the authorities and of mass media to provide 'correct information to the public' on issues of general interest. Autonomy is granted to public radio and television services, with the obligation to ensure equitable representation of 'important social and political groups'. Separate organic laws regulate the public media services and the parliamentary control exercised over them through the National Council of the Audio-Visual.

Freedom of association and freedom of assembly are guaranteed by separate constitutional texts. Freedom of assembly (under Article 39 CR) has a pre-eminent place among the fundamental rights, due to its historic role in the establishment of the new constitutional order. The protection of this freedom aims specifically at facilitating the exchange of ideas and the collective manifestation of social and political life. Like all political rights, the freedom of assembly may be limited, on the grounds prescribed by Article 53.[27] The most usual limitation is the obligation to obtain authorisation from the local authorities prior to the assembly. On the other hand, the authorities have the positive obligation to protect the authorised assembly from any disturbance or forms of violence.[28]

Freedom of association protects all collective entities established according to the law. Alongside freedom of expression and assembly, freedom of association forms the core of any democratic society. According to Article 40 CR, citizens may freely associate in political parties, trade unions, private employers' associations and other forms of association. This freedom also implies the right not to associate: nobody can be forced to become a member of any association, nor are the associations obliged to admit any person as a member. Certainly, the principle of non-discrimination as set out in Article 4 §2 must be applied in these cases. Besides the negative obligation not to preclude the exercise of this liberty, the state must at the same time ensure the legal framework to allow the creation and functioning of the organisations. Magistrates and members of the police and military are not allowed to be members of political parties.

---

[27] See above, II.C.
[28] According to Law no 60/1991.

C. Personal Protection: Rights to Freedom of Conscience and Religion

Religion, churches and religious groups experienced rapid growth and attained importance in post-communist Romanian society. Even in recent polls, the Church is, alongside the army, the institution most trusted by the general public. However, although this is the general impression, the term 'Church' here does not always mean the Orthodox Christian Church ('Greek Orthodox'), which is the principal religion in Romania. Over 80 per cent of Romanians declare themselves to be Orthodox Christians, the rest being divided between the Roman-Catholic Church, Protestant religions, neo-Protestant cults, the ancient-style Orthodox Church, Islam, Judaism and atheists.

Religious freedom is established in Article 29 CR, and includes the freedom of religious cults, the principle governing the relationship between state and Churches and between religious cults themselves, as well as the right to religious education.

In Romania, there is no official Church, but neither is there a strict separation between Church and state. Religious cults are declared autonomous from the state by the Constitution, but the state assumes the duty to support religious assistance in public institutions such as hospitals, prisons, asylums and orphanages (Article 29 §5 CR). Romania is not a secular state. Some religious references can be found in public life, such as the oath taken by dignitaries and civil servants. The law on religious freedom expressly established the 'neutrality' of the state towards all religion or ideology. Neutrality also means the possibility for the state to cooperate with religious cults in fields of common interest. The central public authorities may conclude partnerships with religious cults.

In 2006 a new Law on religious freedom and general regime of cults was enacted, 40 years after the previous regulation. The new law updates and clarifies some controversial issues. First, it gives a formal definition of religious freedom, being the right of a person to have or to adopt a religion and to manifest it individually or collectively, in public or in private, by specific rituals and practices, including by religious education, as well as the right to keep or to change his or her religion. Secondly, it recognises certain religious cults as 'public utility legal persons', whereas the other collective religious entities ('religious associations' and 'religious groups') are either private law legal persons or associations without legal personality, respectively. Religious cults were given rights and privileges by law, including tax privileges, the ability to seek financial support from the state (funding used under strict state control) and the right to organise educational institutions. As regards the 'private' or individual freedom of religion, there has been no practice of particular importance so far, such as a strong debate on religious symbols, signs and clothes (like the debate on wearing the burqa in France, for instance). There have been some controversies regarding the presence of Orthodox icons in schools, but no significant jurisprudence has come out of it so far. Recently, however, the Constitutional Court has ruled that religious education classes should not be compulsory in schools *ex officio*, but only by written request of the parents.[29]

D. Personal Freedoms: Rights to Liberty and Security of the Person, Respect for Private Life

The *right to liberty and security* is recognised by Article 23 CR under the heading 'Individual freedom', inspired by French law. The constitutional text comprises in reality the classic *habeas corpus* guarantees. Historically, this right has been found in all modern Romanian constitutions, including the communist ones (albeit seriously violated by the totalitarian authorities in terms of actual guarantees). The present Constitution sets out detailed coverage of individual freedom and security, listing a set of guarantees against the arbitrary behaviour of authorities as regards individuals in state custody (eg a limitation on the length of detention, specific guarantees concerning searches, the right to be informed of the reasons for the restrictive measures in the presence of a defence lawyer, the presumption of innocence, the *nulla poena sine lege* rule, etc).

Article 23 was amended in 2003 under the influence of the case law of the ECtHR on Romania, regarding the guarantees against the arbitrariness of pre-trial detention. Thus, in the original version, the period of pre-trial detention could be ordered by the public prosecutor, which the Strasbourg Court found to be in breach of the guarantees of independence and impartiality required by Article 5(1) of the Convention.[30]

---

[29] RCC, Decision no 669/2014.
[30] *Pantea v Romania* App no 33343/96 (ECtHR, 3 June 2003).

After the amendment, a decision on pre-trial detention can be taken only by a judge.

Respect for private and family life is provided for in positive terms: 'The public authorities shall respect and protect intimate, family and private life' (Article 26 §1 CR). Clearly, this does not exclude the 'horizontal effect' of this right, ie the protection of private and family life against breaches by other individuals, as a positive obligation of the state. Personal freedom is specifically guaranteed, as 'the right of the natural person to dispose of himself' (Article 26 §2 CR).

Other rights involving personal freedoms are the right to freedom of movement (Article 25 CR), and the inviolability of a person's home and correspondence (Articles 27 and 28 CR).

E. Minority Protection and the Right to Identity

Minority issues constantly feature on the agenda of human rights protection in Romania. The problem of minorities entered the constitutional arena in Romania after World War I, with the creation of the Romanian national state following unification with Transylvania, Bessarabia and Bukovina in 1918. The fall of the multinational European empires led to the creation of large minority groups in the territories of the newly established national states (Poland, Romania, Czechoslovakia, Yugoslavia, Greece, Bulgaria), therefore clauses regarding the protection of the rights of persons belonging to these groups were included in the peace treaties of 1919–20.

The 1923 Constitution was the first to refer to the 'equality of all Romanians', without distinction of ethnic origin, language or religion, without using the notion of *minority*. These provisions applied the Treaty on minority protection signed in Paris on 9 December 1919, which, in its Preamble, stated that 'Romania … wishes to offer certain safeguards of freedom and justice to all inhabitants … without distinction of race, language or religion'. The Treaty referred to the general principle of non-discrimination, and to respect for the individuality, personality and distinctive ethnic character of those citizens belonging to ethnic, religious and linguistic minorities. At the same time, Romania engaged to recognise, by fundamental laws, the provisions of the Treaty. The 1923 constitutional provisions imposed by way of international law were applied in the subsequent legislation of the time: the Law on administrative unification (1925), the Law on primary education (1924) and the Law on the general regime of religious cults (1925). The 1938 Constitution partially restated these provisions. The times and terminology changed with the establishment of communist rule in 1947. Thus, the 1948 Constitution recognised the rights of 'co-inhabiting nationalities',[31] while the 1952 and 1965 Constitutions used the expression 'national minorities', although in everyday language the term 'co-inhabiting nationalities' survived.

The 1991 Constitution recognises the existence of national minorities (unlike France, for instance), and guarantees the right of persons belonging to them to preserve, develop and express their ethnic, cultural, linguistic and religious identities. It follows an individual rather than a collective approach to minority rights, inspired by the wording of Article 27 ICCPR.[32] The Constitution-drafters chose to maintain the expression 'national minorities' due to its presence in the international legal documents in the field and to its clarity by reference to the notion of 'citizenship'. During the Constituent Assembly's work on the draft Constitution, in the context of a discussion on using 'ethnic minorities' instead, one of the prominent specialists on the constitutional committee stated that 'ethnic origin expresses a mainly biological relationship, whereas belonging to a national minority means more, a socio-political, cultural, spiritual, linguistic relationship'.[33] However, the term is not defined in the constitutional text, therefore its interpretation according to international documents helps in inferring the meaning and elements of the 'right to identity of persons belonging to national minorities': the right of these persons to enjoy their own culture, to practise their own religion, to learn and use their native language, including in relationships with the authorities, and education-related rights. In 2003, there was a proposal to replace the expression 'national minority' with 'minority national community, constituent element of the state', but although the proposed text was sustained by the Venice Commission

---

[31] The term 'nationality' was used with the meaning of 'national or ethnic origin', not in the sense of 'citizenship', as in other systems.

[32] 'In those States in which ethnic, religious or linguistic minorities exist, persons belonging to such minorities shall not be denied the right, in community with the other members of their group, to enjoy their own culture, to profess and practise their own religion, or to use their own language'.

[33] *Geneza Constituției României* (Bucharest, RA Monitorul Oficial, 1998) 158.

as a reinforcement of the minorities' position,[34] it was not included in the final draft law. In 1990–91, another minority-related controversy surrounded the possibility to found political parties based on ethnic criteria. Initially, the Constitution drafting committee proposed an indirect prohibition on ethnic parties, but after a firm opinion to the contrary from the President of Romania, the final draft did not include it.[35]

As regards the content of the state's obligations towards the protection of the right to identity, it is set out in the subsequent legislation and refers to 'preserving, developing and expressing the ethnic, cultural, linguistic and religious identity of minorities', covering the obligation to grant persons belonging to national minorities the right to learn their native language in schools and to be educated in that language. Within the Education Ministry there is a General Directorate on Education in Minority Languages, which has competence in organising this aspect of education. National minorities also enjoy the following: political representation rights granted to organisations of national minorities, which have the right to be represented in Parliament *ex officio* by a place in the Chamber of Deputies; the right to use native languages of minorities in relationship with their public authorities (Articles 120 §2 and 128 §2 CR; and the Law on Local Government). The state is also obliged to adopt a law on the status of national minorities (a constitutional obligation granted by Article 73 §3 CR), the draft of which is still pending in the Parliament.

Other institutions with competence regarding issues concerning national minorities are the Department on Inter-ethnic Relations (which functions within the Government) and the Council of National Minorities (a consultative organ of the Government).

Not all of these generous constitutional and legal provisions are always reflected in the actual context of minorities and their problems. Currently, the most controversial issues in this respect are: the right to education in the native language (including teaching the Romanian language as foreign language, and the teaching of Romanian history and geography in the native language of minorities), the requests for cultural autonomy of the 'Szekely county' (a region inhabited mainly by a Hungarian population), the social and economic inclusion of gypsies,

[34] CDL-AD (2003)4, *Opinion on the Draft Revision of the Constitution of Romania*, at 8.
[35] A Iorgovan, *Odiseea elaborării Constituţiei* (Tg.Mureş, Vatra Românească, 1998) 83.

Table 2: Ethnic structure of the Romanian population (percentages)[36]

Total number of stable population	21,680,974
Romanians	89.47%
Hungarians	6.60%
Romani (Gypsy)	2.46%
Ukrainians	0.28%
Germans	0.27%
Russians (Lipovans)	0.16%
Turks	0.14%
Tatars	0.11%
Serbians	0.10%
Slovakians, Bulgarians, Croatians, Greeks, Jews, Czech, Polish, Italians, Armenians, others	under 0.10% each

the compulsory education of gypsy children and the illegal customs of the gypsy community (such as 'marriages' of young children).

In practice, the Roma minority raises the most issues. Traditional Roma culture is not always in accordance with legal requirements, especially as regards children's rights. The social and economic situation of the Roma population (largely affected by poverty and unemployment), and the nomadic culture of some of the Roma groups, complicate the whole picture. Due to poor management of Roma issues by the Romanian authorities, but also to the characteristics of the minority groups (especially their nomadic character), large numbers of Roma migrated into the developed European countries and provoked public outrage (the most relevant being the Italian response in 2011, the French authorities' repeated attempts to pay off Roma immigrants so that they would return to their home countries, not to mention the recent reactions of the British media), which led to even less acceptance of this 'unfavoured minority' all over Europe. It is also true that Romanian society is very conservative and prejudiced against those anti-social actions that are statistically more frequent within the Roma minority. The major issues expressed within the public internal discourse are the criminal actions of wealthy individuals within the Roma minority

---

[36] Available at http://www.dri.gov.ro/documents/ds_etniesilbmaternamedii.pdf.

(especially in businesses involved with metal recycling), the reluctance of Roma parents to send their children to school, the use of children for begging and other criminal activities, and marriages between children (especially in the wealthy layer of Roma society).

The authorities tackle these problems differently at the local, national and international levels. Local authorities are predominantly trying to address the social-economic issues of the Roma groups, through specialised departments organised in the local councils. At the national level, the National Agency for Roma was established in 2004, a specialised agency subordinated to the Government, defined as 'the governmental structure of representation of Roma people at national level'. The Agency is responsible for structuring and developing social measures contained in the Government's 'strategy of social inclusion', through programmes developed in cooperation with NGOs. The Agency's programmes especially target access to education, access to and conditions within employment, and the creation of a national network of Roma experts, intended to assist the authorities in their efforts at Roma social inclusion.

F. Economic, Social and Cultural Rights

Economic and social rights were 'cherished' under the communist rule, occupying privileged positions both in the constitutional texts and in practice, within the centralised economic system. After the fall of the regime, following international and European trends, economic and social rights were maintained in the Constitution, with a different position and in a different context. Although not expressly mentioned, the '*status positivus*' rights were given a secondary level of protection. All constitutional texts establishing these rights make reference to subsequent legislation (eg 'state education is free of charge, according to the law', a provision that was interpreted as allowing state universities to introduce tuition fees for a number of places).

The Constitution provides for the main social and economic rights: right to education, right to medical assistance; right to work and to social protection; right to strike; right to property and right to inherit property; right to a healthy environment. A purely economic right, newly introduced in 2003, is the right to 'economic freedom', which guarantees free access to an economic activity, as well as the provision and actual possibility to exercise the right to the free economic initiative. The free exercise of this right is hindered by excessive fiscal and bureaucratic burdens, imposed on national and foreign investors, as well as by high-level corruption.

G. The Right to Property

From the post-1989 transitional context to the present day, the right to property has been one of the rights most hotly debated, by individuals, civil society, the courts and the ECtHR. The constitutional text itself underwent some changes in 2003, with a view to strengthening the protection: 'Private property is to be equally protected and guaranteed by law' (instead of the previous, 'Private property is equally protected by law').[37] Certainly, the main issue concerning the right to property, in the context of the new constitutional order, was reparation following the serious breaches of this right perpetrated by the communist authorities in the late 1940s and 1950s, involving nationalisation of buildings and enterprises, and the 'collectivisation' of land and other agricultural assets. The main goal of the constitutional text protecting the right to property was to limit possible future deprivations of property, rather than to ensure reparation for past encroachments. Expropriation is only permitted for reasons of public utility, and only on payment of 'just and prior' compensation. Nationalisation or any other measures involving the compulsory deprivation of private property on the basis of the social, ethnic, religious or political features of the owners, or for other discriminatory reasons, are strictly forbidden by Article 44 §4 CR.

Interference with the right to use property is regulated only from the point of view of 'works of general interest', which allow the public authorities to use the subsoil of any property, with the duty to compensate the owner for any damage caused. General confiscation is forbidden as regards property acquired in accordance with the law. Only property and goods resulting from a criminal offence may be confiscated, according to the criminal law.

---

[37] Another change was determined by Romania's accession to the EU, which required foreign citizens to be allowed to acquire land ownership, under the conditions resulting from Romania's accession to the Union and from other international treaties, in terms of reciprocity, as well as by legal inheritance.

In the context of property protection, dealing with past violations was the most controversial issue over the last 25 years. In the early 1990s, Romania hesitated as to which model to adopt when dealing with nationalised properties: the restitution model, adopted in Czechoslovakia, or the compensation model, as in Hungary.[38] This hesitation led to uncertainty and confusion in the courts, especially following political pressure.

In its early case law (from, say, 1993) the Supreme Court upheld judgments of lower courts asserting their jurisdiction to deal with claims concerning nationalised immovable goods,[39] but in 1995 it radically reversed its jurisprudence, quashing lower courts' decisions on the ground that they had exceeded their jurisdiction and that nationalised property might only be acquired by way of legislation. This change was determined by political pressure,[40] especially a famous speech by the former President of Romania, Ion Iliescu, made in 1994, in which he said, inter alia, that 'judgments adopted by courts do not have a legal basis to decide the restitution of property, as long as a law does not say in what context and how such a restitution can be made to a nationalised owner'.[41] The Supreme Court rapidly acquiesced in supporting the political will expressed in the speech:

> Courts do not have jurisdiction to impugn Decree no 92/1950 or to order that property nationalised under its provisions be returned ...; legislation alone can bring the nationalisations carried out under Decree no 92/1950 into accord with the provisions of the present Constitution concerning the right to property.[42]

The consequence was the submission (by the General Prosecutor) and admission (by the Supreme Court) of dozens of appeals for annulment of lower-court judgments that had found in favour of the restitution of property. The General Prosecutor had exclusive competence to submit an appeal for annulment, which was not subject to any time limit so that final judgments could be challenged indefinitely.

---

[38] D Bogdan & A Mungiu-Pippidi, 'The reluctant embrace: the impact of the European Court of Human Rights in post-communist Romania' in D Anagnostou (ed), *The European Court of Human Rights: Implementing Strasbourg's Judgments on Domestic Policy* (Edinburgh, Edinburgh University Press, 2013) 80.

[39] SCJ, Judgment of 9 March 1993.

[40] Bogdan & Mungiu-Pippidi (n 38), at 80–81.

[41] Available at www.adevarul.ro/2002-10-23/Societate/.

[42] SCJ Judgment (full court) of 2 February 1995.

Subsequently confronted with hundreds of individual applications, the ECtHR delicately avoided the subject of the political origin of the Supreme Court's jurisprudential volte-face. It noticed, however, that by allowing appeals lodged by the General Prosecutor under the above-mentioned power, the Supreme Court of Justice 'set at naught an entire judicial process which had ended in a judicial decision that was "irreversible" and thus *res judicata*—and which had, moreover, been executed'.[43] The Strasbourg Court stressed that the Romanian Supreme Court of Justice had infringed the principle of legal certainty, thus breaching the applicants' right to a fair hearing under Article 6(1) of the ECHR, and considered that the exclusion from the jurisdiction of the courts of restitution of property cases was contrary to the right of access to a tribunal. Although the ECtHR's case law on this matter started in 1999, the annulment appeal was removed from legislation only in 2003.

Despite an abundance of legal provisions on this matter, changed and 'improved' by successive governments, the Strasbourg Court continued to be confronted with a large number of similar cases until October 2010, when it issued the first pilot judgment concerning Romania—*Maria Atanasiu and others*—in which Romania was urged to take general measures in order to prevent further violations:

> [T]he Court considers imperative that the State take general measures as a matter of urgency capable of guaranteeing in an effective manner the right to restitution or compensation while striking a fair balance between the different interests at stake.[44]

Due to financial shortcomings, the measures were taken belatedly, after an extension was requested by the Romanian Government.[45] In 2015, the case was still pending within the supervision procedure of the Committee of Ministers of the Council of Europe.

H. Fundamental Duties

A specific feature of the Romanian Constitution is the establishment of 'fundamental duties', considered a natural consequence of citizenship

---

[43] *Brumărescu v Romania* App no 28342/95 (ECtHR, 28 October1999), §62.

[44] *Maria Atanasiu and others v Romania* App nos 30767/05 and 33800/06 (ECtHR, 12 October 2010).

[45] For details, see Bogdan & Mungiu-Pippidi (n 38), at 81–83.

and a counterpart to the fundamental rights explored above. There are four such fundamental duties, two of a general kind (the duty of fidelity to the country, and the duty of good faith in exercising the rights and freedoms) and two more specific ones (the duty to defend the country and the duty to contribute to public expenses by means of taxes). The duty of fidelity is stronger in the case of persons occupying public office, who are bound by an oath, while in the case of the military obligations, changes to the constitutional text in 2003 allowed for the introduction of alternative service, as opposed to the compulsory military service in force until then.

IV. INSTITUTIONAL GUARANTEES OF RIGHTS

A. Fundamental Rights in Romanian Courts

For the post-communist Romanian courts, it was at first difficult to understand the role of the Constitution and of individual rights seen as an 'objective legal order'. Instead of integrating into the desired constitutional culture (assumed not only at the superficial level of the 'black-letter Constitution' but also at the level of society as a whole)[46], Romanian courts created their own 'transitional constitutional culture', dominated by relativity, insecurity and mistrust. Assuming the role of sole 'implementers of laws', incapable of carrying the burden of transitional problems (adaptation, harmonisation with European standards, interpretive tasks), it was difficult for these 'transitional' judges to think outside the box. The first reaction of Romanian judges, including Supreme Court judges (with few exceptions), to the case law of the Constitutional Court and the ECtHR was resistance.

In the early 1990s, the Constitutional Court gave a series of rulings, following unconstitutionality referrals, in which it repeatedly explained that its decisions, according to the Kelsenian model of constitutional review, had *erga omnes* effect. The Court also explained how an ordinary court should react when faced with a situation in which a legal provision would be declared unconstitutional: it should not passively await the intervention of the legislator but should directly apply the relevant

---

[46] See also M Guțan, 'Transplantul constituțional și obsesia modelului semiprezidenţial francez în România contemporană (I)' (2010) 5 *Pandectele Române* 35.

constitutional provisions.[47] However, many Romanian ordinary courts simply ignored the Constitutional Court decisions, arguing 'the lack of legal provisions in the matter submitted to litigation'. This reaction of the courts led to the consequence that many decisions of the Constitutional Court, especially in the field of fundamental rights, were deprived of effect.[48]

Considering this mindset, it is no surprise that the courts' resistance towards constitutionalisation was also in evidence as regards the standards laid down by the ECHR. It suffices to refer once again to the case of the nationalisation of buildings: it took seven years, a Constitutional Court decision, the entire jurisprudence of the ECtHR and, finally, a belated change of legislation[49] to convince Romanian judges that the appeal for annulment procedure did not comply with the principles of access to justice, legal certainty and a fair trial, whereas, according to Article 20 CR, they could have acted directly against any legal provisions that were inconsistent with the ECHR.

In 2000, the Constitutional Court started to base its decisions on the judgments of the Court in Strasbourg. Although this was not always done in an inspired way, it seemed to give a lead to the other courts. The HCCJ followed rather belatedly in the steps of the Constitutional Court, by also basing its decisions, as well as on the Constitution and Constitutional Court decisions, on the Strasbourg case law.[50] Its position was timidly followed by other lower courts—the courts of appeal and departmental tribunals. However, at this point, there was no actual 'dialogue', in the sense of interpreting and adapting the reasoning of the ECtHR judgments to that of the Romanian courts, but rather a parallel approach: the courts merely invoked European judgments without always developing their arguments, and without making a true interpretative effort as regards those European judgments.

---

[47] RCC, Decision no 186/1999.

[48] See, eg, RCC, Decision no 279/1997.

[49] The position of the ordinary courts towards the Constitutional Court decisions necessarily (if not forcefully) changed after the constitutional revision of 2003. Thus, the modified provisions regarding the effect of these decisions expressly mention their *erga omnes* application and the deprivation of legal effect of legal provisions declared unconstitutional by such decisions.

[50] See HCCJ, Panel of 9 judges, Decision no 39/2005. See also HCCJ, Decision no 1414/2005, Decision no 3221/2005.

Steps have been taken in recent years to eliminate these shortcomings, but almost entirely under external pressure resulting from Romania's accession to the EU and/or strong critical views emanating from the European institutions, and sometimes with the obvious opposition of the judicial forums. To conclude, the ECtHR jurisprudence regarding Romania proves that some fundamental rights and their interpretation are still a challenge for Romanian courts, at all levels. In a judgment from 2013, the Strasbourg Court noted that although the power of national courts to apply the Convention directly has been available for almost 20 years, 'none of the decisions submitted by the respondent Government showed that a litigant had successfully relied on the relevant provisions of the Convention in order to obtain the acceleration of his or her court action'.[51]

The most recent changes to the procedural legislation gave a special place to the ECtHR case law in the relationship with national courts.[52] The New Code of Civil Procedure provides, as regards two of the most important instruments for jurisprudential unification—the extraordinary appeal on points of law and the preliminary request for the interpretation of the law[53]—for the obligation of the judge-rapporteurs to present the relevant case law of the ECtHR on the subject matter in issue. Thus, the decisions of the HCCJ in these two procedures, which are binding to the inferior courts, will be vectors for integrating the supranational European law of human rights into the national law and jurisprudence.

B. The Ombudsman

One of the specific safeguards of fundamental rights provided by the Constitution is the Ombudsman (*Avocatul Poporului*—in a more literal translation, 'the People's Advocate'), an office drawing inspiration from the old Swedish institution and its various avatars in different European countries. It is an entirely new institution in Romanian law, created by the 1991 Constitution and functioning since 1997 when the organic law

---

[51] *Vlad and Others v Romania* App nos 40756/06, 41508/07 and 50806/07 (ECtHR, 26 November 2013), §§115–116.

[52] See for details B Ramaşcanu, 'Direct Application of the ECtHR Case-Law by Romanian Domestic Courts' in Guţan & Selejan-Guţan (eds) (n 13), 181.

[53] See Ch 5.

was enacted. There had been no proposals or attempts to introduce such an institution in the past, and there is no clear source of inspiration from elsewhere: it is rather a mixture of features from different but similar bodies. The reception of this highly popular institution has been seen as the expression of Romania's will to assume all aspects of fundamental rights protection, including by the means specific to this type of organ: negotiation, mediation and conciliation.

The structure and functions of the Romanian Ombudsman follow, therefore, the general pattern present in other legal systems: a non-jurisdictional organ, with rather limited methods of acting, and independent from all other public powers. Unlike other systems (such as that in Finland)[54], the Romanian Ombudsman is not considered a part of the legislative or executive powers. Even in the constitutional text, it is included in the last part of the second title on fundamental rights, due to its main purpose according to the Constitution: defending individual rights and freedoms.

The Ombudsman is appointed for five years by Parliament, but is not subordinated to the latter. Its aim is 'to protect rights and freedoms of individuals'. As an independent body, the Ombudsman cannot replace any other public authority, and cannot be compelled to submit to any instructions or provisions of any authority.

The institution is specialised in the following fields of action: human rights, equality of opportunity, equality between men and women, religions and national minorities; children's rights, family rights, rights of young people, of retired people, of persons with disabilities; the military, justice, the police, penitentiaries; prevention of torture in places of detention; property, labour, social protection, taxes. Any individual can bring a complaint against the administration before the Ombudsman. The Ombudsman is thus characterised as an instrument of parliamentary control over the administration. Acts of other state powers are excluded from its competence: acts of Parliament and of MPs, acts of the President of Romania, and acts of the Constitutional Court, of the President of the Legislative Council and of the judiciary.

The Ombudsman may also act *ex officio*. The other public authorities must ensure that the Ombudsman has the necessary support to exercise its attributes. As means of action, the Ombudsman pursues

---

[54] Husa (n 18), at 155.

investigations, holds hearings, takes statements, and requests information and documents.

By successive changes of the Constitution and the organic law, the Ombudsman has been given additional powers in relation to constitutional review. The Constitutional Court has an obligation to request the Ombudsman's opinion in cases based on referrals of unconstitutionality that deal with fundamental rights. The Ombudsman can refer matters to the Constitutional Court in two direct ways: challenging legislation before its entry into force and, after 2003, challenging legislation after its entry into force, thus being the only entity that can bring a case directly to the Constitutional Court against positive legislation. In 2010, the Ombudsman was given the power to introduce an appeal on points of law at the HCCJ, alongside the General Prosecutor, the Steering College of the High Court and the Steering Colleges of the courts of appeal. The Ombudsman also has the power to address administrative courts for illegal administrative decisions.

The Ombudsman's final acts cannot be challenged either in court or before Parliament. However, a person may file a court action simultaneously with a complaint at the Ombudsman.

As regards individual complaints, after investigation the Ombudsman issues recommendations. When it finds a violation of the rights concerned, it asks the authority responsible to take action to revoke the impugned act, to repair the damage and to restore the applicant to his or her original position.

If the authority found in violation of an individual right does not reverse the illegal acts within 30 days, the Ombudsman may address, in this order, and within different time limits, the superior authorities, the Government and Parliament. Annually or on request, the Ombudsman will present reports to Parliament, in which it may recommend changes of legislation, or the taking of certain measures in order to improve respect for individual rights.

The most vivid discussion concerning this new institution concerns the fact that its recommendations and other acts are not binding, which is deemed to be the cause of the Ombudsman's alleged low efficiency. However, these commentators overlook the fact that, by its very nature, the institution does not need decision-making power: it is based on the idea of conciliation rather than constraint. But this is also a matter of mentality. Romanian authorities are not familiar with the exercise of conciliation. Whenever a rights violation occurs, the most effective means of dealing with it is by the decision of a court, even by forced execution. The role of the Ombudsman is specifically to challenge this kind of mentality, and to try to solve such cases by appealing to the goodwill of the authorities as regards the law and the available rights. On the other hand, as little as the citizens trust the judiciary, they trust the Ombudsman even less, because it cannot impose sanctions, although the number of requests is increasing. Sanction is, in the public's view, the ultimate victory against an adversary, more effective than any amiable settlement. But sanctions can be applied only by the courts, so giving any such power to the Ombudsman would essentially alter the institutions fundamental nature. Nevertheless, the Ombudsman remains an important instrument of parliamentary control over the administration.[55]

V. CONCLUSION

Although, formally, fundamental rights are a normative system under the Romanian Constitution, they have not yet fully permeated into the legal system, and especially into legal and social consciousness, even after 26 years since the fall of the dictatorship. The knowledge of having and using rights is strengthened by the fame of the ECtHR and its jurisprudence, while the attitude of the authorities at all levels—legislative, executive and judicial—is also moulded by the relationship with EU law. But human rights are not yet an organic part of the Romanian constitutional and judicial culture.

The international—mainly European—influence is still a very important factor for change as regards both norms and mentalities, but there is a long way to go towards full acknowledgement of the human rights culture. In November 2011, it was still possible to discuss the possibility of passing a law enabling secret service and intelligence officers to decide on criminal investigations. The 'general measures' regarding property cases, requested in 2010 by the ECtHR in a pilot judgment,

---

[55] 'In 2014, the Ombudsman fulfilled its constitutional and legal mission on protecting personal rights and freedoms ... There were registered 10,346 petitions, 137 investigations were made, there were 56 ex officio cases and 33 recommendations were issued. The Ombudsman gave 909 opinions to the RCC, raised 3 referrals of unconstitutionality, 1 objection of unconstitutionality and one appeal on points of law.' (*Annual Report on 2014*)

were pending for over two years, and the final outcome was not satisfactory. The case law of the Strasbourg Court was 'enriched' in 2010–14 by many repetitive judgments on ill-treatment in Romanian prisons and by Romanian authorities,[56] and these may continue. Comparative law plays little part, unfortunately, in the approach of the Romanian courts towards human rights, no other country exerting any influence in this respect. The dialogue between constitutional courts[57] is also very limited, and the precedential value of ECtHR judgments has started to be recognised only recently in legislation and by the national courts.[58]

However, the influence of the European law of human rights on Romanian law cannot be denied: significant constitutional and legal changes have occurred as a result of Strasbourg case law, but there is more to be done. Romania is still among those countries with serious human rights issues pending before the ECtHR, involving conditions of detention, the length of proceedings and the rights of persons confined in psychiatric hospitals. The reinforcement of judicial dialogue at the European level through Protocol 16 to the ECHR will probably improve the perception of Romanian courts regarding human rights and the direct application of the Convention. The Constitutional Court, as well as the HCCJ and the courts of appeal. will have the right to address the Strasbourg Court with requests for advisory opinions, which will contribute to a higher quality national jurisprudence.

FURTHER READING

D Bogdan & A Mungiu-Pippidi, 'The reluctant embrace: the impact of the European Court of Human Rights in Post-communist Romania' in D Anagnostou (ed), *The European Court of Human Rights: Implementing Strasbourg's Judgments on Domestic Policy* (Edinburgh, Edinburgh University Press, 2013) 71.

---

[56] *Archip v Romania* App no 49608/08) (ECtHR, 27 September 2011) and subsequent case law on Art 3 ECHR.

[57] ES Tănăsescu & Ş Deaconu, 'Analogical Reasoning as a Dialectical Instrument' in T Groppi & M-C Ponthoreau (eds), *The Use of Foreign Precedents by Constitutional Judges* (Oxford, Hart Publishing, 2013).

[58] See, for details, B Selejan-Guţan, 'Human Rights as a European Judicial Culture' in Guţan & Selejan-Guţan (eds) (n 13), 202.

M Guţan, 'Comparative Law in Romania: History, Present and Perspectives' (2010) 1 *Romanian Journal of Comparative Law* 9.

—— & B Selejan-Guţan (eds), *Europeanisation and Judicial Culture in Contemporary Democracies* (Bucharest, Hamangiu, 2014).

I Raducu, 'Report on Romania' in G Martinico & O Pollicino (eds), *The National Judicial Treatment of the ECHR and EU Laws* (Groningen, Europa Law Publishing, 2010) 369.

B Selejan-Guţan, 'Transitional Constitutionalism and Transitional Justice in Postcommunist States—the Romanian Case' (2010) 2 *Romanian Journal of Comparative Law* 283.

——, 'Romania and the European Court of Human Rights: Highlights of the Recent Case-Law' in G Gornig, B Schöbener, W Bausback & TH Irmscher (eds), *Iustitia et Pax. Gedächtnisschrift für prof. Dr. Dieter Blumenwitz* (Berlin, Duncker & Humblot, 2008) 331.

—— & R Bercea, 'La Roumanie à l'heure de l'intégration européenne—défis posés par l'Union Européenne pour la protection des minorités' in L Trocsany & L Cognard (eds), *Statut et protection des minorités: Exemples en Europe occidentale ainsi que dans les pays mediteranéens* (Brussels, Bruylant, 2009) 173.

ES Tănăsescu, 'Le traitement des nationaux par leur État-parent—le cas de la Roumanie' in DC Dănişor (ed), *Dreptul la identitate. Le droit à l'identité* (Bucharest, Universul Juridic, 2010) 207.

M Voican, 'Le rôle des autorités locales dans l'implémentation de la stratégie pour les roms' in DC Dănişor (ed), *Dreptul la identitate. Le droit à l'identité* (Bucharest, Universul Juridic, 2010) 341.

7

The Process of Constitutional Change: Mechanisms, Limits and Future Developments

⟶◆⟵

Constitutional Amendment – Informal Changes – Trends – Eternity Clauses

I. CONTEXTUAL MECHANISMS AND DYNAMICS OF CONSTITUTIONAL CHANGE

THE ASSERTION THAT constitutional change 'reveals the deep nature of a constitutional system'[1] is confirmed by the dynamics of constitutional change in the Romanian system. This concluding chapter offers a general overview of the main themes of Romanian constitutionalism, from the points of view of past and future constitutional changes. All the contextual elements that determined the existence and the functioning of the system are faithfully reflected in its mechanisms of change: history, the trend towards Europeanisation, legal transplant. To these can be added an important factor: the inner characteristics of Romanian politics, which are essentially influential when it comes to constitutional interpretation and change. In the presence of a 'weak' Constitution, which lacks clarity here and there, the Romanian political class is tempted to circumvent it, trying to interpret and apply its provisions in that class's favour. Moreover, if, in doing that,

---

[1] S Boyron, *The Constitution of France. A Contextual Analysis* (Oxford, Hart Publishing, 2013) 236.

a political party or politician has the Constitutional Court on its side, by cleverly and constitutionally manoeuvring the appointment of judges, a favourable reading of the Constitution is assured. These phenomena are characteristic of the Romanian constitutional system.

It has been said that constitutions are made for the people, and that they should be designed to serve future generations and should display stability. To this end, mechanisms of constitutional change are designed in favour of that stability, although it has been established that contemporary constitutions are 'organic and evolutionary: they reflect or respond to changes in society'.[2] The given society within which a constitution is enacted and produces its effects is determinative:

> the concept of *living constitution* stems from recognition that any written legal text and any set of constitutional provisions, however introduced, at the end of the day produces different normative outcomes when the context in which they are embedded and to which they are to be applied significantly changes.[3]

This is why it is sometimes difficult to draw a line between what is constitutional and what is not in matters of constitutional change. In this chapter, I aim to assess the degree to which the living constitution influences the need for constitutional change in post-communist Romania, the actual needs, sources of inspiration and tools used to achieve these goals, and the future prospects for this process.

In 1991, the Constitution was the response, after the fall of the dictatorship, to the emergence of a new political and social reality: the desire to change the orientation of the country towards democracy and the rule of law, as 'ideals of the 1989 Revolution'. Therefore, while stressing the importance of a stable fundamental law, its drafters established a very formal and restrictive amendment procedure. They did this not only to secure their work, but also to imply that constitutional change should be made only when essential, and when truly necessary in a wider context. The post-communist constitutional change itself must be understood as the result of two strict needs: breaking with the communist past and establishing a brand new constitutional order.

---

[2] C Fusaro & D Oliver, 'Towards a Theory of Constitutional Change' in C Fusaro & D Oliver (eds), *How Constitutions Change* (Oxford, Hart Publishing, 2011) 4.
[3] ibid, at 406.

Thus, constitutional emotion has been channelled more negatively than positively, the future constitutional design being a relevant instrument to exclude everything that past experience had shown could lead to anti-democratic lapses. From a more formal perspective, rigidity in this case went hand-in-hand with the Constitution's supremacy. However, no formal requirements and rules for the adoption of a new Constitution are provided. If such a decision were ever to be made, informal constitutional action would be necessary—the organisation of a referendum, the dissolution of Parliament to create a 'new' Constituent Assembly— all under the supervision of the Constitutional Court.

The debate around the problem of the constitutional change in post-communist Romania was dominated, on one hand, by the necessity to manage a constitutional identity crisis caused by the abrupt change of the political and constitutional landscape, and, on the other hand, by the necessity of conferring internal and external political legitimacy on the post-communist regime. Therefore, the 1989–91 'constitutional moment' was marked by two main tools of constitutional reform: the appeal to the pre-communist democratic traditions and the use of constitutional transplant.[4] In the following years, constitutional changes were primarily formal, influenced by a series of factors, such as European integration, the malfunctioning of state institutions, political interests and an appeal to history.

A. Formal Changes

Since its adoption in 1991, the Constitution has been amended once, in 2003. Further amendment draft laws were initiated in 2011 (by the President and Government) and in 2013 (by the Parliament), but none has been adopted so far.

Constitutional change after 1991 was determined by multifarious factors, in the context of experience during the transition years and of Romania's accession to the EU. One such factor was external European pressure, which came from two sides: accession to the EU and judgments of the ECtHR. Romania was scheduled to join the EU in 2007, but in order to do so it had to make so-called 'Euro-amendments'

---

[4] See Introduction and Historical Overview.

to its fundamental law, confirming the supremacy of EU law over domestic law. Romania's joining NATO was also invoked as an incentive to change. This led to the introduction into the Constitution of a new title—'Euro-Atlantic Integration'—which, first, provided for the relationship between EU law and domestic law, and, secondly, regulated the country's accession to the North Atlantic Treaty by a ratification law similar to a 'constitutional law', ie adopted with a two-thirds majority by Parliament.

The judgments of the Court in Strasbourg influenced the dynamics of the 2003 constitutional change: the rewriting of Article 23 as regards preventive detention was entirely a consequence of the Court's judgment in the *Pantea* case, which found Romania in breach of Article 5 of the ECHR.[5] In addition, several new rights were introduced, but not in direct connection with the Convention: the right to a healthy environment, access to culture and economic freedom.

History has also played a significant role in the dynamics of constitutional change: the concept of 'aversive constitutionalism'[6] is rooted in fear of past institutions—the communist regime and even the monarchy—although the question of the form of government and whether to change it is more frequently reopened for further consideration. In the same context, there are more voices—in academic texts and on the political scene—that claim to be in favour of radical amendment of the whole political system by reintroducing the classical parliamentary model, with changes suggested as 'lessons from history', in order to avoid the troubles and inconveniences shown by the current semi-presidential regime.

As to democratic constitutional history, the appeal to constitutional democratic traditions has been rhetorical, without any serious interest in defining and correctly evaluating the reality and strength of past constitutional institutions and practices. The provision, in Article 1 §3, for compulsory interpretation of the main constitutional principles through the lens of Romanian 'democratic traditions' becomes a strange method of binding constitutional future developments to a hazy

---

[5] See Ch 6.

[6] KL Scheppele, 'Aspirational and aversive constitutionalism: The case for studying cross-constitutional influence through negative models' (2003) 1 *International Journal of Constitutional Law* 300. See Ch 1, section III.B.ii.

constitutional past, which is very feebly reflected in actual constitutional texts and practices.

Another set of changes was rendered necessary by the malfunctioning of some institutions, or simply by an incorrect understanding and implementation of their mechanisms. This was the case regarding the bicameral structure of Parliament, which was strongly criticised by commentators for its egalitarian and parallel nature, so a partial solution was offered by amending the Constitution. The binding effect of the Constitutional Court's decisions also falls into this category: due to the lack of precision of the initial text, the ordinary courts failed to recognise the Court's decisions as compulsory, therefore the Constitution needed to include an express reference to the effect of an unconstitutionality decision. Equally, the new version of the Constitution corrected a malfunction within the executive branch: as a response to previous vagueness, which led to serious controversies, it was expressly provided that the President of Romania cannot remove the Prime Minister from office.

Constitutional change may also be triggered by purely political incentives. This was the case, in the constitutional amendment process initiated in 2013, regarding the attempt to exclude the President from the executive branch (by introducing an express reference to the fact that the executive branch only includes the Government) or to forbid the President from refusing the nomination of the candidate for the office of Prime Minister proposed by the majority.

In the category of 'innovative' changes can be included the extension, in 2003, of the presidential mandate to five years, with the declared purpose of avoiding presidential and parliamentary elections at the same time. However, this adversely affected political stability. Cohabitation occurred as a result of this time difference, and its inconveniences are presently triggering discussions on a return to the initial four-year mandate.

In this context, political conflicts, especially those created in periods of cohabitation, have greatly influenced the dynamics of constitutional change. Such a conflict took place between 2008 and 2013, having constitutional amendment at its centre. In 2008, President Băsescu convened a 'Presidential Commission for the Analysis of the Political and Constitutional System of Romania', with the purpose of identifying the 'political and constitutional limits of the governing system', and suggesting a 'framework for the debate regarding the amendment of the Constitution and the State's institutional reorganisation'. The Commission was composed of professors of law across the country and from abroad. After its work ended, the President used the Commission's report to draft a constitutional amendment initiative, but he did not follow all the expert opinions expressed in the report.

The initiative was referred to the Constitutional Court on 9 June 2011, and the Court issued its decision on 17 June 2011, deciding that six points of the proposal were unconstitutional on the ground that they exceeded the substantive limits of the amendment (suppressing elements of fundamental rights guaranteed by the Constitution) and suggesting revision of other proposed changes. The project was sent, together with the Constitutional Court's decision, to the Romanian Parliament, with the express requirement that it examine it and make the changes suggested by the Constitutional Court. In Parliament a surprising thing happened: the parliamentary group of the Chamber of Deputies belonging to the 'presidential' party (PDL) assumed the project as its own and submitted it as initiator. Although it was registered and introduced on the agenda of the Legal Committee, the project was not discussed in the plenary chamber at once, but it was eventually rejected in 2013.

After the change of the political majority in May 2012, and especially after the elections in December 2012, a new process of amendment started, triggered by the new political majority. The new initiative was drafted in May–July 2013.[7] Following political changes in the spring of 2014 (the break-up of the governing coalition and the loss of the two-thirds majority necessary to amend the Constitution), the amendment process was put on hold.

B. Informal Changes

In Romanian constitutionalism, constitutional changes made without amending the Constitution are rare. Constitutional conventions and 'informal constitutionalism' do not have the chance to become established, as they will always be contested for not being written into

---

[7] See European Commission for Democracy through Law (Venice Commission), *Opinion no 731/2013 on the draft law on the review of the Constitution of Romania*, CDL-AD(2014)010, Venice, 21–22 March 2014, available at http://www.venice.coe.int/webforms/documents/?pdf=CDL-AD(2014)010-e.

the Constitution. The formal nature of constitutional change is a consequence, on the one hand, of the formalism of the Romanian legal system (which includes, inter alia, the primacy of written sources of law and the refusal of the courts to acknowledge judicial precedent) and, on the other hand, of the state's seeming inability to innovate without 'models'. New institutions and practices were adopted mainly because they had proved to be successful elsewhere. The role of history in this context is significant: virtually all constitutional changes in Romanian modern history were made under external pressure and/or by legal transplant. Therefore, the need for models has become an innate feature of Romanian constitutionalism. The above-mentioned appetite for formal change is deeply connected to the evaluation of constitutional transplant as a 'magical panacea', by continuously appealing to constitutional models with universalist claims, and with a never-ending, faithful attachment to the French 'constitutional ingredients'.

Informal constitutional change by means of judicial interpretation of decisions of an activist Constitutional Court is also very unlikely to happen. As has been shown throughout this book, and especially in chapter five, the Constitutional Court is far from enjoying an image as a strong and coherent constitutional interpreter. Its inclination towards politicisation and its jurisprudential inconsistency make it (still) a weak link in the balance of powers chain. Unless context-generated changes occur, especially as regards the appointment of judges,[8] the Constitutional Court will find it hard to become a stable and neutral pillar of the rule of law, with a credible role to play in informal constitutional changes.

This does not mean that attempts at informal change have been completely absent. For example, in its Decision no 682/2012, the Constitutional Court suggested that, given the silence of the constitutional text, the consultative referendum initiated by the President in 2009, regarding the adoption of the unicameral Parliament, might have binding effects as regards any future amendment of the Constitution. Another example is the constitutionalisation of the Court's new competences introduced by law, which were declared by the Court itself, in the decision regarding the constitutional amendment draft, as having a 'constitutional rank'.[9]

---

[8] See Ch 5.
[9] RCC Decision no 80/2014.

II. LIMITS

Ever since 1866, Romania has had rigid Constitutions in times of democracy. During the communist era, this rigidity was subject to political decision, as was proved by the 'revision' in 1974, when the function of President of the Republic was introduced.[10] The 1991 Constitution stipulates a rigid amendment procedure, which demands a high level of political consensus among the parliamentary political parties. It also imposes formal and substantive constitutional limits on the constitutional amendment, which reflect the influence of Romanian ethnocentric constitutionalism. However, this rigidity is not as unyielding as in other constitutions. The dissolution of Parliament and new elections are not required for the constitutional revision process to start. The elements of rigidity may be found in the formal adoption procedure for a constitutional amendment law, in the limits of any amendment and in the involvement of the people, who have the final decision.

A. Formal Limits

The formal rigidity of the Constitution is expressed in the actual procedure for amendment and also in the temporal limits provided by Article 152: the Constitution may not be revised during a state of siege or emergency, or in wartime.

As for the procedural limits, they apply to both the conditions of any initiative and the parliamentary procedure. Thus, amendment of the Constitution may be initiated by the President of Romania on the proposal of the Government, but also by parliamentarians (at least a quarter of the total number). A popular initiative is also possible (supported by at least 500,000 voters), but subject to more special requirements: the voters who are signing the initiative must come from at least half of the counties, and in each of those counties, or in the capital city, Bucharest, at least 20,000 signatures must be recorded in support of the initiative. In practice, all amendment initiatives so far have been formally initiated by Parliament. A peculiar case was the 2011 proposal, which, although it was drafted on the initiative of the President, who referred it to the Constitutional Court, was then

---

[10] See Ch 3.

introduced into Parliament by a parliamentary group belonging to the party that supported the President. The 2013 project was also initiated by the parliamentary majority. As for the presidential initiative, the proposal of the Government is only a formal requirement, as was demonstrated in 2011, when the President exercised the first step of his initiative practically alone.

The examination of the initiative by the Constitutional Court is a compulsory step, as is the advisory opinion of the Legislative Council. After the Constitutional Court has adopted its decision, the initiative is referred to Parliament, where it will be debated in separate sittings by the two chambers. The proposal must gather at least two-thirds of the votes of each chamber's members, therefore a high level of political consensus is necessary. The law must be adopted by both chambers in the same form. Should any disagreements appear, a mediation committee is formed, which will comprise an equal number of members from each chamber and will have the mandate to discuss only the divergent opinions. If no agreement is reached in the mediation committee, the chambers will come together in a joint sitting and shall decide by the vote of at least three-quarters of the total number of MPs. Therefore, in the event of disagreement, an even higher level of consensus is required. So far, there has been no recourse to mediation during the amendment procedure.

Although the Constitution does not stipulate it, after the adoption of the final version by Parliament, the Constitutional Court is called to decide *ex officio*, over a five-day period, on the text. If the Court finds that there are aspects that infringe the Constitution, the law is returned to Parliament to be corrected.

The final step in the amendment procedure is the compulsory referendum,[11] by which the sovereign people are called to give their consent. The referendum must be held within 30 days from the adoption of the law in Parliament, if the Constitutional Court hands down a constitutionality decision.

In 2013, the Constitutional Court, called to re-examine the new changes to the referendum law proposed by the new parliamentary majority, established that the lowering of the validity quorum of participation to 30 per cent was constitutional, as the legislator may introduce

---

[11] See Ch 1.

any conditions through silence on the matter in the constitutional text. However, invoking the stability of electoral legislation, advocated by the Venice Commission, the Court considered that the validity quorum, although strongly discouraged by the Commission, was a part of the 'European electoral heritage', and therefore any change to its status should not enter into force earlier than a year from the date of enactment.

B. Substantive Limits and 'Eternity Clauses'

Article 152 CR provides an extensive package of substantive limits on constitutional amendment. The first set of limits are the 'eternity clauses' regarding the core features of the state, which determine its very existence and the constitutional identity of the nation: the national, independent, unitary and indivisible character of the state, territorial integrity and official language. Another set of eternity clauses concerns the principles of democracy and rule of law.

It is perhaps odd to find the republican form of government in this list. Although the Republic was not part of traditional Romanian democracy, and it was introduced and identified with the communist regime, in its case aversive constitutionalism did not function. At the constitutional moment in 1991, maintaining the Republic was considered necessary, responding to the wish of the people to elect the head of state. Therefore, the choice was read in a 'popular' key. Moreover, preservation of the republican form of government was included in the limits to amendment of the Constitution. The opponents of the idea of a republic, who supported the reinstatement of the old monarchical dynasty, were in a minority within the Constituent Assembly, and the approval of the final text of the Constitution by referendum was seen as the legitimisation of the Republic's privileged status, that has come to be seen as set in stone. After the presidential authoritarian tendencies in 2009–12, a stronger pro-monarchical movement formed within civil society, but, despite some support within the political sphere, no consensus was reached to change the Constitution radically in this respect. At any rate, a decision to change the form of government would mean a decision to adopt a new constitution, as the constitutional system would become parliamentary and the balance of powers would dramatically change.

The 'national' character of the state has remained a permanent topic of discussion in the context of proposals for constitutional amendment. In 2003, as well as in 2013, the political representatives of the Hungarian minority came up with suggestions to remove this feature of the state from the constitutional text, but these attempts and/or amendments were systematically rejected by the different constitutional committees as contrary to the spirit of the constitutional design.

Another category of strong limits on constitutional amendment concerns fundamental rights as part of the democratic heritage: no amendment shall be made if it results in the suppression of the fundamental rights and freedoms of the citizens, or of the safeguards thereof (including institutional safeguards, such as the Ombudsman or the Constitutional Court).

III. FUTURE DEVELOPMENTS

A. Major Themes of Debate in the Context of Post-Communist Constitutional Change

The 1991 Constitution is, for different reasons, continuously and intensely criticised by specialists, the political class and civil society. Constitutional change is a recurring theme in political debate, as the system is seen to be in permanent need of reform. In this context, debate about constitutional change revolves less around how we could make the present Constitution work than around how the Constitution should be formally amended. There are also those who argue that there is no need for formal change,[12] and supporters of a change in political practices rather than of the constitutional text itself:

> [T]he present Romanian Constitution has the irrefutable merit of not having allowed any political actor, be it President, Government or Parliament, to dominate political life, to have the ability to annihilate its opponent, to obtain excessive power, [or] to abuse its power.[13]

---

[12] See, for instance, ES Tănăsescu, 'Trebuie revizuită Constituția României?' (2014) 5 *Dreptul* 3.

[13] D Apostol Tofan, 'Primele reflecții cu privire la Raportul Comisiei Prezidențiale de analiză a regimului politic și constituțional din România' (2009) 4 *Curierul Judiciar* 216.

Nevertheless, although the constitutional text would not, theoretically, allow such a concentration of power, in practice this has happened by 'forcing' the Constitution, especially in the period 2009–12, when a strong President, backed by a weak Prime Minister who was politically obedient to him, was able to dominate the whole of public life, including by interfering with acts of government and, indirectly, with judicial power.

Current experience shows that the need for constitutional revision has never been assessed in an objective manner: constitutional change has been triggered either by purely political reasons or interests, or by direct or indirect external pressure. Where the amendment was the result of doctrinal criticisms and proposals, the proposed version was not justified by serious doctrinal studies (eg the changes in the functioning of bicameralism). Even the latest constitutional amendment initiative was permanently enmeshed in political negotiations. For example, in 2013, President Băsescu publicly affirmed that he would offer his resignation if the new power modified the Constitution according to his initiative.[14]

Therefore, apart from the constitutional moment in 1991, when a major choice was made for democracy in order to fill the constitutional void created by the abrogation of the 1965 Constitution, post-communist Romania did not have a coherent plan for improving its constitutional system. Equally, informal changes were subject to political interests, and therefore lacked coherence, especially as regards the interpretations given by the Constitutional Court. From this conundrum, one can detach some major themes to be discussed in the context of future constitutional change.

i. Parliamentarism v Semi-presidentialism

A change to the constitutional system's structure was envisaged and discussed by civil society, as well as in liberal political circles. Presidentialism was not considered, by some voices, to be an adequate option,[15] and neither was the current semi-presidential system. A 'rationalised'

---

[14] Obviously, neither of these events ever happened.
[15] B Dima & ES Tănăsescu (eds), *Reforma constituţională: analiză şi proiecţii* (Bucharest, Universul Juridic, 2012), at 36.

parliamentary regime was proposed,[16] but none of the amendment initiatives took up that view, as the majority opinion still supported semi-presidentialism.

Instead of radically changing the system, during the last constitutional amendment process attempts were made to curtail the powers of the President and to strengthen the Government within the executive. A trend towards parliamentarisation can therefore be identified. However, the current constitutional arrangement of powers offers a solution with the possibility of a moderate president, having the function of mediator and less involved in actual governance. Thus, formal constitutional change would not be necessary in order to obtain a 'weaker' president. Informal changes would be more appropriate, especially given the mentality and self-positioning of those who occupy the presidential seat.

Another trend is to reinforce the parliamentary majority by trying to prohibit political migration, and therefore to reduce the risk of cohabitation. However, the Constitutional Court declared the proposed text unconstitutional for violating the representative character of the parliamentary mandate.

As for more radical parliamentarisation of the system, two possibilities were envisaged: a parliamentary republic with a more powerful parliament and a president with symbolic representative powers and the adoption of a new form of government, that is, a parliamentary monarchy. The latter is a topic that comes on and off the agenda of civil society and politicians when talking about revising the Constitution. The reintroduction of the monarchy would certainly mean a shift to a purely parliamentary regime, and the Constitution would have to be almost entirely rewritten. A legitimate question can thus be raised whether it would not be wiser to adopt a brand new Constitution to this end, as both envisaged changes would exceed the current limits of constitutional amendment.

The latest draft constitutional amendment included certain attempts to lessen the possibility of the President's becoming a dominant institution, including the return to the four-year presidential term of office (with the clear intention to limit the probability of cohabitation). The draft also included the express provision that 'the President of Romania cannot reject the proposal of the Prime Minister to revoke

---

[16] ibid, 39 at 43.

and appoint Government members' in the reshuffle procedure,[17] and the breaking of the presidential 'monopoly' on initiating national referendums by introducing the possibility for citizens (minimum 250,000) to exercise this power (the latter proposal was welcomed by the Venice Commission in its Opinion).[18]

ii. Other Themes of Debate on Constitutional Change

Apart from the major problems involved in a radical change of the system, some other issues have constantly made the agenda in the constitutional change debate over the last decade.

The most visible by far was the debate on *unicameralism versus bicameralism*. It started in the context of the referendum organised by President Băsescu in 2009, aimed at 'consulting' the nation about changing the structure of Parliament and reducing the number of MPs to a maximum 300. The referendum was convened simultaneously with the presidential elections in November 2009, and its result was positive, the proposal being supported by over 77 per cent of voters. However, on the one hand, the Constitution does not grant direct binding effect to referendums convened by the President, as it does with the other type of binding referendum.[19] On the other hand, Romania does not have a 'legislative referendum', like France, established by the Constitution. Even more doubtful would be a referendum aiming at amending the Constitution, as Parliament is the sole legislator and, moreover, all actors involved (President, the people) have in their turn the right to initiate constitutional change in other ways. Therefore, the obligation of Parliament to follow the result of such a referendum is debatable. To date, the proposal for a unicameral Parliament was rejected as part of the 2011 presidential initiative of constitutional amendment, and the reduction of the number of MPs to a maximum 300 was included in the 2014 parliamentary constitutional amendment.

Reducing 'governmental law-making', or the abuse of legislative delegation, was also a recurring topic in successive proposals for amendment. The first attempts were made in 2003, when the constitutional texts regarding legislative delegation were modified in order to bring more

---

[17] Venice Commission (n 7), §107.
[18] ibid, §150.
[19] See Ch 1, section II.B.iv.

clarity to and impose limits on this controversial institution. However, it seems that these amendments were not sufficient as long as the abuse of Government Ordinances (GOs) continued. This was recently highlighted by the European Commission and the Venice Commission, who explained this excessive use of ordinances by the 'cumbersome legislative procedures in Parliament'.[20] In the 2013 draft constitutional amendment, no significant change was proposed, which, exacerbated by the continued excessive use of GOs in practice in 2012–13, led the Venice Commission to conclude that this practice 'involves risks for democracy and the rule of law in Romania'.[21]

Additionally, starting in 2008, governments started to 'abuse' the right to impose laws through the responsibility engagement procedure.[22] This was covered by the 2013 draft constitutional amendment law, which reduced the exercise of the prerogative to once only during one parliamentary session.

The role of the Constitutional Court was the subject of constant debate, especially regarding consolidation of the Court's independence. The present system of appointing constitutional judges, although classic within the Kelsenian model of constitutional review, does not seem to cope with the Romanian political context of permanent doubts regarding the fairness of the appointments and the political past of the appointees. Proposals were made to supplement the criteria for appointment, or to change the procedure.[23] Recently, enhancement of the transparency of the selection procedure has been proposed, by including the advisory opinion of a special independent professional committee, made up of former judges and prestigious law professors, in order to establish more accurately compliance with the 'high professional competence' criterion.[24] Another idea was to change the appointing authorities: to include the High Court of Cassation and Justice alongside the political authorities, and at the same time to impose

---

[20] CDL-AD(2012)026, Venice Commission, *Opinion on the compatibility with constitutional principles and the rule of law of actions taken by the Government and the Parliament of Romania in respect of other state institutions* [...], 17 December 2012, §79.

[21] Venice Commission (n 7), §173.

[22] See Ch 3.

[23] See Ch 5.

[24] Ş Deaconu, 'Necesitatea reformării Curţii Constituţionale a României prin revizuirea Constituţiei' (2013) 1 *Revista de Drept Public* 114.

a quota of career judges or legal academics, as in Austria, Croatia, Germany, Italy and Portugal. During the debates of the constitutional amendment committee in 2013, the experts in the advisory group also proposed such changes, but the amendment law, submitted to the Constitutional Court in January 2014, did not contain any change regarding the appointment of Constitutional Court judges.

Another point of debate on changes regarding the Constitutional Court was its jurisdiction. The main target was the removal from the Constitution of the paragraph that permits the introduction of new competences of the Court by organic law. Since 2003, two competences have been introduced in application of this paragraph: the power to review laws on constitutional amendments after their adoption by Parliament (and not only the amendment initiative, as the Constitution provides in Article 146 a); and the power to review Parliament's Resolutions (introduced in 2010)[25]. The 2013 amendment project contained this proposal, but the Constitutional Court declared it unconstitutional in Decision no 80 of 14 February 2014, by informally adding all matters relating to the Court's jurisdiction to the list of amendments limits [or 'to the unamendable clauses'].

iii. Constitutional Models

In recent years, in debates on constitutional change, the importance of foreign national constitutional models has slightly decreased. The French model seems to have lost its primary influence, although it was used extensively by the presidential committee of 2008 to advocate consolidation of the President's powers following the French model of organisation of the executive power. The committee members struck the other 'classical' constitutional regimes from the potential list of sources of inspiration—parliamentary (UK) and presidential (USA)— and praised the advantages of the French 'model semi-presidentialism', without presenting any of its disadvantages, directly suggesting its adoption by the Romanian Constitution. However, other expert reports from civil society[26] referred to the Austrian model, regarding the political accountability of the President, or to the German model of rationalised parliamentarianism.

---

[25] See Ch 5.
[26] Dima & Tănăsescu (n 15), at 125.

In the current constitutional amendment process, more importance was given to internal developments and problems requiring solutions. Constitutional transplant from a given system has also lost momentum, but if, at some point, a radical change of system or form of government is envisaged, recourse to it will be certainly reactivated.

B. International Benchmarks of Constitutional Change

The international context has maintained its role in the development of Romanian constitutional design. At the constitutional moment in 1991, European integration was an ideal target, which still seemed far from being reached, but which reflected the ambition of the political class of all post-communist countries. Naturally, the criteria that Romania had to fulfil in order to become a member of the European order were not purely constitutional but political and economical too. However, the political and constitutional requirements went on to play an increasingly important role, after Romania's admission as a member state of the Council of Europe in 1993.

In 2007, after a long and painful transition, the target was reached and Romania joined the EU, but European supervision remained in place, in a unique way, through the CVM. It was the first sign that, although the EU acknowledged Romania as a member state, it did not fully trust its dedication to the rule of law: reform of the judiciary and anti-corruption strategies were, and still are, central to the CVM, which was introduced onto the EU supervisory circuit only when Romania and Bulgaria joined the Union. Although in the first period, 2007–12, the European Commission examined particularly the achievement of its own benchmarks, and refrained from making references to the constitutional system of the country, since 2012–13 it has expressed serious concerns regarding the 'stability of the constitutional order'. However, the European concerns primarily revolve around constitutional practices rather than the Romanian Constitution itself: respect for Constitutional Court decisions, the practice of EGOs and the appointment of a new Ombudsman were all mentioned. In the end, the European Commission concluded that

> while the Constitution and the Constitutional Court's role and decisions have been respected, commitments regarding the protection of the judiciary against attacks, the stepping down of Ministers with integrity rulings against

them and the resignation of Members of Parliament with final decisions on incompatibility and conflict of interest, or with final convictions for high-level corruption have not been fully implemented.[27]

The Venice Commission was a constant presence in successive Romanian constitutional moments, being one of the main advisers of the Constitutional Drafting Committee in 1991. In 2003, the unfinished draft was the object of an advisory opinion of the Commission.[28] Likewise, in 2013, the amendment project was submitted to the Venice Commission, especially given its involvement in advising the Government after the events of July 2012. The Opinion of the Venice Commission on the 2012 crisis also contained a section on 'Proposals for amending the Constitution and laws in order to avoid similar situations in the future',[29] in which the following improvements were envisaged: more clarity in the President's suspension procedure; streamlining the legislative procedure; clear provisions in the Constitution on the dismissal of the Ombudsman; and clarification of the competences of the President and the Government. However, not all of these changes would need to be of a formal kind: some of them could pertain to the interpretation of the existing constitutional provisions and to good state practice.

To sum up, the international benchmarks for constitutional change in Romania aimed primarily at changing the 'living Constitution' rather than the black-letter instrument. Certainly, more clarity in the constitutional text is desirable: sometimes incorrect interpretations lead to improper practices. However, even in the presence of a clear text, inadequate mentalities and conduct at the institutional level can affect the whole functioning of the system. As the Venice Commission rightly said in closing its Opinion:

> [R]espect for a Constitution cannot be limited to the literal execution of its operational provisions. The very nature of a Constitution is that, in addition to guaranteeing human rights, it provides a framework for the state institutions, sets out their powers and their obligations. The purpose of these

---

[27] COM(2013) 47 final, p 12.
[28] CDL-AD (2003) 4, Strasbourg, 18 March 2003.
[29] Venice Commission (n 20), §88.

provisions is to enable a smooth functioning of the institutions based on their loyal cooperation ...[30]

C. Conclusion

The 1991 Romanian Constitution and its evolution over the last two decades illustrate an interesting phenomenon: although it was intended as a new start on a clean slate, the established constitutional system embodies all three phases of the Romanian constitutional development in modern times. The pre-communist tradition, the communist past, and the post-communist present and future can all be identified in both the constitutional text and the living Constitution. The pre-communist age, especially the period 1866–1938, created a 'democratic nostalgia', especially for the 1923 Constitution, which was reflected in the debates on the new 1991 Constitution. The heritage of this period can be found especially in the option for a bicameral Parliament, and in the belated recognition of a privileged status for 'the democratic traditions of the Romanian people'. The contribution of the communist age is the fear of stepping back towards dictatorship and the wish for a democratic European future. The post-communist transitional period is the most relevant for the development of the 'living constitution', for the dynamics of the constitutional change and for the existence—or not—of a Romanian constitutional culture of democracy. Romania's accession to the EU formally marked the end of the transition; and, seemingly, despite continuous monitoring through the CVM, Romania has managed to prove its European orientation.

Nevertheless, the events of 2012 and 2013 demonstrate that, after 25 years of 'new democracy', the Romanian constitutional culture is still in transition. Apparently, the constitutional system did not use its full capacity to find self-regulatory channels able to avoid major crises. This was a consequence of multifarious factors: political and economic corruption, economic backwardness, the lack of a culture of respect for political opponents (coming from the lack of the democratic exercise for more than 50 years), an overly fragmented Parliament (due to the inability to achieve cohesion in the political scene and to frequent

---

[30] ibid, at 18, §87.

political migration)[31], the abuse of governmental delegated legislation and the distorted role of the President, which generated a too conflicted cohabitation in the last decade. As emphasised before, true constitutional change in Romania, one that will matter in the future, at all levels of the system and at all levels of society, should be an informal one:

> Romanian constitutionalism, both in its institutional and in its cultural-identitarian meaning, will establish its limitations according to the perception of the Romanian people about the legitimacy and functionality of political practices. The anxiety regarding the head of state's authoritarianism can remain, under these circumstances, an axiological referential which marked a certain historic moment.[32]

This means that formally changing the Constitution will not lead to the desired results, unless they are consciously assumed as a change of mentality.

Although now a member state of the EU, and seemingly embarked on the road to democracy, Romania is still a 'backslider' in many respects, a form of 'unconsolidated' democracy. In 2011 it occupied fifty-ninth place out of 167 in the Economist Intelligence Unit Democracy Index,[33] but in the latest index from 2013[34] it had dropped a place, to sixtieth out of 167, and remains in the category 'Flawed democracies'.[35] In the DEMOS EU Democracy Index, Romania constantly occupies the last place.[36]

This brings us back to 1993, when the following remark was made in a monitoring report on Romania's accession to the Council of Europe:

> It is in fact comparatively easy to transform a dictatorship into a democracy overnight. It is more difficult to alter attitudes and habits. Sometimes, this

---

[31] See Ch 2, section II.C.ii.

[32] M Guțan, 'Transplantul constituțional și obsesia modelului semiprezidențial francez in România contemporană (II)' (2010) 7 *Pandectele române* 67.

[33] J Birdwell, S Feve, C Tryhom & N Vibla, *Backsliders: Measuring Democracy in the EU* (London, DEMOS, 2013) available at www.demos.co.uk/files/DEMOS_Backsliders_report_web_version.pdf, at 42.

[34] Available at www.eiu.com/Handlers/WhitepaperHandler.ashx?fi=Democracy_Index_2013_WEB-2.pdf&mode=wp&campaignid=Democracy0814.

[35] The indicators used in this classification are mainly: democratic malaise and public distrust, corruption and organised crime, the justice system, media freedom, human rights and the treatment of minorities.

[36] Birdwell et al (n 33), at 96–113.

takes a whole generation, and certain Western countries already belonging to the Council of Europe are no exception.[37]

More than two decades later, this observation is still valid to define the relationship between the written and the 'living' Constitutions of Romania.

FURTHER READING

P Blokker, 'Constitution-Making in Romania: from Reiterative Crises to Constitutional Moment?' (2012) 2 *Romanian Journal of Comparative Law* 187.

B Dima, 'The Commission for a New Constitution: A Civil Society Perspective on the Process of Constitutional Revision' (2011) 1 *Romanian Journal of Comparative Law* 151.

M Guţan, 'Romanian Semi-Presidentialism in Historical Context' (2012) 2 *Romanian Journal of Comparative Law* 275.

B Iancu, 'Separation of Powers and the Rule of Law in Romania: The Crisis in Concepts and Contexts' in A von Bogdandy & P Sonnevend, *Constitutional Crisis in the European Constitutional Area* (Oxford, Hart Publishing, 2015) 153.

---

[37] A Spielmann & J Frowein, 'Report on Human Rights in Romania', Parliamentary Assembly of the Council of Europe, Doc AS/Bur (44) 94 of 25 January 1993, (1993) 14 *Human Rights Law Journal* 136.

Index

abortions, 204
access to justice, 186, 194, 206, 217–18, 232
Ad Hoc Assemblies, 7–9, 65
Adenauer, Konrad, 200
administration *see* public administration
Adrianopolis Treaty (1929), 5
anti-Semitism, 16
Antonescu, Crin, 125
Antonescu, Ion, 16
Apostol Tofan, D, 249
armed forces: political neutrality, 46
Audit Authority, 98
Austria: Romanian territories, 2, 3, 13
autonomous administrative agencies, 141–4
aversive constitutionalism, 59–60, 102,
    203–4, 242

Băsescu, Traian, 48–50, 79, 108, 110,
    111–12, 113–17, 121–2, 178n32, 193–4,
    243–4, 250, 252
Belgium, 11, 147, 156
Berlin Peace Treaty (1878), 209
Berthélemy, Henri, 164
Black Tuesday (2013), 86
Boc, Emil, 108, 110, 113
bribery, 76, 86, 138, 185
Bucharest Treaty (1812), 3
budget: adoption, 96–7
Bulgaria, 40, 223, 255

caesarism, 8
Carol I, King, 9–13, 25
Carol II, King, 15–16, 25
case law:
    Constitutional Court *see* Constitutional
        Court jurisprudence
    ECtHR *see* European Court of Human
        Rights
    source of law, 38
    stare decisis, 165, 197, 198
Ceaușescu, Nicolae, 18–20, 60, 102–3
censorship, 18, 219
Chamber of Deputies
    see also Parliament
    Black Tuesday (2013), 86
    constitutional change, 244

Constitutional Court judges and, 169
electoral process, 77
immunities, 86–7
minimum age of deputies, 78
minority representation, 225
President: interim state President, 125
Question Time, 93
children:
    illegitimacy, 45, 210
    Roma, 226–7
Chiuariu, Tudor, 82–3
Christianity, 11, 209, 221
citizenship:
    1991 Constitution, 206
    acquisition, 45
    Christianity and, 11, 209
    citizens v nationals, 43–5
    concept, 43–52
    dual citizenship, 46
    equality, 45
    fundamental duties, 230–1
    referendums, 47–52
    rights, 45–6
    terminology, 211
    voting rights, 46, 73, 209–10
civil service *see* public administration
Colombia, 74, 198
communist period:
    1948 Constitution, 17, 210, 224
    1952 Constitution, 17–18, 224
    1965 Constitution, 18, 102, 103, 204, 224
    1989 Revolution, 19–21, 55, 204, 207
    centralisation, 148, 149
    constitutional change, 246
    constitutional dynamics, 27–8
    deportations, 18
    elections, 72
    functionarism, 149
    fundamental rights and, 204, 205
    history, 1, 17–19
    judicial review and, 164
    judicial system, 181–2
    legacy, 257
    local government, 149
    political parties and, 67
    president, 102–3

Securitate, 139–40, 166, 204
Supreme Tribunal, 189
unicamelarism, 61, 66
conscience, freedom of, 221–2
Constantinescu, Emil, 108, 110
Constitution (1991)
   see also specific elements
   amending *see* constitutional change
   codes, 35
   constitution-making process, 22–4
   constitutional sentiments, 207
   Council of Europe and, 208
   dynamics, 29–30
   formalism, 33, 34, 241
   French model, 34, 36–7, 58, 60
   horizontal effect, 218
   legislation *see* legislation
   models, 57
   political context, 240–1
   Romano-Germanic system, 33
   source of law, 34–40
   Spanish model, 37
   structure, 58–62
constitutional change:
   dynamics, 241–5
   eternity clauses, 248–9
   formal changes, 241–4
   formal limits, 246–8
   future, 249–59
      bicameralism, 252
      constitutional models, 254–5
      debate, 249–50
      delegated legislation, 252–3
      international benchmarks, 255–7
      major themes, 249–55
      role of Constitutional Court, 253–4
   informal changes, 244–5
   initiatives, 246–7
   limits, 246–9
   process, 239–59
   referendums, 47, 49–52, 247–8
   substantive limits, 248–9
Constitutional Court:
   achievements, 198
   budget, 168
   case law *see* Constitutional Court
      jurisprudence
   chairman, 168
   decision-making process, 168
   delay mechanism, 174
   ECtHR advisory opinions, 237
   feebleness, 29
   High Court and, 191–3
   historical foundations, 163–7

independence, 62, 68, 165, 169–71
judges
   appointment, 109, 168–9, 253–4
   composition, 166, 167–8
   immunity, 171
   political neutrality, 46
   term of office, 168
jurisdiction, 62
   a priori review, 172–3, 198
   abstract review, 171, 172–3
   changing, 254
   concrete review, 171, 173–6
   constitutional review, 88, 171–6
   electoral litigation, 172, 179
   international law, 172
   limits, 192
   parliamentary resolutions, 92–3,
      176–8
   political conflicts, 172, 179–81
   popular legislative initiatives, 90
   reform proposals, 197–8
   survey, 171–81
   unconstitutionality of legislation, 88,
      118, 171, 172–3
   models, 165–6
   new institution, 62
   overview, 163–81
   politicisation, 30, 62, 110, 167, 168–9
   pre-communist tradition and, 28–9
   presidential complaints, 112, 118, 172,
      179
   role: debate, 253–4
Constitutional Court jurisprudence:
   ANI constitutionality, 142–4
   binding decisions, 37, 197, 198, 231,
      243, 255
   Code of Criminal Procedure, 186–7
   constitutional change and, 86, 245, 246–7
   CSM mandate, 196
   early years, 166
   ECtHR jurisprudence and, 232
   electoral system, 74–5
   emergency government ordinances, 132,
      133, 215
   engagement of responsibility, 136–7,
      180–1
   equality principle, 211
   fundamental rights, 214–16, 244
   institutional conflicts, 180–1
   international law and, 212
   legal certainty principle, 75
   lustration, 140–1
   parliamentary conflicts of interest, 84
   presidential immunity, 120

presidential powers, 109–11, 112, 114–15
presidential suspension, 121–4
property rights, 167
recent decisions, 167
referendums, 50–2, 245
regionalisation, 159–60
same-sex relationships, 166
Securitate records, 166
source of law, 37
status of EU law, 39
constitutional history *see* history
constitutional models:
19th century, 2, 4–5, 8, 9, 11
1991 Constitution, 34, 60
Belgium, 11, 147, 156
Constitutional Court, 165–6
France *see* France
future, 254–5
Germany, 57, 254
Portugal, 57
pre-communist era, 25, 26
Spain, 37, 57
trend, 2
United Kingdom, 254
United States, 254
contraception, 204
corporatism, 62, 194, 196
corruption:
DNA, 87, 188–9
local government, 148–9, 159, 160
members of parliament, 85–7, 99
political parties, 72
prevalence, 144–5, 200
Costa Rica, 74
Council for Academic Diplomas and
Degrees, 141
Council of Europe, 208–9, 255, 258–9
Council of National Minorities, 225
Court of Auditors, 71, 95, 97–8
Court of Cassation *see* High Court of
Cassation and Justice
courts
see also specific courts
continental system, 62
fundamental rights in, 231–3
hierarchy, 183–4
mistrust of, 217–18, 236
New Code of Civil Procedure, 233
organisation, 183–5
transitional constitutional culture, 231
Crimean War (1853–6), 7
Cuza, Alexandru Ioan, 9–10, 12, 25, 147
Czech Republic: EU membership, 199
Czechoslovakia, 223, 229

death penalty, 204
defence policy, 119–20
democracy:
1991 Constitution and, 21, 22, 40
communist period and, 17
Constitutional Court and, 176, 178
constitutional principle, 54–5, 56, 57
democratic nostalgia, 257
democratic traditions, 42–3, 54, 56–7, 66,
77, 104, 134, 242, 257
eternity clause, 248
free association and, 220
free expression and, 218–20
Golden Age, 15
government ordinances and, 253
post-communist period, 28–9
referendums and, 47, 49–50, 52
rhetoric, 242–3
right to information and, 220
unconsolidated democracy, 258
DEMOS, 258
Denmark: bicameralism, 77
Diaconu, Mircea, 84
dignity, 54–5, 192, 204, 206, 218
disability discrimination, 46, 210
doctrine: source of law, 38

economic, social and cultural rights, 215–16,
227–8
Economic and Social Council, 58
Economist Intelligence Unit, 258
elections:
bribery, 76
Constitutional Court powers, 172, 179
historical development, 72
negative vote, 99
parliamentary elections, 72–6
party-list system, 75–6
proportional representation, 73–5
supervision, 76
Elkins, Zachary, 178–9
emergency government ordinances (EGOs),
35–6, 126, 131–3, 159–60, 215, 255
engagement of responsibility, 135–7, 180–1
equality:
citizenship, 45
constitutional principle, 206, 209–11
gender equality, 45, 210, 234
historical development, 209–10
minorities, 223–7
property rights, 167, 210
ethnic minorities:
constitutional change, 249
language, 14, 154–5, 183

local government and, 159, 225
national minorities, 41–2, 53, 71
political parties and, 69, 70
protection, 223–7
right to identity, 23, 206, 224–5
Romanian ethnic structure, 226
terminology, 224
European Charter of Local Self-
Government, 153
European Commission for Democracy
through Law *see* Venice Commission
European Convention on Human Rights
see also European Court of Human Rights
access to justice, 218
derogations, 214
detention rights, 187
importance, 203, 207–8
priority, 213
Romanian accession, 186
Romanian monism, 36
Romanian violations, 212–13
European Court of Human Rights:
advisory opinions, 237
international benchmark, 188
political parties and, 69
Romanian cases
CSM and, 196–7
effect, 192, 205, 212–13, 232–3, 237,
241–2
free expression, 192, 219
mistrust of domestic courts and,
217–18
Pantea case, 187, 209, 222, 242
pre-trial detention, 209, 222–3, 242
prisoner treatment, 237
property rights, 230, 236–7
repetitive judgments, 237
Romanian judges, 179
source of Romanian law, 37
European Union:
1993 Association Agreement, 38
ANI and, 142, 143–4
council summit representatives, 109–10
CVMs, 257
corruption, 144, 145, 159
CSM, 195
DNA, 189
EGOs, 36
emergency government ordinances,
133
evidence, 21
free expression, 219
judicial system, 190, 193, 195, 200
major concerns, 255–6

objectives, 39–40
Parliament, 84–6, 92
eastward enlargement, 21, 40, 200
legal supremacy, 38–9
origins, 200
Romanian judicial system and, 199
Romanian membership, 21, 24, 188, 207,
233, 241–2, 257
source of Romanian law, 38–40
executive *see* government

fair trial, 186, 206, 209, 217–18, 232
family life, 204, 224
federalism, 53–4
fidelity to country, 231
Finland, 234
foreign policy, 119–20
France:
aversive constitutionalism, 60
cohabitation, 106, 116
constitutional model
19th century, 2, 4–5, 6, 8, 9, 205–6
1814 Constitutional Charter, 6
1852 Constitution, 8
1958 Constitution, 60, 104
1991 Romanian Constitution, 34, 36–7,
58, 60
Conseil Constitutionel, 168
Conseil Supérieur de la Magistrature, 62
Constitutional Court, 166
Court of Cassation, 189
importance, 254
judicial system, 181, 184, 189, 193
legislative process, 89
local government, 147, 148
organic laws, 34
pre-communist era, 25, 26
Prefects, 156
President, 106, 107
public law, 163–4
semi-presidentialism, 104, 105, 109,
119
minorities, 224
presidential term of office, 106
Roma, 226
rule of law theory, 55
free association, 204, 220
free expression, 204, 218–20
free movement, 224
Frowein, Jochen, 208
functionarism, 148–9
fundamental rights
see also specific rights and freedoms
1991 Constitution, 206

communist period and, 204, 205
constitutional change and, 249
constitutional principles, 209–16
constitutional rights, 216–31
derogation clauses, 214
domestic protection, 205–6
economic, social and cultural rights, 215–16, 227–8
fundamental duties, 230–1
international law, 207–8
judicial proceedings, 231–3
proportionality of limitations, 214–16
protection, 203–37
Fusaro, C, 240

Garoupa, N, 195
gender equality, 45, 210, 234
Germany:
constitutional model, 57, 254
human dignity, 206
judiciary, 254
post-war transition, 199–200
social state, 57
WWII and Romania, 16, 17
Gheorghiu-Dej, Gheorghe, 102
Ginsburg, Tom, 178–9, 195
good faith duty, 231
Gorbachev, Mikhail, 19
government:
bureaucracy, 141
constitutional structure, 61
criminal accountability, 137–9
functions and competences, 128–30
parliamentary relations
engagement of responsibility, 135–7, 180–1
ordinances, 131–3
overview, 131–7
political accountability, 93–5, 133–4
supervision and control, 93–5
President *see* President
presidential relations, 112–17, 126–7
appointments, 112–17, 127
cohabitation, 116–17, 124
meetings, 128–9
reshuffles, 114–16
Prime Minister *see* Prime Minister
structure, 128
survey, 126–39
vacancies, 130
Venice Commission and, 256
votes of no confidence in, 61, 94
government ordinances:
challenging, 174

constitutional change, 252–3
EGOs, 35–6, 126, 131–3, 159–60, 215, 255
excessive use, 66, 137, 258
fundamental rights and, 215
mechanism, 35–6, 91–2, 131–3
Greater Romania, 13–14
Greece: minorities, 223
Groza, Petru, 17

habeas corpus, 222
High Court of Cassation and Justice:
composition, 189
Constitutional Court and, 191–3
constitutionality of legislation and, 175, 176, 192–3
ECtHR advisory opinions, 237
fundamental rights and, 232
historical development, 189
jurisdiction, 62, 184, 189
jurisprudential consistency, 190–1, 200
origins, 164
overview, 189–93
President, 194
renaming, 189
superior court, 183
high treason, 124–5
history:
communist period, 1, 17–19, 27–8
Constitutional Court, 163–7
constitutional dynamics, 24–30
communist period, 27–8
post-communist period, 28–30
pre-communist period, 25–7
creation of Romanian state, 52
equality principle, 209–10
High Court of Cassation and Justice, 189
liberal constitutionalist period, 1, 2–16, 25–7
local government, 147–50
parliamentary development, 65–6
post-communist period, 1, 19–24, 28–30
presidential function, 102–3
human rights *see* fundamental rights
Hungary, 13, 21, 199, 229

identity right, 206, 224–5
Iliescu, Ion, 20, 21, 22, 107, 108, 110, 166, 229
illegitimate children, 45, 210
independence of Romania, 13, 53, 209
information rights, 220
innocence: presumption, 142, 222

International Covenant on Civil and Political
    Rights (ICCPR), 214, 218
international law:
    constitutional review, 172
    fundamental rights, 207–9, 211–14
    monism, 36–7
    subsidiarity, 37
Iohannis, Klaus, 42n17, 110
Italy, 166, 173, 199–200, 254

Jèze, Gaston, 164
judicial system
    see also specific courts
    communist period, 181–2
    Constitutional Court *see* Constitutional
        Court
    constitutional principles, 182–3
    continuing concern, 200
    French model, 181, 184, 189, 193
    judges *see* judiciary
    organisation, 183–5
    overview, 181–97
    prosecutors, 185–9
    transitional period, 199–200
judiciary:
    accountability, 185
    appointments, 61–2, 109, 184
    communist period, 181–2
    Constitutional Court *see* Constitutional
        Court
    constitutional structure, 61–2
    CSM, 179, 184, 185, 186, 189,
        193–7
    disciplinary sanctions, 185
    High Court, 189
    independence, 61, 62, 182, 183, 184
    irremovability, 184, 185
    mistrust of, 217–18, 236
    qualifications, 184
    women, 184

Kelsenianism, 24n17, 30, 34, 164, 165, 169,
    171, 175, 197, 231, 253

language:
    citizenship and, 45
    French, 5
    non-discrimination, 210, 223
    official language, 183, 248
    pluralism, 14, 154–5, 183
    right to identity and, 224–5
    Romanian, 3n1
legal certainty principle, 75, 133, 174, 198,
    230, 232

legality principle, 222
legislation
    see also Parliament
    constitutional review, 33, 88, 118, 171,
        172–5
    delegated legislation *see* government
        ordinances
    instability, 52
    international law *see* international law
    organic laws, 34–5, 132
    post-communist practice, 66
    process, 77–8, 88–92
        adoption, 91
        committee stage, 90–1
        competent chamber, 90
        initiative, 88–9
        Legislative Council, 89–90
        length, 91
        plenary debate, 91
        presidential role, 118
        promulgation, 118
Legislative Council, 89–90
libel, 192
liberal constitutionalist period:
    1866 Constitution, 9–15, 33, 65–6, 97,
        134, 148
    1923 Constitution
        bicamelarism, 65–6
        communist period and, 17
        constitutional review of legislation,
            24, 33
        Court of Auditors, 97
        democratic nostalgia, 15, 257
        equality principle, 210, 223–4
        fundamental rights, 205
        government accountability, 134
        judicial review, 164
        Legislative Council, 89
        overview, 14–15
    1938 Constitution, 16, 210
    Ad Hoc Assemblies, 7–9, 65
    Belgian model, 11
    Carol I, 9–13, 25
    constitutional dynamics, 25–7
    Constitutional Monarchy (1866–1938),
        9–15
    Cuza reign, 9–10, 12, 25, 147
    dawn, 2–5
    French model, 2, 4–5, 8, 9
    golden age, 15
    history, 1, 2–16
    independence, 13, 53, 209
    inter-war period (1918–38), 13–15
    legacy, 257

Organic Regulations (1831–58), 5–7,
    67, 147
political parties, 67
right-wing dictatorships (1938–44),
    15–16, 149
liberty and security: right to, 222–3
life: right to, 204
local government:
    centralisation trend, 148
    constitutional principles, 149–55
    decentralisation, 150–2
    deconcentration, 149, 152
    corruption, 148–9, 159, 160
    delegated competences, 152
    financial autonomy, 157–9
    functionarism, 148–9
    historical development, 147–50
    legislation, 153
    linguistic pluralism, 154–5
    local autonomy, 152–3, 155–9
    overview, 147–60
    politicianism, 148–9, 160
    Prefects, 151, 153, 155–7
    regionalisation, 159–60
    secondary legislation, 153
    shared competences, 151–2
    structure, 155
lustration, 139–41

mentally disabled persons: voting
    rights, 46
Michael I, King, 16, 17
migration, 215, 226
miners' riot (1990–91), 207
models *see* constitutional models
monism, 36–7
Monnet, Jean, 200
motions of censure, 93, 94, 133–4
multiculturalism, 206

Napoleon III, 9
Năstase, Adrian, 72
nation:
    citizens v nationals, 43–5
    concept, 41
    national state, 52–3, 249
National Agency for Integrity (ANI), 83–4,
    139, 142–4
National Agency for Roma, 227
National Anti-Corruption Directorate
    (DNA), 87, 188–9
National Bank, 139
National Council Against Discrimination
    (CNCD), 112, 209, 211

National Council for Studying the Former
    Securitate Archives (CNSAS), 139–40
National Council of Broadcasting, 139
National Day, 53
National Institute of Magistrates (INM),
    184, 195
national minorities *see* ethnic minorities
nationalisation, 228–30
NATO, 21, 188, 242
Nazism, 16
negative legislator, 175
negative vote, 99

Oliver, D, 240
Ombudsman:
    1991 Constitution, 216
    appointment, 95
    dismissal, 256
    initiating review of legislation, 172, 174
    new institution, 62, 90, 165
    overview, 233–5
    political neutrality, 68
    Venice Commission and, 255
organic laws, 34–5, 132
Organic Regulations (1831–58), 5–7, 67, 147
Orthodox Church, 2–3, 11, 26, 221, 222
Ottoman Empire, 2, 3, 4, 6, 7, 11

Paris Convention (1858), 8, 9, 65
Paris Treaty (1919), 223
Parliament
    see also legislation
    appointment powers, 94–5, 168
    bicameralism, 48–9, 61, 65–6, 76–8,
        243, 252
    budget adoption, 96–7
    bureaucracy, 81
    Chamber of Deputies *see* Chamber of
        Deputies
    committees, 78–9
    committees of inquiry, 93, 94
    constitutional change: initiatives, 246–7
    Constitutional Court and: judicial
        appointments, 168
    constitutional structure, 60–1
    elections, 72–6
    financial control: Court of Auditors, 97–8
    floor-crossing, 79–80, 122
    government relations
        appointments, 127
        control of executive, 93–5, 133–7
        criminal accountability, 137
        engagement of responsibility, 135–7,
            180–1

motions of censure, 93, 94, 134–5
ordinances *see* government ordinances
overview, 131–7
reports, 130
votes of no confidence, 61, 94
groups, 78–9
historical development, 65–6
interpellations, 94
legislative process, 77–8, 88–92
members
  bribery, 86
  conflicts of interest, 83–4
  corruption, 85–7, 99
  criminal convictions, 82–3
  immunities, 84–7, 98, 178
  incompatibilities, 83–4
  number, 48–9
  resignation, 82–3
  status, 82–7
Opposition, 87–8
overview, 65–99
parliamentarism v semi-presidentialism,
  59, 250–2
political parties, 67–72
presidential relations, 118–19
  dissolution, 61, 95–6, 118–19
  impeachment, 124–5
presidents, 81
questions, 93
referendums and, 95
resolutions, 92–3
  constitutional review, 176–8
Senate *see* Senate
sessions, 81
sittings, 82
unicameralism v bicameralism, 48–9, 252
parties *see* political parties
people's tribunals, 182
Permanent Electoral Authority, 71, 76
personality cult, 16
Phanariots, 3–5, 8, 148
Poland, 21, 199, 223
police:
  political neutrality, 46
  Securitate, 139–41, 166, 204
political conflicts: Constitutional Court
  powers, 172, 179–81
political parties:
  alliances, 70
  constitutionality litigation, 179
  corruption, 72
  dissolution, 69
  ethnicity and, 70
  financing, 71–2

historical development, 67
ideological restrictions, 70
ideological shallowness, 76
main parties, 70–1
membership, 68–9
parliamentary floor-crossing, 79–80, 122
parliamentary opposition, 87–8
pluralism, 67–8, 182
registration, 69
survey, 67–72
politicianism, 148–9
Ponta, Victor, 42n17, 87, 109, 117
Popescu, C-L, 176
Popescu-Tariceanu, Calin, 114
Portugal, 57, 254
post-communist period:
  1989 Revolution, 19–21, 55, 204, 207
  1990 elections, 20–1
  1990 'mini-constitution,' 20
  1991 Constitution *see* Constitution (1991)
  2012–13 crisis, 49–52, 62, 81, 86, 109–10,
    122–4, 169, 255–8
  constitutional dynamics, 28–30
  European Union and, 21
  history, 1, 19–24
  major themes, 24
precedents, 165, 197, 198
Prefects, 151, 153, 155–7
President
  see also semi-presidentialism
  accountability, 95, 120–5
  conflicts of interest, 120
  constitutional amendments and, 246
  constitutional complaints, 112, 118,
    172, 179
  decrees, 125–6
  election, 105–6
  government relationship, 126–7
    2009–12 period, 250
    appointment of Prime Minister, 61,
      113, 130–1, 243
    cohabitation, 116–17, 124
    criminal accountability, 137
    government appointments, 127
    meetings, 128–9
    overview, 112–17
    removal of Prime Minister, 243
    reshuffles, 114–16
  historical development, 102–3
  immunity, 111, 120
  impeachment for high treason, 124–5
  incompatibilities, 120
  institutional design, 104–5
  interim President, 125

judicial appointments, 109, 169, 184
messages, 95
minimum age, 105
national defence decisions, 95
neutrality, 110–12
parliamentary relations, 118–19
　dissolution, 61, 95–6, 118–19
　impeachment, 124–5
referendums and, 95
role and powers, 107–20
　budget, 96–7
　defence, 119–20
　dissolution of Parliament, 61, 95–6,
　　118–19
　foreign policy, 119–20
　guardian of constitution, 107, 110–11,
　　112
　initiating legislation, 88–9
　issues, 258
　judicial appointments, 109
　mediator, 107, 111–12
　representative of the state, 107,
　　109–10, 119
　suspension, 61, 116, 120–4, 243
　term of office, 106–7
　theory and practice, 30
　vacancy of office, 125
　Venice Commission and, 256
presumption of innocence, 142, 222
Prime Minister:
　appointment, 61, 113, 243
　competences, 130–1
　constitutional complaints, 179
　criminal accountability, 138–9
　CSAT member, 119
　government reshuffles, 114–16
　ministerial appointments, 127, 130
　parliamentary relations, 130
　powers, 109–10
　presidential decrees and, 125–6
　termination of office, 130–1, 243
prisoners, 187, 209, 222–3, 237, 242
private and family life, 204, 224
property rights:
　constitutional protection, 228–30
　ECtHR cases, 230, 236–7
　equality principle, 167, 210
　nationalised property, 228–30
proportional representation, 73–5
prosecutors, 62, 185–9, 209
psychiatric hospitals, 237
public administration:
　autonomous agencies, 141–4
　functionarism, 148–9

lack of professionalism, 160
lustration, 139–41
ministerial administration, 141
politicisation, 141
structure, 139
survey, 139–44

referendums:
　1991, 56
　2009, 245, 252
　2012, 123
　consultative and binding, 47–52
　legislative referendums, 118
　parliamentary consultation, 95
　quorum, 49–51, 122, 123, 247–8
　suspension of President, 116
　unicameralism, 245, 252
regionalisation, 159–60
religious freedom, 71, 221–2
republic, 56–7, 102
res judicata, 230
Revolution (1848), 6–7, 26, 67
right to life, 204
right-wing dictatorships (1938–44),
　15–6, 149
Roma, 112, 226–7
rule of law:
　constitutional principle, 54, 55–6
　eternity clause, 248
　European Union and, 255
　government ordinances and, 253
　judicial system principle, 182
　parliamentary tactics and, 80
Russia, 3, 4, 5–7, 13

same-sex relationships, 166
Schuman, Robert, 200
Securitate, 139–40, 166, 204
security: right to, 222–3
self-determination, 52–3
semi-presidentialism:
　absence of legislative referendums, 118
　constitutional structure, 59–60
　dangers, 102
　debate, 250–2
　dissolution of Parliament, 119
　France, 104, 105, 109, 119
　institutional design, 104–5
　parliamentary semi-presidentialism, 59
Senate
　see also Parliament
　ANI and, 142
　conflicts of interests, 83–4
　Constitutional Court judges and, 169

criminal convictions of senators, 82–3
electoral process, 77
mininum age, 78
President: interim state President, 125
separation of powers, 58–9, 61, 95–6,
    101–2, 118
social and economic rights, 215–16,
    227–8
social state, 54, 57–8
sources of law:
    case law, 38
    doctrine, 38
    EU law, 38–40
    legislation *see* legislation
    survey, 34–40
    travaux préparatoires, 38
Sova, Dan, 87
sovereignty: concept, 40–1
Soviet Union, 17, 18, 19, 56
Spain, 37, 53, 57
Spielmann, Alphonse, 208
standard of living, 57
stare decisis, 165, 197, 198
state:
    characteristics, 52–8
    creation of Romanian state, 52–3, 223
    national state, 52–3
    religious neutrality, 221
    republic, 56–7
    social state, 54, 57–8
    unitary and indivisible, 53–4, 149, 182
subsidiarity, 37, 151
Superior Council of Magistracy (CSM), 179,
    184, 185, 186, 189, 193–7
Supreme Council of National Defence
    (CSAT), 119, 124, 130, 139, 141
Supreme Court of Justice *see* High Court of
    Cassation and Justice
Sweden: bicameralism, 77

taxation, 97, 157–8, 222, 231
telephone tapping, 188, 204

territories, 2–3, 13–14, 53, 150, 223
trade unions, 58, 71, 220
transplants *see* constitutional models
travaux préparatoires, 38
treason, 124–5
tribunals, 183, 184
Turkey, 3, 8, 13

United Kingdom:
    constitutional model, 254
    minority national groups, 53
    Roma, 226
United Nations, 23
United States, 163–5, 254
Universal Declaration of Human Rights
    (UDHR), 212, 218

Văcăroiu, Nicolae, 125
Venezuela, 74, 198
Venice Commission:
    on citizenship, 44, 211
    constitutional advice, 23, 37
    Constitutional Court and, 165, 170
    on government ordinances, 253, 255
    minorities and, 224–5
    on parliamentary procedure, 78
    on political parties, 69
    on political shifting, 80
    on referendums, 50, 51n31, 248
    role, 256–7
Vienna Diktat (1940), 16
voting rights, 46, 73, 209–10

Wilson, Woodrow, 52
women:
    communist period, 204
    gender equality, 45, 210, 234
    judges, 184
    political parties and, 71
    voting rights, 210

Yugoslavia, 223